ALEKSANDR BLOK

Between Image and Idea

Number 1

COLUMBIA STUDIES IN THE HUMANITIES

Edited under the auspices of the Faculty of Philosophy

Columbia University

ALEKSANDR BLOK

Between Image and Idea

by F. D. Reeve

Columbia University Press 1962

NEW YORK AND LONDON

The Columbia Studies in the Humanities
is a series edited under the auspices of
the Faculty of Philosophy of Columbia University
for the purpose of making available scholarly
studies produced within the Faculty.

First published in book form in 1962
by Columbia University Press, New York and London

Library of Congress Catalog Card Number: 61-15468

Printed in the Netherlands

Prefatory Note

This book is a critical study of the work of Aleksandr Aleksandrovich Blok (1880–1921), the outstanding writer of the Russian Symbolist movement and the greatest Russian poet in the period from the turn of the century to the end of the First World War. Blok occupies a position of importance in Russian literature roughly comparable to that of Yeats in English or to that of Rilke in German. His work consists of a great number of lyric and narrative poems, verse dramas, critical essays, translations, and reviews. This study is an effort to make Blok's work known in the terms with which we have come to respond to poetry during the last forty years. Blok's poems are cited in Russian and in English translation. The translations are as close to literal as possible.

I thank the Ford Foundation for a Fellowship to Paris in 1955–56, under which the basic research for this book was done; Columbia University and its Department of Slavic Languages for having granted me a leave of absence; the library staff of the École des Langues Orientales and members of the École Pratique des Hautes Études, VIe Section, for courteous and important help; the managing editor and staff of the Columbia University Press; and friends, acquaintances, and correspondents here, in Paris, and in Russia who in one way or another have kindly, warmly helped this book along.

I am grateful to the Columbia Studies in the Humanities Fund and to its Editorial Committee for having given this book a publication award. The very great support extended by the Ingram Merrill Foundation pleases me deeply; the Foundation has generously provided funds toward the publication of this book.

Portions of this book have previously appeared in the *Slavonic and East European Review* and in the *American Slavic and East European Review*, whose editors I thank for permission to reprint.

A microfilm version (1958) of this study has complete footnotes and a more extensive bibliography.

New York, 1961 F. D. REEVE

Contents

Illustrations

ALEKSANDR BLOK

Between Image and Idea

I

An Artistic Method

Symbolism is an artistic method.—V. Briusov

There are moments of intellectual history in which a course of events or a procedure alters substantially, leaving the peculiar impression of a tradition violated by revolt. In our usual thinking, we seem to celebrate the revolt as tradition as soon as we are a little way off from it, although those who revolted insisted that they were fulfilling a unique and inexorable tradition. The Symbolist poets, who announced a seemingly radical poetics, desired to, and did, restore poetry to traditional meaning, if not to its "traditional" place.

The word "traditional" has two easily confused interpretations: in one sense it means habitual, prevailing, or accepted; in the other, more important sense it refers to all that we care to or need to preserve of our history—what of the past is meaningful. The change in poetry that culminated in what is called Symbolism was a revolt against the first interpretation in the name of the second. It was an effort to tie all the worlds of modern bourgeois society into the one meaningful world of its art.

"I am told of a group of Symbolists in Russian literature," Arthur Symons wrote in 1899, noting that the movement which had begun in France had by that time spread throughout Europe. "What...it seeks is not general truth merely, but *la vérité vraie*, the very essence of truth—the truth of appearance to the senses... and the truth of spiritual things to the spiritual vision."

What we seem to have forgotten is what the Russian Symbolists, like the French before them, were sure of: that there is no real difference between what you say and how you say it or, as Baudelaire put it, "What cannot be said does not exist." Despite their divergences the Russian Symbolists, like the French, understood that a word is neither more nor less than what it "suggests," that a word at any moment is the total of all its possible meanings.

Russian Symbolism was that Russian literary movement, manifested mainly but not only in poetry, which from about 1890 to 1910 tried to give new importance to literary activity by demonstrating the interdependence of culture and politics, the dignity of the intellect, and the meaning of formal, artistic creation.

A literary school did exist, of course. There was Briusov, its leader.... There was the decadent movement.... There was, as everyone agrees, a great deal of foolishness, stupidity, and charlatanism.... But there was also something more, and the profound integrity of such men as Blok is the proof of it.... We open *Vesy* or even... *Apollon* not merely with curiosity but with excitement, looking neither for handsome phrases nor for brilliant verse, but trying to draw close to that mystery which hovered namelessly, ineluctably in the air. Exactly what it was no one knew. People talked of "the transformation of the world by art," of "the realisation of spiritual desires"; people even spoke of "mystical anarchism"—words, words, words. But one thing is certain: that there was a sort of vague foreboding, or perhaps memory, of an enormous triumph... and there was a homogeneity among those who "recognised each other" in their community of experiences. Logically all this had no meaning, which is why with time, and looked at in the cold light of reason, it all seems absurd. But even in the final days of symbolism people still felt that symbolist art was by nature really magical, able to reach—and, in its vitality, to transcend—that wall which no one can pierce.[1]

As drama in its development oscillates between meaning and entertainment, so poetry moves between image and idea. Symbolist poetry was a movement away from science, "ideas," and the Romantic and Parnassian poetry of the first two thirds of the nineteenth century toward myth and imagination. The poetry which followed Symbolism moved away from *it* toward irony and idea again, not to create reality, but to *find* it. Just as there is no theater that does not entertain and no theater that does not convey meaning, so there is no poetry without idea or imagination. Blok's poetry, in particular, is characterized by a kind of ambivalence between image and idea as if anticipating the subsequent development of modern intellectual and dramatic poetry, that use of "concrete and meaningful images in terms of which the play of the mind may exhibit itself," as Brooks characterized Yeats's symbols. It moves toward the characterization which Francis Fergusson has applied to Dante's *Purgatorio* (Dante was a sort of hero to Blok)—toward the "drama of the mind."

What is perhaps most perplexing to the "traditional" reader of Symbolist or post-Symbolist poetry is the imagery—the metaphors that link the disparate events of experience into new wholes that ordinary sensibility, confused, rejects. The poet does not want merely to note down a state of mind, and it is not his job to do so. The poet's effort is not to separate himself from experience or to exclude anything, but the opposite—to work out a technique of inclusion of as much as possible, as Mallarmé worked it out, of the intangible aspect of the tangible; to impress reality into behavior and make it sing.[2] Poetry, like music, is regarded as involving a principle of complexity. The Symbolists wanted to work out a system of specific relations among things of this world that would automatically call into being a world of experience and meaning beyond the specific system. The system is the supreme fiction, the embodiment of reality, which is what Blok was talking about when he talked of the essential nature of the "spirit of music." Symbolism is the means to reality and the reality itself.

A literary symbol is a word or group of words that embody by analogy a complex of emotion and thought beyond the references of usual discourse. The embodiment need not be an image; it may be an action, a form, a rhythm, a gesture which contains an "idea." The verbal half of the analogy embodies the "transcendental"; the symbol is what it symbolizes, as words are also the only expression of what lies between them. However, Symbolist literature differs from literature in general, which is symbolic, by its effort to establish a definite, transcendental system.

A symbol is not a definition of a complexity: the simple is not merely exclusion of the complex. Rather, a symbol is a kind of overcoming of the complexity that at the same time preserves the original complex of senses. In a poem or a body of poems it acquires value only by adding new contextual meanings to its first meaning.

> A symbol is the only eternal reality, and the determinist trend which has come about from a more detailed explication of certain series of causality and which, having systematized the functional dependence of appearances, has completely spread across life, admitting only certain formal methods of cognition. In a symbol we have transcendence of the concepts "formal" and "substantial," so that the real artist is a symbolist insofar as he depicts life through the prism of determinism, always necessarily injecting into it an ineffable facility and euphoria.[3]

In this sense, a symbol is the center of the expression of experience. The meaning of a system of symbols lies both inside and outside itself. Given any example, we face the constant difficulty of grasping the reciprocal relation between the notion and its movement (gesture) and the whole context (poem) in which the movement keeps alive.

What the Symbolists showed us is that, whatever the movement is, we need not go beyond the poem; in fact, we should not. The beginnings of French Symbolism in the middle of the nineteenth century were connected, Valéry said in his *Variétés*, with a "remarkable determination definitively to isolate poetry from everything except its own essence." Valerii Briusov said that a poem cannot be measured by its logical structure (its ideas)—that it is in no sense allegory because there is no external-internal difference of significance. Symbolism, he said, "*has desired to be and has always been only art*."[4] He believed that all life—and all history—was properly the poet's subject and that the meaning of life and of history was expressed in the forms of art. The Symbolists' poems were involved in historical relevance, but that relevance is not a criterion of the poems nor a particularly satisfactory guide to the total complexity of any poem. A poem is a moment of reality in which tradition and culture have complete and simultaneous being and the meaning of which is accessible less in terms of tradition and culture than in its own terms. It is, after all, the given case; it is all we have.

The Russian Symbolist poets, like the French, saw an intimate connection between a poet's work and his behavior, but they saw the meaning of that behavior adequately explained and significantly expressed by his poetry alone. Against the restive and revolutionary—the partial because progressive—tendencies of society, they valued that understanding which transfixed a moment in a hierarchy of time, which gave meaning to being by locating it in a real, philosophical system. They knew the corruption of urban life and the boredom and alienation of bourgeois society. They knew that anything could be said and that nothing would matter. They knew they were expected to produce exotic mysteries or lyrics of mood And they refused: to the degree that they refused, they wrote poetry we still value, they restored to poetry its roots in rhythm and total understanding.

The factions in the Russian Symbolist movement were not clear-cut until the beginning of its decline (what V. F. Asmus called "the loss of confidence in the power of art alone to resolve the contradictions of Russian life"). In general there were two factions almost from the start: one, with Briusov, arguing for freedom in and for art, in the sense of what Eliot has called "autotelic art"; the other, with Belyi, Ivanov, and, partly, Blok, associating art with what might be called the generative forms of life, the evangelical aspect of Symbolism. Briusov believed that

Art is autonomous: it has its own method and its own task.... Symbolism is an artistic *method*... by means of which art is set off from both the rational understanding of science and all the supra-rational attempts at understanding of mysticism.

Belyi, on the other hand, believed that

The rise of the Symbolist school of art... was an answer to the increasingly widespread vulgarization of art. The aristocratic heights of eternal Symbolism rose before the crowd in bright, prophetic form.... Out of art will come a new life—and the salvation of mankind.[5]

Blok's work shows that out of an iconoclastic romanticism, out of the incompatibility of social theories and personal values, and out of concern for the specifics and vitality of poetry he built a poetry of drama, or at least verging on drama, in the sense that it is a poetry of symbols which function as correlatives of two hypostatized notions of what is real—the natural and the supernatural. A poem is itself the reality of both, all the possible positions of the moving elements. It is the whole drama, the idea of the theater. As such, it lives its life between gesture and meaning, between image and idea. This poetry is the bridge between the two periods of nineteenth-century Russian poetry and the poetry that followed the Revolution—between, on the one hand, the Romantic poetry of the first half of the nineteenth century and the "Parnassian" poetastering of the second half, and, on the other hand, the modern, self-conscious, terse, mimetic Russian poetry written shortly before and during the 1920s; between the old poetry consciously built around "meaning" either applicable or ideal, and a new poetry self-consciously built into meaning around imagery.

Blok, usually called a Romantic poet, was not. Blok used the devices of "traditional" poetry to return poetry to its meaningful tradition. Of great significance was his extension of the frames of reference of Russian poetry. Attracted to the mystical German Romantics and fascinated by the state of mind of the French Symbolists and their precursors, especially Baudelaire, he turned also to American and English poets. He celebrated neither Kipling nor Whitman, then fashionable in Russia, but reflected Byron, Coleridge, and most particularly Poe and Shakespeare. The excellence of Blok's poetry and his deep understanding of these writers in large measure opened them up in a new way to the poets who followed him, especially Pasternak.

II

A Biographical Sketch

Perhaps somewhere a poet stands
Reflecting sadly in a garden:
Why do I, as my years run out,
Disturb him with my hazy dream?
—N. Zabolotskii

August 10, 1921, was a hot day. At 57 Ofitserskaia Street, Petrograd (or Petersburg, now called Leningrad), apartment 23 was filled with wreaths and flowers. Poets, writers, leading literary figures and Russian intellectuals moved through the rooms. The acrid smoke of incense filled the air. Aleksandr Blok, 40 years old, his head wreathed in chrysanthemums, lay shaved and washed in an open coffin, pale and emaciated, worn out by life and the final months of terrible pain. A chorus from the Mariinskaia Opera sang. When the singing was over, Blok's closest and oldest friends themselves carried the open coffin out, down the stairs, to the Smolenskoe Cemetery, where he was to be buried beside his grandfather, under an old, spreading maple. (In 1944 Blok's remains were moved to the writers section of the Volkovo Cemetery, and a black marble obelisk was erected over the grave.) In the church in the cemetery they sang the Tchaikovsky Mass. A long line of people brought flowers. A girl ran up and kissed the dead man's hand. A thousand people watched and wept as the cover was locked on the coffin and the coffin lowered into the ground. They now watched and waited as one evening in April, four months before, they had watched and waited for Blok to come out of the Theater of Drama in Petrograd after a special program of readings—waited for Blok, waited for what remained of the old literary tradition.

Blok had died on Sunday, August 7, 1921. He was born on Sunday, November 16, 1880, in the home of his maternal grandfather, A. N. Beketov, the rector of St. Petersburg University. His forty years of life spanned the period from the Russo-Turkish War (1877–78) to the establishment of the undisputed hegemony of the Soviet government following the Russian Civil War (1917–21). They covered a period of extraordinary intellectual vitality and accomplishment in all phases of science, mathematics, history, creative art and literature, economics, and politics. They were coincident with radical transformations and reversions in ideas and habits of thought in all spheres of life.

Blok was born the autumn before Dostoevsky died. He died in the middle of the great famine of 1921–22, five months after Lenin's famous speech introducing the New Economic Policy. Almost each year of his life—certainly each year of his mature life—witnessed some crisis, some catastrophe, some turning point in history. The crises were failures of the government to satisfy the actual requirements of the country or were changes of tradition, if under such headings one can lump those political events and events involving intellectuals which deeply moved Blok. He carried a red flag in a demonstration during the 1905 Revolution. The success of the 1917 Revolution at first gave him much hope. He regarded his work on a committee investigating certain tsarist ministries and on the supervisory board of the new Soviet theater commission as very important. He saw that the deaths of Tolstoy, Kommissarzhevskaia, and Vrubel in 1910 were signposts, even symbols, of the collapse of Symbolism and of that cultural unity which he had lived under for thirty years and in terms of the values of which he thought and wrote his poetry. His own death was a mark of the end of the period of transition from the old to the new, even as his life was a symbol of the transition itself—a transition in which men's efforts and manners changed but their values and habits did not. His short life was filled with an emotional and intellectual intensity and a sense of dreadful despair ascribable only to the extreme pressures of his environment and to the violent alterations which his society and most of the Western world were going through. Despite the continual fickleness of literary coteries and the fluctuations of history, the loss of friends and the failures of reform, Blok held to his convictions and kept his convictions in accord with what he believed the essential understanding of his time, as if he were himself a living illustration of Stockman's phrase in *The Enemy of the People:* "The strongest man is he who stands most alone."

Blok's father, Aleksandr Lvovich, graduated from the law faculty of St. Petersburg University in 1874 and remained there to prepare for appointment as Professor of Public Law. He soon received an appointment at the University of Warsaw, then in the Russian section of Poland. From Warsaw he returned to St. Petersburg in the early fall of 1880 for the public defense of his Master's degree. His defense was brilliant, like the man himself. His friends regarded him as a poet manqué, and he knew hundreds of lines of poetry by heart. When playing the piano he seemed to forget his usual sense of discipline and severity and would excite his listeners by the deep feeling and almost mystical intensity which filled his music. Ladies adored him; men admired his intelligence; and Dostoevsky, who used to meet him at Filosofova's gatherings, wanted to portray him as a character in a novel. Blok himself, who scarcely knew his father, suggests something of this man's magic in his poem *Vozmezdie* (Retribution):

> Once (as he was walking through the living room)
> Dostoevsky noticed him,
> "Who's this swain?" he asked
> Vrevskaia quietly, leaning toward her;
> "He looks like Byron." The catchy
> Phrase was seized upon by everyone,
> And everybody turned his attention
> To the unknown face.
>
> . . .
>
> He did resemble Byron,
> As sometimes a sick brother
> Resembles a brother who is well:
> That same reddish reflection,
> And the same expression of power,
> And the same longing for the deep.

Blok's father was clever, extremely able, unusually talented, and severe; he was a stern idealist who was hard on himself and on others—including his wife, who, unfortunately, could not endure it. Their life together was miserable. Their first child was born dead. Moments of delight together reading or chatting were no compensation for wild outbursts, fights, and serious incompatibility. As a result, they divorced in 1889. Both soon remarried. Blok, who had spent most of his life up to that time in his mother's care and surrounded by aunts and nurses and maids, moved into the household of a sometimes hostile step-father. He was thrown all the more on his mother for affection and attention. It was his mother who introduced him to the work of Tiutchev, Grigor'ev, and Flaubert. It was she who placed him in a special secondary school, she with whom he went abroad in 1897 to Bad Nauheim, she who each summer took him to her family's *dacha* "Shakhmatovo" outside Moscow. Blok was the center of her life and her reason for being from his birth until the day of his death. All through his life she was never far from him.

The milieu in which Blok was brought up was that of a cultured, intellectual family, the members of which had over the years been professional people. Blok's great-great-grandfather, Johanna von Blok, was a doctor who became a medical officer in the Russian Army in 1755. His mother's father, A. N. Beketov, was not only Rector of St. Petersburg University but also an outstanding botanist and scientist, known also for having established the "Petersburg Advanced Classes for Women." Blok's maternal grandmother spent her life translating and editing scientific and artistic works. His own mother translated French verse and prose and even wrote and published some poems of her own. One of his aunts, M. A. Beketova, published several volumes of translations of French literary works; his mother's other sister, E. A. Krasnova, translated from French, Spanish, and English and was known for her posthumously published *Rasskazy* (Stories) and *Stikhotvoreniia* (Poems). Their influence, and the influence of his father's admiration for Flaubert's work, are evident in Blok's later translating *St. Julien l'Hospitalier* and publishing an edition of selected Flaubert letters.[1]

It is not at all surprising that, in such surroundings and with such a background, Blok began writing at an early age. He started writing compositions, he said in his autobiography, when he was five years old. Later, he and his cousins put out a family magazine, at the rate of one copy by hand per month, called *Vestnik* (The Messenger). During the summer at Shakhmatovo, he put on plays and excerpts from plays (he was fond of "declaiming" Hamlet's famous soliloquy) with his family, a few friends, and the neighboring peasants as audience. The peasants, needless to say, were mystified and impressed by a handsome young man leaning in a doorway, his hand raised to his forehead, reciting Shakespeare. Later, at the university, Blok took active and enthusiastic part in dramatic presentations under the pseudonym Borskii, but subsequent first-hand opportunities to see actors' bickerings disillusioned him, and he, with growing confidence in his ability as a poet, gave up all thought of a professional theatrical career.

Blok began to write seriously when he was about eighteen. Most of his work was lyric poems, of which he had written about eight hundred by 1904 when his first book, *Stikhi o Prekrasnoi Dame* (Verses about the Beautiful Lady), came out, containing about one hundred poems. The book did not cause a furor; it was not in line with the new Symbolist principles that Briusov and others had introduced from France, and it was not the sort of "Romantic" poetry that was characteristic of the end of the nineteenth century. The concept of the Lady and her cult, as established in Russia in the late nineteenth century by Vladimir Solov'ëv, was introduced into the Russian Symbolist movement by Blok, enthusiastically supported by Andrei Belyi, and was for a while an aspect of the development of Russian Symbolism, but the book which introduced it was at first neither understood nor accepted by the public. One professor even suggested that a newspaper editor pay someone 100 rubles to translate Blok's poems into comprehensible language.

Blok's background was not involved with contemporary literature as such or with problems and theories of literature. Rather, the work of his aunts and mother and of their mother was educational, or generally cultural, as much as literary. As Blok himself said, the poetry he first knew and which first moved him was that of Zhukovskii and of Polonskii. At St. Petersburg University, in 1899, Blok came upon Zinaida Gippius's story "Zerkala" (The Mirrors), his introduction to "decadent" literature. He read Solov'ëv's philosophy and experienced a real change in his intellectual life. He called that summer his mystical summer and spent the next couple of years working on poems almost all of which treat some aspect of his approach to or understanding of the Beautiful Lady. Presumably under his father's influence, he had entered the law faculty of the university in the fall of 1898; now, unhappy about "practical sciences" and deeply moved by the new world of thought and imagination that Solov'ëv's work and the work of the early Russian Symbolists had opened to him, he transferred to the philological faculty, from which he graduated in 1906. He wrote his thesis on Bolotov and Novikov under I. A. Shliapkin, who warmly praised Blok's work for its scholarship and sensitivity and who at one point almost persuaded Blok to accept a university appointment and prepare for a Master's degree.

Summing up the life of his family, Blok commented that, "As Verlaine would put it, *éloquence* prevailed." This, along with his mother's support of his interest in and sense of music, established his basic frame of reference, which he later transformed but never entirely abandoned. As a result, he never pledged allegiance to any one faction or school in the general "modernist" literary movement and frequently did an about-face when no one was expecting him to. He was in the literary current but not of it. Vladimir Solov'ëv's brother Mikhail and his wife, Blok's mother's cousin, encouraged Blok enthusiastically. Through them his poems reached Dmitri Merezhkovskii and his wife, Zinaida Gippius, who, with Pertsov had founded the magazine *Novyi Put'* (The New Way). The Solov'ëvs also sent some of Blok's poems to Briusov for an anthology he was compiling, *Severnye Tsvety* (Northern Flowers). Neither of the Merezhkovskiis nor Briusov was particularly astounded by Blok's work, but they recognized a serious talent, and all three editors accepted some of his poems. Blok met these "literary giants" in the fall and early winter of 1901–02. By the middle of the following summer, however, in August 1903, Blok had moved away from the Merezhkovskiis (although some five years later they drew closer again) with the support and affection of Belyi. In a letter to his mother that August, Blok announced: "I finally and fully feel, after all, that *The New Way* (the interesting August issue *without* my note has arrived) is *junk*. Bugaev [Andrei Belyi] seconded this completely."

He endured extreme intellectual ups and downs under the seemingly placid exterior of a well-ordered, quite usual, leisured, university student's life. At one moment he could not make his sense of mysticism fit Gippius's religious argument for development of an extensive, national, cultural renaissance, and yet he knew that he, at the beginning of a career, could not bypass her. At another moment his intellectual turbulence and agitation made him fascinated with his own dilemmas and the echos and interpretations of them he read in Dostoevsky. He made a Dostoevsky-like reference to suicide—"the end lies in ecstasy"—in his diary in March 1902, and, in November 1902, actually left a pre-suicide note. And at still another moment he was almost enchanted by his correspondence with Gippius, an exchange of letters which he called "extremely interesting, completely mystical."

The family summer house Shakhmatovo was next to Boblovo, the summer house of D. I. Mendeleev, the great scientist. Mendeleev's daughter, Liubov' Dmitrievna, a year younger than Blok, took part in Blok's amateur theatricals—playing Ophelia to his Hamlet—and studied drama seriously in St. Petersburg, after finishing her secondary education. In August 1903, she and Blok were married. The wedding itself was very much as one would imagine it between two people of their social position and inclinations, except for this: Blok's friends, with deep seriousness and intensity even in joking, believed that Blok's wife was the incarnation of the Beautiful Lady to whose cult they all had become attached. Blok and his wife—whose first name was "Love"—became the center of a rather fantastic cult among the little group of friends. In time, the game was played too seriously: Belyi's intensity and Liubov' Dmitrievna's response went too far. Blok and Belyi argued violently—Blok even challenged Belyi to a duel—and separated with rancor. Although they subsequently overcame their mutual bitterness, their work and poetic theories carried them away from each other, and the old, very close friendship never returned. Blok's wife continued acting and made something of a small career for herself as an actress in provincial towns and occasionally in "off-Broadway" productions in St. Petersburg. In the spring of 1909 she gave birth to a boy, of whom Blok was not the father. Blok, nevertheless, looked forward eagerly to the child's coming. His disappointment and grief were real and great when the child died after only eight days.

Blok and his wife had drifted apart. They enjoyed reading together and traveled abroad twice, but Liubov' Dmitrievna spent much of her time on tour in the provinces. Blok lived alone for the most part, began to drink heavily, slept with prostitutes, and had several affairs with actresses. Through all this he regularly wrote his mother, even telling her of his drinking, his sorrow, and his nights spent with "beautiful women." He became a kind of legendary figure, an embodiment of a stereotyped picture of a poet, with his curly hair, long lean face, dark coat and flowing tie, and his mournful, penetrating, intelligent eyes. Gippius said of him: "He has a look of surprised, evil exhaustion. And of a loneliness neither resigned nor agitated, just plain tragic."

His rise was rapid. He was barely twenty-two when his first poems were published. He was twenty-four when his first book of poetry appeared. By the time he was thirty, the most important Symbolist magazine *Vesy* (The Balance) had failed, the Symbolist movement was in decline, and he had become one of the outstanding poets of his day. He had written some of his most beautiful poems—for example, "Blagoveshchenie" (The Annunciation)—and had been invited to join the new and very select Society of Devotees of the Literary Language, which had been set up in conjunction with the new Acmeist magazine *Apollon* (Apollo). He was at the height of his intellectual and artistic activity and literary popularity. In the next eight years he established himself as a major poet—chiefly with the long poems *Retribution* and *Dvenadtsat'* (The Twelve)—and began to fall from favor with the intellectuals. He had an active literary life of only fifteen years, yet managed to crowd into that short period a half-dozen dramas, numerous critical articles and countless reviews, and well over a thousand poems. Not all of the material repays study, nor was it all even in Blok's day considered valuable or, for that matter, acceptable. In 1920

Aleksandr Blok, 1907

Blok annoyed his warmest admirers by publishing two volumes of poems, *Za gran'iu proshlykh dnei* (Behind the Border of the Past) and *Sedoe utro* (The Grey Morning), composed entirely of previously uncollected or unpublished early poems. The definitive text of Blok's work, comprising all that he wished to be preserved of his lyrics, includes some 760 poems. His play *Roza i krest* (The Rose and the Cross) was given over two hundred rehearsals by the Moscow Art Theater but was never presented. During the last ten of the fifteen years of his active literary life he was accorded all the respect and subjected to all the gossip, diatribe, and parody that attend a major writer. As soon as he was dead, the critics and the biographers and the memoirists took over, trying to describe what he had been and trying to explain what his poetry meant.

Blok was honest and kind. Although he became fashionable—and in Russia has become fashionable again—he was never modish. He never asserted allegiance to any particular group or school and seems never to have cultivated or to have encouraged any special faction for his own advantage. Although it was he who sponsored the Beautiful Lady and he who, with Belyi and his friends, first exploited her as an aspect of Symbolist poetry, it was also he who first moved away from such a cult. A few years after that mystical summer of 1901 he began to de-emphasize mysticism altogether. When Anna Schmidt presented herself to him as the incarnation of the Lady, he would have nothing to do with her, regarding her as an absurd, harmless fraud. Although he was less interested in the technical innovations in versification introduced chiefly by Briusov, following the French Symbolists, than in the general use or meaning of poetry as an instrument of understanding, as argued by Belyi and Viacheslav Ivanov, he regularly protested being listed on either "side." When Semënov in his "Russian Letters" in the *Mercure de France* in 1907, classified the Russian poets as divided in three camps—viz., the Parnassian decadents Briusov, S. Solov'ëv, M. Voloshin, and others, and the pure decadents Bal'mont, Sologub, and Kuz'min; the Neo-Christian romantics (really Symbolists) Merezhkovskii, Gippius, and Belyi; and the mystical anarchists Viacheslav Ivanov, Chulkov, Gorodetskii, and Blok—Blok sharply protested. Nothing he had ever written had anything to do with "mystical anarchism," which, he said in his notebooks, was nothing but foolish enthusiasm. The 1917 Revolution, which Blok is generally acknowledged to have caught up in art as aptly as art can catch a particular historical time, and for which he himself hoped and worked, he came to see as a failure, the product of abstract economic theories and bourgeois intellectuals who, like himself, had no real contact with or understanding of ordinary people.

From the start, Blok was an enigmatic figure. Some people though him brilliant and perceptive; others, kind and conventional. Some felt he was a great poet; others, a mere poetaster, or even, as one man felt in connection with *Verses about the Beautiful Lady*, a hack who had deliberately contrived to insult Russian womanhood. In general, the public was cautious, as the public usually is. As Abramovich characterized the reaction, in a review of Blok's work in an issue of *Obrazovanie* (Education) in 1907:

> The author's [Blok's] first volume, *Verses about the Beautiful Lady*, with its peculiar commingling of V. Solovëv's "Divine Eroticism" with the gentle, naturalistic mysticism of the artist Nesterov, immediately established the originality of the themes which agitated the poet.

Summing up Blok's work after his death, Mandel'shtam said that it was from beginning to end intensive, concerned with over-all cultural values—unlike the poetry of the Symbolists, of Bal'mont, Belyi, and Briusov especially. Blok in 1903 had sent Briusov a letter, à propos of Briusov's book *Urbi et Orbi*, in which he said he had no hopes of ever being as good a poet as Briusov and deeply praised Briusov's accomplishment. At the performance of Blok's play *Balaganchik* (The Puppet Show) in Kommissarzhevskaia's Theater in 1906 some in the audience screamed and whistled in outrage and some equally warmly clapped and shouted. Izmailov called Blok's poems "the flowers of a new Romanticism." Kornei Chukovskii labelled Blok "the poet of the Nevskii Prospekt." Briusov hailed him as the poet "of day, colors, and sounds." Abramovich said that, even among the poets themselves in 1906–7, Blok, just twenty-six years old, was considered one of the leaders of the new movement along with the "old guard"—Bal'mont, Briusov, and Viacheslav Ivanov. People only ten years younger than Blok, Annenkov later said, grew up "under the sign of Blok." In 1908, however, Belyi, who had split with Blok, called Blok "a talented portrayer of nothing" and said that "The Beautiful Lady turned out to be the most venomous caterpillar, later decaying into a whore and an imaginary quantity something like the square root of minus one." In 1911 Blok first read parts of *Retribution* to a literary audience at Viacheslav Ivanov's. Gorodetskii was impressed by the poem's fresh insights and the richness and variety of details of everyday life. Ivanov, on the contrary, saw the poem as a decomposition, a decline or ruination following from apostasy, a product of nominalism.

The legend of Blok grew up around the view that Blok himself was a romantic symbol of suffering. It was known that Blok earned little by his literary work, and this was rather widely and very sympathetically discussed in certain liberal circles. It was also known that Blok had received some money from his father and that he, unlike others, was, as Piast put it, systematically spending capital. He would dine and drink late, watch variety shows, spend long evenings with prostitutes, for whom his affection is also legendary. Gorkii tells the story told him by one girl of how she was with Blok one night when she was tired, how she slept in his lap and he caressed and comforted her. Blok noted in his diary in the late fall of 1911 what he felt remained of one wild night. Who reads it now can sense the loneliness and the unhappiness involved and the pathetic absurdity:

> I'm not myself at all.... I tear her lace and batiste, in these coarse hands and pointed heels there is some sort of force and mystery. The hours with her—tormenting, fruitless. I take her back. Something sacred, a daughter, precisely, a child. She disappears in the alley.... It's cold, sharp, the water in all the branches of the Neva is high, everywhere the night at 6 in the morning when I return home is like 6 in the evening.
>
> Today is lost, of course. A walk, a bath, something in my chest is painful, I feel like moaning because this eternal night preserves and multiplies ten times the one and the same feeling—to madness. I almost want to cry.

Blok could not find any faith or construct any system which by activity would have provided an avenue of escape from his isolation. His integrity and idealism and fervor set him apart from most people's behavior. He was disaffected and disillusioned by the world. He was tormented that men were satisfied with being less than men, that a kind of acceptable profanity, sometimes even of animal savagery, characterized social life. Once on a streetcar with Chukovskii, Blok remarked that he often shut his eyes not to have to look at the monkeys. "Are they really monkeys?" Chukovskii asked. "You mean you really don't know this?" Blok said. Blok called one cycle of poems "Strashnyi mir" (The Terrible World), but the world of his life then, which he said it was still too early to quit, he called terrible *and* beautiful.

Blok and his wife went abroad together twice before the First World War, traveling through Germany, France, and Italy. Neither trip particularly influenced Blok, although both trips temporarily assuaged his restiveness and dissatisfaction with himself. One of the "results" of the first trip was the cycle of beautiful poems called "Ital'ianskie stikhi"

(Italian Verses), and from the second trip came the full-length play—much in the manner of a medieval morality play—*The Rose and the Cross.*

Blok was apprehensive that war would come, but when it finally came, in 1914, he was indifferent. He had no desire to fight in what seemed to him a senseless struggle leading to mutual destruction for both sides. He did finally enlist as a kind of company clerk and served with a forward engineers' company. His wife worked behind the lines as a nurses' aide. Blok greeted Soviet termination of Russian participation in the war sympathetically.

The 1917 Revolution at first found him excited and hopeful, but he never joined the Communist Party. He worked for the Provisional Government's commission investigating the records of tsarist ministers, and he was a member of the Soviet government's board of directors of the State theaters. He also served as chairman of the Petrograd division of the All-Russian Union of Poets and as a director of the Petrograd division of the All-Russian Writers' Union.

In January 1918, Blok completed his poem *The Twelve*, printed in *Znamia Truda* (The Banner of Labor) in March 1918, given a public reading by Blok's wife, and published separately as a little book in May. The poem not only went through several printings and editions in a few years but also was translated into Italian, French, German, English, and other languages. It was and is Blok's best-known work, considered by most to be an extraordinarily suggestive and effective poem expressing the essence of the Russian Revolution and its time. Its appearance caused a sensation. Some said it was blasphemous hooliganism; others, the beginning of a new literary age, the Bolshevist credo. Whether for or against the poem, reaction was strong. Blok was incontrovertibly famous. On April 25, 1921, he was honored enthusiastically with a "personal" evening in the Theater of Drama in Petrograd.

Blok had followed his time as best he could and had tried, as best he could, to see beyond it. In January 1918, the month in which he wrote *The Twelve*, he remarked to Chukovskii: "But I see the wings of an angel behind the shoulders of each Red Guardsman." He was disappointed by the opposition of Merezhkovskii, Gippius, and the Social Democrats. He sincerely believed that he, not they, understood what was happening in Russia and what had to happen, but he valued their good opinion and feared the consequences of the misunderstanding of so many intelligent people. The very censure Briusov had leveled at the poetasters of the late nineteenth century, that "technical barbarism" (tekhnicheskoe odichanie) which he had said they were guilty of, was leveled at Blok by Zinaida Gippius herself. Others, such as Osip Brik, sat in the middle, arguing that poetry was too important for a poet to allow it to be given over to partisan political hassles. Trotsky felt that he cut through the controversy by his understanding that Blok, of course, was not "one of us," but that *The Twelve* was "the most significant work of our time."

After *The Twelve* Blok produced nothing of comparable value except for several critical and theoretical articles. The two volumes of poetry that he published, *Behind the Border of the Past* and *The Grey Morning*, were collections of early poems. People said that he was as good as dead. He was, in fact, terribly ill. Toward the end of 1920 and the beginning of 1921, it became clear that he was dying. However, he worked until the very end, filled with plans and versions of the unfinished chapters of *Retribution* and of new plays and articles and with a sense of a new poetry.

Whatever he and others then felt his future could have been, in the beginning of the twenties, as Western literature was on the verge of an unusual brilliance, his past had been remarkable. After his death the romantic legend around him continued: that he was the long-suffering poet of the Beautiful Lady, lost and foundering in a hostile age. Now that some forty years have passed since his death, we can see that he was the chief—possibly the only—Russian Symbolist poet, the poet whose work extended the great tradition of Russian poetry and from whose work, albeit in sundry and even contradictory ways, modern Russian poetry followed.

III

Blok's Critical Position

CULTURE VS. CIVILIZATION

> Sooner or later you have to answer for every step you take, and to take a step now is difficult, most difficult of all, I suppose, in literature.—A. Blok

The Russian Symbolists, missionaries in the sense that they were representatives of a cult, poets working out a program, tended to distort literary history to satisfy their convictions of its future. Their surveys of the historical moments of literary symbolism were usually realignments of the past designed to emphasize the cogency of their then present theory. Perhaps this kind of argument, interesting for its indication of what the Russians took to be their chief sources, is most satisfactorily summarized in Briusov's article "Toward a History of Symbolism." He proceeds from the viewpoint of Maeterlinck's phrase, "With us the *I* is more profound than the 'I' of passions and of reason," to distinguish in the history of Western culture two poetic traditions or lines of development. One he associates with Sophocles, Shakespeare, Goethe, and Pushkin; the other, with the occult choruses of Aeschylus, the mystics of the Middle Ages, William Blake's prophetic books, and the "incomprehensible verses" of Edgar Poe and Tiutchev. This second line he calls "the lyric," and he defines lyricism as that poetry which provokes in the reader "completely particular movements which I call *frames of mind*." The success and hegemony in art of the hermetic movement he identifies historically with Egypt, India, Hellenistic Alexandria, the "height" of the Middle Ages in Europe, and contemporary Russia. Neither Neo-Classicism, which as generalization he identifies with Racine and as a picture of life with Molière, nor Romanticism, he says, brought the development of poetry closer to the essence of the soul. He calls Lessing, Goethe, and Schiller semi-Neo-Classicists who opened up the way for Romanticism by their criticism. He calls Tieck, Hugo, and Byron outstanding Romantics, "destroyers of the old order," whose essential work was to destroy.

"Baudelaire completed this revolutionary bacchanalia by raising his voice in song to the Devil." The way to French Symbolism was opened by the pre-Raphaelites. He takes Rossetti's "Proserpine" as a typical example. Rossetti, he says, extended Romanticism through consciousness of artistic devices, insisting that "figure and color are only intermediaries between the spectator and the artist." Symbolism proper was inaugurated by Rimbaud, Verlaine, and Mallarmé, "each of whom made an original contribution to the reform of the language of poetry."[1]

Seen in these terms, Symbolism was, Briusov thought, like other literary schools, only a stage in the evolution of poetry:

> I have no hope of Symbolism developing farther. It is only a transition to a new poetry. It even seems that it has already finished its business. The old poetry is in pieces.... Symbolism has created a completely new, still untested instrument for transmitting the innermost movements of the soul.... When you get deep into Maeterlinck's drama... you begin to feel the air of a new era in the history of man.

It is this "deeper drama," the drama of language, characteristic of several poets who came after Blok, that Blok tried to work out in his poetry. It is this tension in Blok's poetry which distinguishes it from the poetry of Symbolists contemporary to him, which, in fact, suggests that only Blok's poetry is, among that of all his contemporaries, successfully Symbolist.

The nineteenth-century Russian poetic tradition had become corrupted in the last part of the century. The powerfully imaginative poetry of Tiutchev and the skilled, emotionally impressive and socially significant poetry of Nekrasov were bowdlerized into sentimental or sententious poetastering, as in Surikov's "The Poor Man's Fate," Pleshcheev's "My Little Garden," Nadson's "At a Fresh Grave," Apukhtin's "I've No Regrets that I Wasn't Loved by You," or made into a kind of effete exoticism, as in the work of Fofanov and Lokhvitskaia. Not that these poets did not want to be "realists"; rather, they had little talent and enjoyed what prominence they did chiefly by default. Historically, their work is squeezed in between that of Pushkin, Tiutchev, Fet, Nekrasov, and the important lyricists of the first half of the nineteenth century and that of the Symbolists, the Acmeists, and the brilliant lyricists of the first third of the twentieth century. Their influence on the poets who came after them, the Symbolists, is rather small: one can find certain similar figures and rhetorical devices, for example, but, unlike deliberate Symbolist use of Nekrasov's or Fet's dactyllic meters or of Tiutchev's images, the similarity is the result of a partial coincidence of attitude.

Unlike so-called Parnassian poetry, Symbolist poetry did not involve rejection of the sense of a poet's social obligation. In fact, the transition in Merezhkovskii's work from poetry of a "civic" character to poetry of a "symbolist" character is connected with his elaboration of a system of belief which he thought more nearly adequate to reality than mere political opinion or agitation. Blok himself, generally apolitical, not only took part in the 1905 revolutionary demonstration but also from time to time throughout his life wrote patently political verse, of which *The Twelve* is usually taken as an extraordinary example.

An analogous transition characterizes the poetry of Vladimir Solov'ëv from whom Blok derived the other side of his early poetic "theory," the notion of a mystical Lady. Solov'ëv gradually but discernibly moved away from a sensitive but slack kind of love poetry to an explicitly mystical poetry celebrating the existence of a heroine and a world—Sophia, Divine Wisdom, and the reality of the metaphysical context—inaccessible except through the lustrations of his own poetry. There is a kind of absurd, high seriousness in the cult of Sophia emphasized by Anna Schmidt's maintaining that she was She. Solov'ëv cajoled her; Blok later, when she importuned him, refused to have anything to do with her. But when Blok married, his friends Belyi and Sergei Solov'ëv, as mentioned before, apparently seriously believed that the marriage was mystical, all the more because Blok's wife's first name was Liubov' (Love). All this was the absurdity; the rest was in its way sensible, as one understands from Vladimir Solov'ëv's letter to Romanova in 1873:

> Ever since I began to think seriously, I have realized that the existing order (chiefly the social and civil order...) is not what it ought to be.... The present condition of mankind... must be changed, transformed.

That attitude which fashioned a transcendental philosophy dominated by a female figure of beauty and wisdom—whom Solov'ëv asserted he had actually seen three times—began from social disaffection and offered its discoveries as social reform, ultimately to be consummated in revelation of the Heavenly Kingdom through the offices of the Lady of Wisdom. She was "the substance of the Holy Ghost hovering over the watery darkness of the world coming into being."

Early in his life Solov'ëv was a follower of Slavophilism; subsequently, he was for a time involved with the Roman Catholic Church, but he finally believed in a fusion of all the Eastern and Western Christian churches. His ideas were much influenced by various German philosophers and idealists and by Tiutchev's philosophy of history. His poetry, associated by its attitude with the work of Aleksei Tolstoy and Tiutchev, worked its wonder on the young Blok, on Belyi, and on other Symbolists. Blok said in a letter to E. P. Ivanov that he considered Solov'ëv's poetry about the Beautiful Lady a "unique *revelation*" but Solov'ëv's theologizing "intolerable *boredom*."

In the period following the stage initiated by Briusov (1894–98) and preceding the stage coincident with the publication of *The Balance* (1904–09), the Russian Symbolists were engaged in consolidating in poetry the hypostatized antithetical worlds of actuality and metaphysics, as if everything came really in pairs of opposites to be composed into poetry. One finds this kind of thinking in Merezhkovskii's work and even in Solov'ëv's, for whom meaning lies only in a final, mystical apotheosis. It is this sense of real contradiction and real conciliation (through the figure of the Lady), implying always social transformation and the discovery of meaning, for which Blok admired Solov'ëv and which Blok borrowed from him. Solov'ëv suggests this opposition in a poem, "Milyi drug" (Dearest Friend), which begins:

> Dearest friend, don't you perceive
> That everything seen by us
> Is only shimmering, only shadows
> Of what's invisible to eyes?

The poem ends by declaring that the only correspondence, the only communication, is the dumb welcome of heart by heart.

Blok did not begin with Solov'ëv's convictions. Rather, he appropriated only an aspect of them, and even that aspect he did not keep for very long. In June 1901—in what he called his mystical summer—he wrote the poem "I Apprehend You," the epigraph to which is the last two lines from Solov'ëv's poem "What Are Words For?":

> And you'll shake off the painful drowsiness
> Of ordinary consciousness in longing and in love.

The actual condition which Solov'ëv's poem assumes is one of pain, from which the desired relief is obtained by a beauty that will perfectly realize emotion as meaning. Blok's poem goes on to attempt to realize the vision in the pain, that is, to dramatize what Solov'ëv's poem promises and to substantiate the faith. Blok's poem gives the drama of the present against the future and suggests, dependent on the actualization of the vision, the real drama of the past against the future in the present moment.

Предчувствую Тебя. Года проходят мимо —
Всё в облике одном предчувствую Тебя.

Весь горизонт в огне — и ясен нестерпимо,
И молча жду, — тоскуя и любя.

Весь горизонт в огне, и близко появленье,
Но страшно мне: изменишь облик Ты,

И дерзкое возбудишь подозренье,
Сменив в конце привычные черты.

О, как паду — и горестно, и низко,
Не одолев смертельные мечты!

Как ясен горизонт! И лучезарность близко,
Но страшно мне: изменишь облик Ты.

I apprehend You. Despite the passing years
I apprehend You still in a constant form.

The horizon's all on fire and intolerably clear,
And I wait in silence—*in longing and in love.*

The horizon's all on fire, and the coming's near,
But I'm afraid: You'll change Your form,

And arouse an irreverent suspicion,
Finally altering Your accustomed lines.

O, how I'll fall, sorrowfully and low,
Not having conquered the deadly dreams!

How clear the horizon is! The radiance is near.
But I'm afraid: You'll change Your form.

The drama is nascent. We do not feel it so much as we expect it. What is important is that our attention is drawn to it, to the agony between the "I" and the real form which the "I" figures vaguely in dreams. We are given the sense of ecstasy involved in simultaneous foreboding and enthusiastic expectation of a mystical, ultimate moment in which everything will either finally succeed or finally fail. Meanwhile we are moved by the poem as the poet is moved—"in longing and in love." Solov'ëv's poem applies the phrase to the savior-symbol itself.[2] In Blok's poem, the phrase characterizes the present activity of the poet or his persona. It moves us toward drama but does not initiate us into the particular rites of love which the poem is about. We have a present fear of conflict; we do not actually have the conflict. Until the drama comes about really, we do not know quite where we are, and neither does the poet. Perhaps that is why to end the poem he used the formal device of returning to the middle words and, through them, to his "middle" feeling, what comes between the dream and the irreverency. The favored "Symbolist" word *luchezarnost'* (radiance) in the last two lines suggests that the best way out of the dilemma is to take the poem as more seriously mystical than we are prepared to admit from a reading of the first ten lines. The poem is not preamble to dream. The poet wants to come awake, to get to reality whatever it does to him, to *be* even though the present is continually shunted off toward the future. Probably the difficulty is that the poet cannot count on the substance of his vision; at least, he does not.

The figure he wants to symbolize creeps back into his own state of being or total emotional attitude. The Lady (assuming the "You" is the Beautiful Lady) matters here less as consummation than as contemporary perception. However you "see" her, you do see her; unfortunately, you have no way of being sure that she "sees" you, that is, that your perception is reciprocated and is, therefore, a viable activity.

The difference between Blok's understanding here and the understanding carried in Verlaine's "Familiar Dream" is clear:

> Je fais souvent ce rêve étrange et pénétrant
> D'une femme inconnue, et que j'aime et qui m'aime.

Verlaine's lady is known by the charm and power of the verse. This is quite adequate. She does not otherwise exist. The lines invoke the substance of the dream; they conjure up the lady who, committed to the poet, we are told, must come. The poet says he does not know her but loves her and that she loves him. That is, she *is* the verse which names her. She is generated by the verse. What happens in Blok's poem is that the symbols are tilted: because in his poem of love we do not know how much the lady loves, we are left with the impression that she does not do anything; but a symbol must define its analogy if it is to preserve itself, to keep reality in the poem. We are told that the Lady lies ahead, but that is not enough; the poem is not about that. We know that a symbol must always lie really ahead, but from the experience or content of faith, not from principles of faith.

Blok's poem is closer to drama and to that irony which ultimately involves drama than is Solov'ëv's. We are offered a conflict between aspects of the author's understanding, a lyric or Romantic attitude which adumbrates a dramatic resolution. We can get the idea of the poem fairly easily, but a symbolic image is not yet there.

Turning to Blok's critical work, one sees that Blok understood that one does not just put it there, as in pastiche. Blok also understood that to keep the symbols working the poet needs a system. Although he never elaborated a system as powerful as Mallarmé's or as workable as Yeats's, still he moved toward one. That is what all his critical articles are about. Most of his book reviews in magazines or newspapers are only pleasant: they suggest what sort of book they are dealing with and take up a moderate or an enthusiastic tone, depending on Blok's likes or dislikes. But his articles go farther: their subjectivity is not arbitrary response. Their subjectivity follows from a sense of personal obligation to work out adequately a particular kind of poetry. Many of the terms used are conventional or unsatisfactorily abstract, but even these terms seem clearly to work toward a system of real, poetic meaning. One sees in them a further elaboration of that poetics which the French Symbolists introduced, a continuation of the modern revolution in poetry.

It is not always continuation in the way a line is geometrically continued. Changes of place and time and of habit of mind altered and extended what had previously been discovered. Blok's mother, for example, had translated Rimbaud's sonnet on colors and vowels. Synesthetic perception of color in verse had become important to the Russian Symbolists. Writing in *Epopeia* (Epopee) Belyi insisted that:

> In Goethe's theory of colors there is a splendid passage about the moral perception of colors, by which color becomes transformed into a symbol of the moral world... so that the poet comments on himself by his choice of color....
>
> Colors are the substance of a poet's soul: it's not for nothing that Goethe always advocated during his whole life a theory of light.

Blok extended this to a theory of meaning. In his diary he epitomized a significant moment in his life, the early years of his marriage and the 1905 revolution, as a color-change not unlike a sea-change:

> Scarcely had my fiancée become my wife than the lilac worlds of the first revolution seized us and carried us into their whirlpool. First I, who had so long secretly wished to perish, was drawn into the grey-scarlet, silvery stars, the pearls and amethysts of the blizzard. My wife followed me, and for her this transition (from the difficult to the easy, from the impermissible to the permissible) was tortuous, and much more difficult than for myself.

In an early article called "Colors and Words," he emphasizes the importance of a poem's imagery and the unimportance of the critic's label "Symbolist," with which, as he sees it, critics try to dress out poets for their own convenience at the expense of the poetry and, worse yet, with which hopeful poets try to identify themselves to guarantee success. A poet's effort should rather be to return to and to restore that vitality of sensation which Blok says distinguishes children from adults. Children are the people who see, and a poem must see also: "They say that there are more words than colors, but perhaps for the graceful writer, for the poet, those words are sufficient which correspond to colors." He cites a poem by Sergei Gorodetskii called "Heat," to which he adds a footnote that anticipates his own subsequent effort:

I think that there is a very marked tendency in all Russian poetry to break with the abstract and to involve the concrete, the actualized. The odor of a living flower is more refreshing than perfume.

Blok says specifically that "the motion of light and of color is emancipatory," that it even "fathers beautiful thought," for the future development of which there may be found, he says, "means more subtle than ready words." As painting is itself nature, so a poem must be transubstantiation of what is dead in such a social completeness that the aesthetic perceptions are the required moral judgment, as Baudelaire was first to show.

Blok's idea of the poet's place in society followed from his understanding of his time as a time of fear and stupidity, and of people's maniacal devotion to "causes," which they expressed as if performing real rituals but which were actually mock rituals. He sensed a kind of self-subversion which he thought the artist's obligation was to locate within moral perspectives and thereby to end.

Our actuality occurs in a red light. The days get continually louder with shouts and waving red flags; in the evening, the city, dozing for a moment, is blood-red in the sunset. At night redness sings on the dresses, on the cheeks, and in the market-place on the lips of the women for sale. Only the pale morning chases away the last tint from the hollow faces.

Everything we live by and in which we see the meaning of our life does thus flash by in mad hysteria. Set on fire on all sides, we gyre in the air like the wretched masks Edgar Poe's revengeful Fool caught unawares. But we, children of the age, fight with this vertigo. Some sort of devilish vitality helps us to burn but not burn up.[3]

The poet, as Rimbaud said of himself, is the one who "alone has the key to this barbaric parade."

Much of Blok's critical writing is incomprehensible because it is deliberately impressionistic. For example, in the article "Russkaia literatura" (Russian Literature), he separates Lermontov and Gogol from

Dostoevsky in this way: waking from a dream of eternal harmony, Dostoevsky can no longer discover it and burns up, but Gogol and Lermontov unconsciously and non-actually fly toward it and burn brightly but do not perish. It is impossible to understand what Blok means by the phrase that cyclones have always hovered over Russian literature, or by the phrase, "May the rider's happiness noiselessly flow on, the rider who on a tired horse is wheeling around the swamp under a great, green star." This kind of approach reproduces the imagery then in vogue, as if literary judgment were equivalent to a drawing by Vrubel or Roerich, but it does not lead us into literature so much as it leads us into Blok's poetry. It indicates that Blok considered the greatest difficulty was to work out a visual understanding, a picture of the motion of emotion which would catch up the age and its people.

Blok's judgment was acute. He argued that art had to contain the public conscience and not some particular religious doctrines, that popular Symbolist imitators would for lack of talent disappear as quickly as they appeared, and that there was nothing wrong with lyric poetry which a good poet could not cure. He was also right that art is "for nothing" in practical terms but that the artist cannot work from that assumption or even from that skepticism. It is understanding of art as illustration of beauty and of meaning, Blok says in "Tri voprosa" (Three Problems), that "shows the contemporary artist the joyful, free and obligatory way through the abyss of contradictions to the summits of art. The voice of duty draws one on to tragic catharsis." His language is not precise, as we ask critical language to be, but he is clearly trying to categorize a precise complex of understanding in all its complexity.

That he understands the complexity clearly, in both its technical and historic aspects, is articulate in this article, which he wrote as a response to Filosofov's attack on his article "On Lyric Poetry." In the first number of *Zolotoe Runo* (The Golden Fleece) in an article called "Tozhe tendentsiia" (This, Too, Is Tendentiousness), Filosofov accused Blok of deliberately escaping from life by, and into, art and asked if the title "man" were not higher than the title "poet." Blok, he said, evidently regards "poet" as superior to "man."

Blok's reply appeared in the following number of the same magazine. At the time, Blok said, when the new Russian art was still persecuted, almost all serious artists waited out the storm of opposition. For these men, Blok said, the "how" of art, the problem of form, was a "fighting word."

By great effort and ability a sense of form was evolved. The finest example of the effort and the power involved, Blok noted, was Briusov's work, in particular his introductions to his *Urbi et Orbi.*

The success of the new art meant also the traducing of it by talentless imitators. The problem of the serious artist then became the "what" of art, an issue of content raised by the imitators who lacked the talent adequately to handle the form. It was Belyi, Blok said, who, in his early articles, first advanced the problem of "what" over the problem of "how."

Among the pile of lyrics published by high-school students in the magazines and newspapers (all, Blok says, written in the new manner) and among the unnoticed work of the real, serious artists there arose the third problem: "In times like these there arises a third, most tempting, most dangerous, but especially most Russian question: 'what for?' *The problem of the necessity and the usefulness of art.*" Even if it be a journalistic question, Blok insists, it is one that a great artist will respond to—precisely as Ibsen responded, Ibsen whom he calls the "standard of our epoch, the last universal writer." Given Ibsen's talent, social consciousness is an impetus and a vehicle for thematic expansion, as in Ibsen's *Catiline.* Blok quotes Mikhailovskii with approval: "Each artist, I think, must be a publicist at heart." He adds that no kind of Symbolism can avoid joining issue on this point. The artist who fails to acknowledge a social obligation commits himself to barbarism, to beating his head against the wall of his own irresponsibility.

The problem behind this problem is another "how": how may the seemingly useless and the obviously useful be meaningfully coordinated? Recent research, Blok says, indicates that folk art, particularly folk-song, commingled the two: "Thus the connecting link between art and work, between beauty and usefulness was rhythm." Ibsen's work, Blok adds, indicates that that rhythm for Blok's time is *duty,* the acceptance of the responsibility of defining the meaning of all social activity. It is a treacherous, narrow, but direct route between the Scylla and Charybdis of the beautiful and the obligatory. It is the tormenting problem that lies behind Verlaine's lines in "Le Ciel est, par-dessus le toit," which, Blok wrote Sologub, were for him "one of the first clear revelations of the new poetry":

—Qu'as-tu, fait, ô toi que voilà
  Pleurant sans cesse,
Dis, qu'as-tu fait, toi que voilà,
  De ta jeunesse?

A miracle is wanted, Blok says, a Demiurge to put together the halves—the butterfly of beauty and the camel of utility—to make the word flesh, to make the artist a man. Behind the present contradiction stands, and through tragic catharsis will come, the "errant hero" in the "theater of the future."

In this article Blok lucidly states what he believes art should be and should be about. Neither in his poetry, his articles, nor in his letters, however, can one find any instructions or any specific "method" worked out. One finds, instead, a sense of drama, bright images, and charm.

One of Blok's attributes was warm generosity, a generosity apparent also in his criticism: when he differs from another's point of view, he is polite; when he has no respect for a pose, he is firm; when he talks of the composition or values of art, he is modest in order to do as little violence to art as possible. This generosity is all the more remarkable because of Blok's intellectual independence. He endured the blandishments of his friends but declined to work through doctrines other than those he considered necessary for himself. He lacked, as he knew, intellectual discipline, a lack which other people often mistook as candor and naïveté, or, as Makovskii mistook it, stupidity.[4] A closer reading of his critical prose would have shown them not merely that Blok was an honest man but mostly that Blok had a sensitive and honest mind. He could not reduce a complex to any other terms.

In his article "Ironiia" (Irony), for example, Blok tries to move toward a complete social understanding through irony, the disease of the age. He locates the concept historically in Russian poetry and life by using as epigraph some lines from Nekrasov, which begin "I do not like your irony." As Blok sees it, people are to be characterized in one of two ways: either they are possessed by the demonic laughter of self-abdication or they are frighteningly serious about life and about themselves, not only incapable of distinguishing between Dante's Beatrice and Sologub's furry fictional halucination the *nedotykomka*, but, worse, in the amorality of what Blok calls their drunken conception of truth, capable of asserting that Beatrice and the *nedotykomka* are identical. Irony is not a new phenomenon, and its social use and meaning are not new either. Blok points out that Dobroliubov discerned three main kinds: naively candid, cunningly placid, and discreetly bitter. But Dobroliubov himself, Blok says, suffered from the contrary disease in an age to which the natural reaction was the work of Koz'ma Prutkov. Moreover, Dobroliubov was pre-Revolutionary; he never anticipated, as Blok puts it, Andreev's "red laughter" or Dostoevsky's piercingly deep irony.

Blok's article is not adequate to our understanding of irony or the literary use of irony in modern novels or even in Sologub's *Melkii bes* (The Petty Demon), to which Blok refers, but it is adequate announcement of Blok's consciousness of the need for response to what he calls the disease of individualism, the disease of irony. He cites Gogol, Ibsen, and Vladimir Solov'ëv to the effect that one must abjure oneself to find oneself, to get beyond the game of self-consummation. One must play through the mask of self to reach what Blok believes is the sacred reality behind it. One must so work the marionettes that the real and other meaning comes clear. What he refers to is the dramatic conflict in a man cut off from society between his experiences and the perdurable aspect of himself. In "Stikhiia i kul'tura" (Environment and Culture), he says explicitly that mankind is revenging itself on itself, alienating itself from its necessary environment and its members from the whole society. The individual lives, he says, between immolation and purification. The airplane that tries to fly from choosing flies simultaneously to its own destruction, just as the machine that rebuilds the earth builds its own catastrophe.

The artist's obligation, Blok says in "O sovremennom sostoianii russkogo simvolizma" (The Present State of Russian Symbolism), as if following Belinskii, is "to show and not to prove." Each artist desires, he says, quoting Fet, "to report himself through his soul without a word." Blok argues that Symbolism is the necessary artistic method of apprehending reality and is therefore chronologically unspecifiable. The idea of Symbolism as potentiality and method Blok calls the "thesis." It is, to cite Briusov, the attitude that the artist "is free in this magic world filled with correspondences"; that the artist creates as he wills, for the world is his; that, as Sologub put it, the world itself is the substance of the artist's dreams. The artist, Blok says,

> ...is the solitary possessor of a hidden treasure; but there are others around [him] who know about the treasure.... Consequently, *we*, the few who know, are the Symbolists....
>
> The Symbolist is from the start a theurgist, that is, the possessor of secret knowledge, behind which there lies secret action.

The poet's job is the elaboration of understanding of this action, of moving from the initial, subjective apperception of mystery to the essential motion of mystery itself, contained in and by the poem, a network of ineluctable images:

He [the poet] sees in it [the mystery] a treasure, over which the fern's flower blooms on a July midnight; and he wants to pick in the light-blue midnight "the light-blue flower."

From these worlds, Blok says, come musical sounds and evocations, which are almost words and which begin to turn color, finally devolving

...into that predominant color which I may most easily term purple-lilac.... The gold sword, piercing the purple of the lilac worlds, flames up dazzlingly—and transfixes the theurgist's heart. A face among the heavenly roses begins to become transparent; a voice becomes distinct; dialogue arises.

Although Blok takes as the starting point of dialogue Solov'ëv's poem about three visions of the Beautiful Lady ("Tri svidaniia" [Three Meetings]), he considers that same point also to be the termination of the thesis. The antithesis is the alteration of the figure of the vision and the self-distortion of the dialogue, the debasement of the indescribable music of pure passion into the catchy tunes of gypsy love-songs, and the ironic mockery of the vitality of the understanding by the mimicry of dead dolls and marionettes. It is the mimetic repetition of the acts of life in terms of the relevancy of an inversion of values, a game played among the devils of one's own consciousness, the reduction of life to a joke.

The inevitable has occurred: my own magic world has become the arena of my personal actions, my "anatomic theater" or *show-booth*, where I myself play a role side by side with my amazing dolls (*ecce homo*!).... In other words, I have made my own life art (a very obvious purpose in all European *decadence*).

The language of Blok's criticism gives phrases to his poetry. His criticism is a skein of ideas in images or of words whose meanings, though insisted upon in the criticism, come clear only in the poetry, if they come clear at all. This article, "The Present State of Russian Symbolism," is coincident with some of his most successful lyrics and with the early work on his long poem *Retribution*. In it he uses certain words that run through earlier poems—words like "secret," "beautiful lady," "roses," "gold sword," "purple-lilac," "darkness," "radiance," "dusk," "apparition," "doll." He refers to Vrubel's work, quotes from Solov'ëv, Belyi, Briusov, Ivanov, and Wilde, and, what is most interesting, he uses lines or variants of lines from his own poems as definitions of the method and principles of verse. Certain concepts touched on in the article are later carried as definitive propositions in his poetry. For example, the opening lines of the prologue to *Retribution* are a description of what he considers the methods by which art achieves permanency; the prologue begins with the line "Life is without beginning or end." In the article, written about a year before the prologue to *Retribution*, he talks about the creation of art as a "self-accomplished fact" and of his impotency before the artistic transformation of his personal life—an artistic transformation which is coincident with his life but which, unlike himself, is neither alive nor dead. "What is created in this way—by the artist's conjuring will and with the help of [his] many petty demons...—has neither beginning nor end; it is not alive, not dead."

Blok here takes beginning and end as terminals of change; in the later poem he takes the same terms as the limits of the definition of permanency. In the article he says that a poem through its symbols is inaccessible to alteration; in the poem he says that the symbols themselves construct the limits of alteration and thereby transfix a poem as continually meaningful experience. It is not, he comes to say, the absence of beginning and end which makes a poem permanent but, on the contrary, the rigid formal imposition of them. He understands a poem to be not an infinite metempsychosis of the poet's personality, a Romantic view, but a special and dramatic interfusion of the symbolic aspects of the general and the individual, in which the merely personal vanishes in the greater circle of organized response.

This greater circle of meaning involves the meaning of social events and the poet's social obligations. However, Blok argues, it does not allow a sociological interpretation of poetry. Poetry proceeds from poetry. A poem is the center of meaning where all appearances commingle, as a theater houses all the figures of a play:

> In counterbalance to the judgment of vulgar criticism that, as it were, "the revolution seized us," we [Symbolists] affirm the exact opposite: the revolution happened not only in this world, but also in others; it was one of the manifestations of the clouding over of the gold and the triumph of the lilac dusk, that is, of those events of which we were witnesses in our own souls.... And Russia herself in the rays of this new civic spirit (by no means Nekrasov's, only by tradition connected with Nekrasov) turned out to be our own soul.

Art, as Yeats said, is a vision of reality. Blok was continually concerned with the precision and the purity of the vision.

> The reality I have written about is the only one which for me gives meaning to life, to the world, and to art. Perhaps those [transcendental] worlds exist, perhaps not. For those who say they don't we are simply "decadents, you know,"

composers of unprecedented sensations, and we talk about death now only because we're tired.

He himself, he says, is not proselytizing. Because his poems are only a detailed elaboration of what his article is about, he requests those who do not understand them not to waste time on them:

> Diligence is as understandable as it is pitiful. The sun of naïve realism has set; to comprehend anything at all outside Symbolism is impossible.... To be an artist is to weather the wind from the worlds of art which are not at all like this world but only bear terribly on it. In those worlds there is neither cause nor effect, time nor space, the carnal nor the incorporeal, and the number of these worlds is infinite....
>
> Art is *Hell*.... The artist painstakingly traces each of his images out of the darkness of this Hell.

In the conflict between the public and the private aspects of himself, an artist should be, Blok says, a simple man politically and a child spiritually. He must not turn art to social use except as art establishes within its own conventions social meaning. Artists, he says in an open letter to Merezhkovskii, are neither scholars nor politicians, but people—people whose duty is to "catch the breath of life."

In a little series of articles—all there is of a projected book of art criticism—in vivid and powerful prose, Blok moves in, like a detective,on the function of art.

> What is art to do? "After all, all that art can do is to make the brute less evil," Flaubert thought. The brute, less; but man, more.[5]

Throughout the articles he implies very much what Pound later said, that art is news that stays news. Aesthetic organization of experience does not involve causal relationships; in fact, it removes the possibility of any.[6] Its object, in the sense of both artifact and aim, is its own perfection.

> ...I serve art, that third term which from any series of facts of the world of life leads me to a series of facts of another, of my own world: of the world of art.

Inevitably, even that vision of reality carried by music moves first from other than formal understanding of actuality. The personality of the poet is properly relevant only as instrument, the agent of the initial aesthetic organization, and of value only in so far as it is expunged in the interplay among a poem's impersonal images. Blok may say that he serves art, because his office seems to him a necessity for which he himself is not responsible. Although at moments he may seem to promote in his poems a personal vision or a personal understanding—that is, the uniqueness of the potentiality of his own personality—what he personally is doing, he suggests, is to become so involved with apprehension of an absolute world or series of interdependent relationships that he is made equivalent to that real vision. He would disappear as a man into the talent of his art. Furthermore, he is trying to show, as with the convincing immediacy of drama, how a gesture reveals the mystery that lies behind it.

Blok began with a different desire, asserting the exclusiveness of his personality in poetry by the adoration of a semi-private, mystical object, the Beautiful Lady. The Lady is not allegorically or analogically symbolic like Dante's, but is symbolic like Baudelaire's. She is an unassigned, unsuccessful symbol, an expression of hope and an extension of awareness. Examined closely, she seems really a sign, not a symbol. Blok tried to keep the Lady located in mind and, as it were, politically active, but because he himself (unlike Dante, as he says) had no allegorical or anagogical ladder to climb, the Lady served simply as a label for his own self-affirmation.

Blok was never much of a politician, but he did work within a general political frame. He admired Strindberg for his social consciousness and his democratic attitude. He esteemed Wagner, not merely for the ecstasy which overcame him when he first heard a Wagnerian opera, but for the fact that Wagner fought in the Dresden uprising of 1849, wrote "the social tetralogy *The Ring of the Niebelung*," tried to establish an universal theater at Bayreuth, and embodied in his art "creative contradictions" which inform on bourgeois civilization and argue for its end. He admired Ibsen for having turned poetry into a dramatic understanding of human relationships and potentialities and for having insisted, as Blok himself insisted, that all his creative work represented a single unity. Blok was aware, for example, that Ibsen revised the ending of his early play *Catiline* in an antiliberal direction, but he perceived clearly that, for all that, Ibsen was a rebel, and he quotes Ibsen's 1871 letter to Brandes:

> What you call freedom, I call liberties; and what I call the struggle for freedom is nothing other than the constant, vital effort to assimilate the idea of freedom.... The very concept of freedom is distinguished by the fact that it continually expands in so far as we endeavor to draw it into ourselves. Consequently, he who in the struggle for freedom stops and says, "I have it," shows that he has forfeited it.

In this article "Katilina" (Catiline) Blok puts Ibsen's play about Catiline against the analyses of Sallust's history, Cicero's arguments, and Plutarch's biography as kin to that understanding which he finds in Catullus' "Attis," a poem that he interprets as being a synthetic understanding of a given historical moment, the completion of which, as of all art, partly depends on the allusive nature of its formal elements. Life cannot be reduced to a scheme, Blok asserts: the very adequacy of any given schematization necessarily indicates the real, internal complexity which it is unable to comprehend. Any analysis other than aesthetic is only partial. The artist is always connected with a specific historical moment which he tries to complete through the perfectibility of form. It is this sense of perfection which prevents an artist from being a liberal, Blok said in response to a questionnaire, and requires that he give himself over, as Pushkin did, to the exigencies of craft, to what Blok calls his "mission," to the expression, as he wrote in "O naznachenii poeta" (The Poet's Job), of the

> ...fathomless depths of the psyche, inaccessible to the state or society, civilization's products,... where waves of sound roll like the waves of the ether that envelops the universe,... where there are rhythmic oscillations like those processes which form mountains, winds, ocean currents and the flora and fauna of the world.

This psychic depth is not more accessible to a poet than to another man, Blok says. On the contrary, he refers to Pushkin, who said that it was concealed from the poet perhaps more than from others: "Among the insignificant people of the world perhaps he is the most insignificant of all." Blok argues that the poet's job moves him initially against the mob, that is, against those agents and instruments of civilization who have not only abdicated their proper selves but also obscured essential human nature and value by imposition of a basically irrelevant superstructure. This is Blok's description of alienation. The distinction Pushkin made between personal and political freedom Blok finds no longer viable: they may be taken only in terms of activity, and in terms of activity they come to the same thing. They are only aspects of that "secret freedom" which one must work toward, which is never actual, and which is contained in all genuine artistic images. The world is really a composition of irreducible analogies, or, as Blok puts it, in terms of a theme which may be called an obsession with him: "A son perhaps in no way resembles a father except in one secret feature, but this feature makes the son and father similar."

What an artist is responsible for, Blok says, is the knowledge of the essence of actuality—what moves that which seems to move. Those values and faiths which moved the Western world from the Renaissance to the twentieth century are, he says, dead. As Rome existed for five hundred years after the birth of Christ, so the modern world may continue merely to exist, rotten and putrid. An artist must angrily oppose whatever would petrify him. That his anger not follow from the corruption of spite, he must keep in mind the knowledge of the greatness of that epoch of which any petty spite is unworthy. One of the best methods for preserving this knowledge is not to forget the fact of social inequality, not to debase it by dealing with it in other terms. "Knowledge of social inequality is exalted, dispassionate and wrathful." The artist must prepare himself ultimately to perceive greater events and, having perceived them, "to succeed in giving way before them,"[7] or, as we would say, to eliminate himself as personality through the formal reorganization of experience into meaning.

This is what Blok argues for in connection with his study of Catiline: not merely the transformation of rebellion into art, but the total view, or *way*, of life which so respects integrity and freedom that it always turns against actual restraint, privilege, or want. Most people, Blok says, simply do not know that things happen, that there are real moments in which real men move. And the few who think and experience are perplexed by the difficulty of adequately comprehending what has happened and is happening. The personal tragedy of the artist follows from this: that, even if he wants to, he cannot change the way he takes the world. The terrible torment is symbolized for Ibsen's Catiline, Blok says, as for all Ibsen's heroes (and, we may add, for Blok himself), by the antithetical, female symbols of the demonic or seductive woman that urges rebellion and the "morning star," the life-figure that leads to peace, both of which exist as simultaneous aspects of experience.

Politically, as Blok understands it, the dilemma may be represented by the antithetical relationship between the individual and the mass. In "Krushenie gumanizma" (The Decline of Humanism), he says the hegemony of the mass is coincident with the decline of those values of culture which distinguished the Renaissance and may be considered the intellectual basis of the structure of Western European society. The opposition between what he calls "culture" and "civilization" (using a dichotomy then current in Russia that followed German influence) is, he says, further complicated by changing degrees of their interdependence. Civilization without the common values of cultural unity is more terrible and more destructive than the raw vitality of barbarism. In such a civilization, in which the individual cannot be defined as part of a vital cultural heritage, specialization atrophies the organic processes of art, reducing art to meaningless pleasure. The rationalizations that constitute the value system of such a civilization by oversimplification deny life, the actual complexity of which, Blok says, responds only to the key of a tragic sense. "Style is rhythm." Having dissipated its style, European culture disintegrated into civilization, making available to the previously unparticipating mob fragments of that intellectual vitality and understanding which had made the human world so great. The equilibrium between man and nature on which human accomplishment had depended had been forfeited. A return of—or perhaps to—value depended, Blok believed, on redefinition of the relationship. This, he said, had been Kant's effort: a fundamentally fresh study of the structure of time and space. Kant was, Blok said, a product of civilization, but he was moreover a "product" who exploded civilization from the inside, a "wild artist," "that most cunning and crazy mystic."

Blok understands two times, two spaces. One he calls historic or calendrical; the other, incomputable and musical. The first is the unalterable condition of man's usual existence—what Blok calls civilized consciousness. The second is the time and space of "the elemental":

> We live in the other only when we feel our own proximity to nature, when we give ourselves over to the musical wave which issues from the universal orchestra. We need no sort of equilibrium of force to live in days, months, and years. This uselessness of the expenditure of creative activity quickly reduces the majority of civilized people to the level of mere inhabitants of the world. But equilibrium is essential to us in order for us to be close to the musical essence of the world—to nature, to the elemental.

Two aspects of the tragedy that is life are the continuation of the repressive force of ignorance and of the repressive force of reason. The third aspect, as Blok sees it, is the incapacity of culture to promote itself, to persuade men to act for their real self-interest. The general conditions under which human life occurs remain constant, although the response to them may be continually fresh. History can be represented in pictures—that is, as essential moments—because these moments are analogous to the real moments of choice or action in which man finds his being.[8] History is not moral. It does not represent the human instinct for perfection. It is indifferent and mysterious, perceptible only as the product of an inscrutable process. It is a series of associations. The present later will itself be taken as an analogy, irrespective of present choice. There is only the fact of movement, of relation, of drama, distinguished, Blok has it, by those actors in the theater and in history capable of the most motion and, consequently, the most meaning. Without the intensity of these heroes, "historical meaning" is lost. The moment loses its identity by becoming analogous only to itself, by becoming tautological. As Herbert Marcuse says, "The individual lives the universal fate of mankind. The past defines the present because mankind has not yet mastered its own history."[9]

Culture and civilization are the two aspects of control of history. By culture Blok means the work of the heroes proper, the best work, an age's understanding of itself, a man's understanding of himself, the fabrication of art and the apprehension of meaning.[10] Civilization is the effective product of culture, the systematic use of tools by which men manipulate their environment and themselves. Civilization means accomplishment; culture means value. Blok predicts hostility between Russian values and European accomplishment, meaning that culture, which explains *more*, is perdurable, that the fashion of a civilization is continually perishing and being recreated by imaginative talent. Only the individual can produce reality, since the given condition of and outside his existence is fragmentary, built into meaning only by the repeated acts of his imagination.

Blok's "General Plan of the *Historical Scenes*" is itself so brief that one may not rely heavily on it.[11] At most, the plan is the outline of a system. As experience is dualistic, referable immediately both to the object experienced and to the aesthetic organization of the act of experiencing, so the world itself may be represented as divided, the halves connected by the activity in each moment of the individual consciousness which guarantees the simultaneous reality of both halves. Culture, associated with imagination, knowledge, and law or symmetry, leads to beauty, perfection, ultimate freedom. Civilization, associated with social custom, manufacturing, and harnessing of elemental forces, leads to social institutions sanctioning justice. History is the total movement of all the individual moments of the conflict between these two antithetical "systems." The historical process might be described as a kind of continual opening and closing of a sphere—open in moments of opposition, closed in moments of discovery, which Blok identifies with the creative acts of the discovery of fire, the acts of Galileo, Newton, and Columbus—acts of culture provoking a fundamental alteration of civilization, that is, acts which establish new kinds of manufacture and social processes. Actuality is the approximate coincidence in any moment of the mutually hostile or indifferent halves. Actual coincidence is symbolic transcendence, when the half itself becomes whole, when the individual participates in the creation of history itself.

Music is taken as the meaningful relation among the fragments of experience; it is the system and the essence of actual revelations. It is the symbol both of being and of becoming, in so far as being makes itself manifest in a historical process. It is symbolic simultaneously of what is communal and anarchic, of the essence of analogy, and of that rebellious force within each individual which in the name of an impossible freedom cuts through all ethical imperatives. It is symbolic of change from what seems stable to what is immovable.

Blok's theory of the function of art hangs, like his poetry itself, halfway between the positions of the Romantics and the Moderns, between, say, the theories of Coleridge and Pasternak. Coleridge says in "On Poesy or Art":

> [Art] is the mediatress between, and reconciler of, nature and man. It is, therefore, the power of humanizing nature, of infusing the thoughts and passions of man into everything which is the object of his contemplation; color, form, motion, and sound are the elements which it combines, and it stamps them into unity in the mould of a moral idea.

And in *Statesman's Manual* Coleridge says:

> [Imagination is] that reconciling and mediatory power, which incorporating the reason in images of the sense, and organizing (as it were) the flux of the senses by the permanence and self-circling energies of the reason, gives birth to a system of symbols, harmonious in themselves, and consubstantial with the truths of which they are the conductors.

Pasternak's theory is found in his *Okhrannaia gramota* (A Safe-conduct):

> Art is realistic, like actuality, and symbolic, like a fact.... Art is also symbolic through the figure of its own pull. Its single symbol is in the brilliance and facultativity of images peculiar to all art. The interchangeability of images is the sign of the condition under which fragments of actuality are reciprocally undifferentiated. The interchangeability of images, that is, art, is the symbol of force....
>
> By nothing except the motile language of images, that is, by the language of accompanying signs, can force express itself, the fact of force, the force protracted in the instantaneous appearance. The direct speech of feeling is allegorical and there is nothing to substitute for it.... The ineluctable language of all art is allegory and symbolically speaks of force.

Blok is the link or the channel between Romanticism and Modernism in Russia.

For Blok, music is the symbol of that extraordinary vitality of the life of the world which, in the name of what is eternal, perishes and returns, drawing man ever closer to his essential self. In "The Decline of Humanism," he said:

> Man is getting closer to what really is; consequently, man is becoming more musical....
>
> In the vortex of the spiritual, political and social revolutions, having cosmic correspondences, a new selection of things is developing, a new man is being formed: man the human animal, the social animal, the moral animal is being rebuilt into an *artist*, to use Wagner's language.

Human gesture, or the total of human activity, to be understood must be taken aesthetically, that is, completely. Only he who does so—the artist—is competent "*passionately to live and to act.*" It is in this sense that the history of an artist is the portrait of a man.

IV

Poems

1898–1904

We met a brother on the road.—A. Belyi
To rise up against materialism.—Z. Gippius

In the preface to the 1911–12 edition of his *Collected Poems*, Blok apologizes for certain weak or childish early poems which in themselves, he says, are worthless:

But each *poem* forms an integral part of its chapter; several chapters form a *book;* each book is part of a trilogy; the whole trilogy I consider a "novel in verse": it is devoted to a unified circle of sensations and thoughts which occupied me during the first twelve years of conscious life.[1]

The principles which inform life as art are specific, self-sustaining patterns, unlike the variegated coincidences which constitute actual life. Blok is explicit about this: in the first, 1909 version of his autobiography he says:

Proof-readers and editors who respect words for what they are must know that there exists a *mathematics of language* (just as there are mathematics of all other arts) and, particularly, *in verse*. Consequently, to change words on a personal whim, whatever they may be, is at least uncivilized.

Once the pattern had been established, once the poem was written, Blok could not radically change it. Words are, he believed, infallible.[2] One may not deny that life which has been written into a poem. All Blok could do to the work that even he no longer wished to support was to locate it historically and leave it. In this 1912 preface he did just that.

However, as if in spite of these beliefs, Blok did edit, reissue, and attempt to revise his early work. In general, the "revision," with some exceptions, is either a reselection of poems or minor alterations that very seldom affect either form or substance.[3] In most of the instances in which, by revision, he eliminated a stanza or two from a poem, in still later "revision" he restored it. Blok felt that his poetry was the substance of himself. In the proposed 1918 introduction to an unpublished reedition of his first book, *Verses about the Beautiful Lady*, he said:

Each new edition of a book gives me an excuse for revising it. In the initial revisions, I meant to reveal its content as widely as possible; in the subsequent revisions, I worried over specifics and technique. But all this labor didn't satisfy me. In the first instance, I got lost in the mountain of material; in the second, I replaced some expressions with others more resourceful in a literary sense at the expense of the essential design. And I felt myself wandering in the forest of my own past while I couldn't think of using Dante's device which he chose when working on the *New Life*.

In *The New Life* Dante deals with his experience on three levels: narration of the experience itself; the poem, which is transformation of the experience; and explication of the poem.[4] Experience supplies material for poetry, of course, but it also moves against poetry. Precisely Blok's failure gives him the greatest possibility for writing successful poetry. The poetry overcomes the life. As Blok wrote his mother in October 1907: "The worse off you are—the better you can write, but one's life and one's calling are incompatible.... I have no real life." What he did was what he wrote—"A poet's words are his acts," he said. Art proceeds from life and leads to it. Symbolism for Blok is the way life is brought to life. As he jotted in his notebook: "Symbolism is poetry's remembering its original ends and efforts... specifically, *practical.* Art is a *practical* goal." Blok repeatedly emphasized the artist's necessary social responsibility *and* social indifference. To succeed the artist must transcend both himself and his society. In his essay "Intelligentsiia i revoliutsiia" (The Intelligentsia and the Revolution), he said that:

An artist's job, an artist's *obligation* is to see what is conceived, to hear that music with which "the air torn up by the wind" resounds....

To redo everything. So to arrange things that everything becomes new.... *This* is *revolution.*

The actuality of a word, in this revolutionary sense, depends for its vitality on the denigration of existing reality. Artistic content is genuine only in so far as it presently denies life-as-it-is in the name of life-as-freedom. Blok said:

Life is worth living only when one makes endless demands on it: all or nothing; when one waits for the unexpected; when one believes not in "what is not of this world" but in what must be in this world.

It is this missionary feeling of the necessity of total revolution—however implausible practically—that moves Blok's poems, even the poems about the Beautiful Lady, who in one aspect may be considered a convenient figure by which to represent the otherwise invisible concept of transcendent but immanent freedom.

In October 1904 Blok's first book of poetry was published: *Verses about the Beautiful Lady*, a collection of 93 of the almost eight hundred poems Blok had written by that time and later incorporated in the second and third sections of the first volume of Blok's *Collected Poems.* It is a book of poems reflecting the literary fashions of the time, a young man's attention to his own sensibilities and his burgeoning craftsmanship.[5] The "complete" text was established by the 1911 edition of the first volume of Blok's *Collected Poems.* This first volume, "Poems 1898–1904," includes over three hundred poems divided in three sections: "Ante Lucem" (1898–1900), "Verses About the Beautiful Lady" (1901–2), and "Rasput'ia" (A Fork in the Road) (1902–4). The definitive edition of this text is the 1922 fifth edition. Taken together, the three sections as they now stand present a development up to and away from the adoration in poetry of a central, mystical, female figure emblematic of another and greater reality than the one to which we are accustomed.

The poems in the section "Ante Lucem" are, in general, imitative of the sentimental and talentless work of such Russian poets of the 1870s and 1880s as Nadson and Apukhtin whom Briusov, Bal'mont and the other early Symbolists had moved against. They are mostly short, conventional lyrics. In them, Blok is given over to expressing a kind of satisfaction with his own emotional capacity. He aims not so much at affecting the reader as at a certain affection. Several of the poems in the section are about, or include reference to, Ophelia (Blok's favorite dramatic role, as previously mentioned, was Hamlet), but Blok's understanding of *Hamlet*, as given in his "Remarks on Hamlet" (1901), points up failures of the poetry written about that time or a bit earlier. The "Remarks on Hamlet," written five years before any of Blok's own plays, shows a sensitive mind and a nice appreciation of the dramatic development of meaning:

> Hamlet thought endlessly. All the questions contain, as the basis of solution, a secret—especially those questions which continually harrass Hamlet. Consequently, the power of thought leads him up against a wall: he must either break himself against it or remain as he was before—either be or not be. And what is most significant is that the wall has long stood in front of him. The problem "to be or not to be" is not new for him. He "knows" it "inside out."[6]

A poem such as "In a Wild Grove by a Ravine" (1898) deals only with the sentimental aspects of the Ophelia-Hamlet relationship:

Есть в дикой роще, у оврага,
Зеленый холм. Там вечно тень.
. . .
Любовники, таясь, не станут
Заглядывать в прохладный мрак.
Сказать, зачем цветы не вянут,
Зачем источник не иссяк? —
Там, там, глубо́ко, под корнями
Лежат страдания мои,
Питая вечными слезами,
Офелия, цветы твои!

In a wild grove by a ravine
There is a green hill. There is always shade.
. . .
Lovers, hiding there, will not
Peer into the cool gloom.
Shall I tell you, why the flowers won't fade,
Why the spring isn't dried up?
There, there, deep down below the roots
My sufferings lie
Nourishing your flowers,
Ophelia, with eternal tears.

Perhaps the source of weakness of this poetry is the immediacy of its connection with Blok's life. For example, a slightly later (1900) poem on the same Ophelia-Hamlet theme, "My Soul Is All Illuminated," is intimately connected with the summer of 1898 when Blok and his wife-to-be, Liubov' Mendeleeva, acted out Hamlet and Ophelia at her parents' summer house. Blok wrote a poem on that performance—and on his love for Liubov'—the next day, August 2, 1898. About two years later he returned to the event again. Twenty years later, in a diary entry for August 17–30, 1918, he returned still another time:

The first poem written at Shakhmatovo ("My Soul Is All Illuminated," May 28 [1900]) shows the sadness of memories of 1898 blew across me again, memories of what seemed (and really was) lost.

This poem, in remembrance of a summer gone by, is interesting for two features which occur, brilliantly successful, in Blok's later poetry: the quotation of poetry, epigrams, or titles in poems (here, a translation of two lines from *Hamlet*, III, i) and the use of imperfect rhyme (here, a consonance of feminine rhymes in which the terminal consonant is disregarded: naprásno—prekrásnym). The quotation is emphasized by the fact that the second of its two lines is the only nonrhyming line in the poem; that is, the quotation is made to stand apart from the poem by its nonrhyming last word. It is also interesting that this occurs before Blok had read Briusov's *Urbi et Orbi*, which he deeply admired, and before he had come temporarily under Briusov's influence.

Прошедших дней немеркнущим сияньем
Душа, как прежде, вся озарена.
Но осень ранняя, задумчиво грустна,
Овеяла меня тоскующим дыханьем.
Близка разлука. Ночь темна.
А всё звучит вдали, как в те младые дни:
Мои грехи в твоих святых молитвах,
Офелия, о нимфа, помяни.
И полнится душа тревожно и напрасно
Воспоминаньем дальным и прекрасным.

My soul is all illuminated as before
By the unfading radiance of days gone by.
But the early fall, pensively sad,
Blew over me with melancholy breathing.
The parting is near. The night is dark.
But still there sounds in the distance, as in those youthful days:
The fair Ophelia!—Nymph, in thy orisons
Be all my sins remember'd.
My soul uneasily and vainly fills
With a remote and beautiful remembrance.

One sees another aspect of the sources of Blok's thinking at this time if one is aware of Vladimir Solov'ëv's influence. For example, the first two lines of Blok's poem just quoted correspond closely to Solov'ëv's—

И прежний мир в немеркнущем сияньи
Встаёт опять пред чуткою душой.[7]

And the world of old in unfading radiance
Again arises before my sensitive soul.

Blok's poem "Luna prosnulas'. Gorod shumnyi" (The Moon Woke Up) (1898) ends with a quotation of two lines from Polonskii, whose work Blok cited in his autobiography as having had a strong lyric affect on him. Zhukovskii, Blok said, was his first "inspirer," through whom he "discovered the spirit of German Romanticism."

The year 1901 marks the end of what we might call Blok's apprenticeship and the beginning of his effort to work out a cycle of poems on a consistent theme. The section "Verses about the Beautiful Lady" includes all of

Blok's poems that he wished to preserve written between January 1901 and November 7, 1902. The title itself was first applied to a series of poems published in *Northern Flowers* in 1903. A group of poems in *The New Way* earlier that year had included references to "The Lady"—to a "Thou" with a capital "T" added after the poems had passed the censor. Blok said: "For poets She [Sophia] is the Muse: She was known by Dante, Goethe, Baudelaire, and Fet".[8] But the collection of poems published in 1904 under the title *Verses about the Beautiful Lady* was not warmly received either by the press, by Blok's father, or by most poets. The cultivation of the Beautiful Lady was successful more as an aspect of the relationship among Blok, Belyi, and their friends than as a poetic doctrine. Everyone knew where the Lady had come from, but no one then noticed what Blok really wanted to make of her. Quite expectedly, even Blok himself gave few signs of knowing. Only as he matured and his talent ripened was he able to see the Lady as having been a figure of that freedom and that permanence which he believed were the ultimate subject and support of art.

The transition in Blok's poetry from the work of his very early period to that of the early period of the Beautiful Lady is perhaps given most satisfactorily by the attitude and highly conscious derivativeness (of a different sort) that lies behind the poem "On a Cold Day, an Autumn Day" (1901):

В день холодный, в день осенний
Я вернусь туда опять
Вспомнить этот вздох весенний,
Прошлый образ увидать.

Я приду — и не заплачу,
Вспоминая, не сгорю.
Встречу песней наудачу
Новой осени зарю.

Злые времени законы
Усыпили скорбный дух.
Прошлый вой, былые стоны
Не услышишь — я потух.

Самый огнь — слепые очи
Не сожжет мечтой былой.
Самый день — темнее ночи
Усыпленному душой.

On a cold, an autumn day
I will go back there once again
To recall this vernal sigh,
To see the image that has gone.

I will arrive, I will not cry;
Remembering, I will not burn out.
I will meet with a song at random
The dawn of the new autumn.

The evil laws of time
Have hypnotized my mournful spirit.
You will not hear my by-gone howl,
My former moaning—I have died out.

Fire itself will not ignite
My blind eyes with a by-gone dream.
Day itself is darker than night
To the man whose soul is dazed.

Seventeen years later, Blok noted in his diary on August 17–30, 1918, that this poem was the result of

> ...walking around "The Islands" in the fields behind Staraia Derevnia [Old Village, a suburb of St. Petersburg] where there occurred to me what I called Visions (sunsets). All this was supported by Vl. Solov'ëv's poetry, a book of which Mama had given me for Easter that year. A. V. Gippius that spring showed me the first just-published issue of *Northern Flowers...*, and Briusov (especially) became tinged with color for me, so that in the "mystical summer" which followed this book continued to play a special role.

The poem is about the poet's fortitude in returning to autumn, the ruins of spring, in those fields and his overcoming, through the poem, the hypnosis of time. Two weeks later in a diary entry for August 29–September 11, 1918, Blok explained the poem this way:

> Here sunsets glow like visions, throwing out *tears*, *fire* and *song*, but someone whispers that I will sometime return to that same field as another—*extinct*, *changed by the evil laws of time*, *singing at random* (that is, as a poet and man, not as a seer and possessor of a secret).

It is in the beautiful, careless song that all magic and all vitality lie, a singing oneself to life.

Blok's poetic development shows a gradual refinement of his self-consciousness from an early, rather awkward use of conventional abstractions representing the self to, later, a dramatic play between images and symbols by which its force invokes or involves a psychic environment. The development is from the self as a posture or series of poses to the self as a real and dramatic figure. Conversely, the development is from ideas reduced to conventional images to images as immediate representations of significant ideas—from love as figure of the Lady to the father as symbol of repression, revenge, and revolution.

Blok's poems of this early period are private in the sense that they are reflections of their author's consciousness as he projects it on actuality. They are characterized by frequent use of *I*. They come from him and lead back to him.

In most of the poems the single center is the poet himself...; association with a second center (thou) developing, along with the first center, a poem's general thematic movement, occurs less frequently.... In the poet's later work the number of instances of a double theme in a poem is greater, but they are less clearly defined, as is the balance among the parts of the poem corresponding to the themes.[9]

The second center or consciousness is posited by analogy to the first. Like the first, but seldom involved with the first, it is what the poem moves around; it does not move the poem. In the poem (1902) that begins

Я вышел в ночь — узнать, понять
Далекий шорох, близкий ропот,
Несуществующих принять,
Поверить в мнимый конский топот.

Дорога, под луной бела,
Казалось, полнилась шагами.
Там только чья-то тень брела
И опустилась за холмами.

I went out in the night to recognize
A distant rustling, a near-by grumbling,
To welcome what does not exist,
To believe in imaginary horses' tramping.

The road was white beneath the moon;
It seemed as if it filled with footsteps.
There only someone's shadow roamed
And sank behind the hills.

the picture is conventional, like the emotion which it depicts. The material of the poem is placed around the protagonist the way scenery is placed around an actor. Both the emotion and the picture are vague, carried by deliberately vague syntax: in this poem, for example—the use of "some-one's," the rhetorical contrast of "distant" to "near-by," the rhetorical question in the fourth stanza, or, most clearly, the quasi-paradoxical lines:

И стало ясно, кто молчит
И на пустом седле смеётся.

And it was clear who was keeping silent
And from the empty saddle was laughing.

Or the device of repetition—in this poem, of repeating the first stanza as the last—a tactical manoeuver to enclose the poem within itself, often used to limit a poem that lives by its song. The device was used in "romances" by Fet, Polonskii, Grigor'ev, for example, and was widely used by the French Symbolists, especially by Baudelaire, Maeterlinck, Verlaine, and Kahn. Most poems that use the device, and certainly this poem by Blok, may end as they began because they lack an organizing crescendo of meaning or elaboration of mind (definition). The stanzaic repetition is then desirable, as under certain conditions of sonata-form, because of the clarity and thematic simplicity with which it encompasses the movement of the poem. Its nonorganic function and its obviousness are often displeasing unless integrated beyond the bounce of meter into the rhythm of meaning as it must be in villanelles or sestinas, for example, forms of poetry which Blok never tried to use.[10]

The convenient, conventional attitude to Blok's work is that the poems in his first book hold together by common reference to the Beautiful Lady, by revelation of a hidden world through the use of common symbols, chiefly of the symbol of the Lady. In a Romantic sense, of course, the Lady is a symbol. In this sense, Blok's work, like the Romantics', is continuation of a very old poetic tradition. But V. M. Zhirmunskii's definition of a symbol in his book *Poeziia Aleksandra Bloka* (The Poetry of Aleksandr Blok) comes much closer to what Blok was doing and to the principles of poetry in general: "By a symbol in poetry we mean a special kind of metaphor—an object or action in the external world specifying a phenomenon in the spiritual or psychical world by means of the principles of analogy." A symbol is a metaphor which is itself the experience it is "about." Applying the sense of the original Greek word, we may say that it is the putting together of the two halves of the bone of experience, the putting together of what has happened to us and of what that means. A symbol defines the event and its meaning simultaneously. A symbol *is* the real experience, as, for example, by this principle of consubstantiation, the symbol of God is God.

The Lady in Blok's poetry often seems to be, but cannot be, a natural sign, which, in *Symbols and Values*, Ernest Nagel said is "evidence of the existence of what it signifies; a symbol is not." Technically, of course, no figure is evidence (art never is), but this figure is taken and offered by the poet as if it were. We are not given any object or action to which it could be analogy or in terms of which its reality could be analogous. We are "asked" to assume its existence in itself. That is, it leads only to itself. Because it calls down no other half, it must be a "sign." Again, we have signs pointing toward drama but want the symbols.

In the twelve-line poem "Zhdu ia kholodnogo dnia" (I'm Waiting for Some Freezing Day), written in 1901, nine of the lines are a stichometric report of what the Lady told the poet and lead to the Lady's promise to admit the poet to his desire, but neither the poet nor the Lady nor the repeated words "twilight," "grey," "winter," "cold," "wait," "roads," "fork in the roads," and so on—words used again and again by Blok with deliberate vagueness—brings us to anything. We perceive only the ambiguity of an inadequately defined but melodically declared emotion. There seems to be some sort of ritual involved—the poem is, clearly, invocation and dialogue—but for all we know it may be merely the optimistic content of a dream. We are not so much tantalized and intrigued by the possibilities as merely left ignorant of real emotion.

Ты говорила: — Приду, —

— Жди на распутьи — вдали
— Людных и ярких дорог,
— Чтобы с величьем земли
— Ты разлучиться не мог.

— Тихо приду и замру,
— Как твое сердце, звеня,
— Двери тебе отопру
— В сумерках зимнего дня.

You said: "I will come,

"Wait at the fork at a distance
Of the crowded, bright roads
So you cannot part
From the grandeur of the earth.

"I will come quietly and will be still,
Like your heart, with the ringing;
I will open the doors for you
In the twilight of a winter day."

Some of Blok's early poems, like the emotions behind them, escape us because they do not inform on the emotion. In many of these poems Blok has not successfully defined a system of correlatives on which to hang his emotions and thereby define them for us. Poetic purity being independent of emotional purity, many of these poems destroy what was clearly a handsome provocation by translating it directly. Others bog down in fantasy or quasi-metaphysical daydreams. Many of Blok's poems cut back on the devices—for example, "aural metaphor"[11]—used as equivalents to the experience Blok wants to convey. Frequently in such poems the intended symbolic aspect of a word vanishes because its function as a symbol is denied. Moreover, the existence of an accessible set of equivalents led Blok himself to manufacture experiences in his poems for which there were no previous attitudes; that is, to attempt the creation of experience in allegorical terms, as if working backward. Consequently, we find in these early poems especially a frequent, improbable overstatement of position, as if mere poeticizing could by itself legislate into being the conditions on which a poem depends for its life.

The two-way trap is illustrated by examination of two poems, neither included by Blok in his definitive edition of his first book, and both written in 1901: "I Understood the Meaning of Your Sorrow," first published in 1926, and "Five Turns Concealed," first published in *Zapiski Mechtatelei* (Dreamers' Notes) in 1919. The first poem reads:

Я понял смысл твоей печали,
Когда моря из глубины
Светила ночи возвращали
В их неземные вышины.

Когда внезапным отраженьем
Небесных тел в земных морях
Я был повержен в изумленье, —
Я понял твой заветный страх.

Ты опечалена природой —
Общеньем моря и светил,
И, без надежды на свободу,
Устрашена согласьем сил.

I understood the meaning of your sorrow,
When from the depths the seas
Returned the night's luminaries
To their unearthly heights.

When by a sudden reflection
Of the heavenly bodies in the earthly seas
I was plunged into astonishment,
I understood your sacred fear.

You are grieved by nature,
By the communion of heavens with the seas,
And, with no hope of reaching freedom,
Frightened by the forces' concord.

The poem tries to be metaphysical by being involved in real and absolute truth ("the music of the spheres," as Pythagoras had it). It lacks any taut structure that could maintain the complex intellectual organization such involvement would require. The effort to contrast or to dramatize the protagonist and his total environment never becomes more than a vague feeling. The poem therefore remains a conspicuously unsuccessful lyric of mood of which we cannot make out the import. Because the terms are not specific they are incomprehensible. Interestingly, Blok's subsequent explication also points out the obscurity of meaning caused by failures of syntax and by improper dislocation of dependencies and references, by which the poet thought to compress or to "poeticize" his understanding. He discusses the poem at some length in his journal for August 29–September 11, 1918, giving background and *explication de texte:*

Then, too, the *meaning of her sorrow* (sorrow, apparently, does not separate events) is to be sought in *nature:* the harmony of forces (of the sea and of the stars reflected in it) *frightens* her and makes the *hope of reaching freedom* vain. There was, as I subsequently discovered, a kinship between this idea and the idea of the captivated World Soul (Origen's Holy Ghost) which Vl. Solov'ëv was the most recent to foster: see [his *Collected Works*, vol.] IX, [p.] 19 [article "The World Soul"] and many other places. I did not yet know all this, but had a feeling for Plato. At the same time, I myself was merely amazed (ϑαυμαξεστο) [sic] by the reflection of *the heavenly bodies in the terrestrial seas*, evidently like the ancient philosopher-artist (heathen). Further, I pray (again to God: *O God* without face, as always) *to lead* me, *an exhausted slave*, out of the *pitiful battle* (evidently, life's, so as not to become fatigued by the phenomenal and more easily to contemplate the noumenal).

Certain phrases in this history of "mystical growth" give us information which the poem does not—for example, the implication of the concept of the World Soul as Plato and Solov'ëv are believed to have interpreted it—but, because the World Soul and the heavenly luminaries do not work the poem—because the poet seems to be only in a planetarium talking to his conscience—the explanation is as irrelevant as they are. It may reveal something about Blok, but it does not inform on his poem. It is an unnecessary note, which even as note is useless because it is not accounted for or included in the poem.

The failure of the other poem, "Five Turns Concealed," is something of the same sort, but it is doubly excessive: the explication itself reduces the poem to absurdity. Its virtue, insofar as footnotes can be virtuous, is that it prevents biographical reading of literature. The poem is a deliberate cryptograph:

And then I wanted to *seal* my secret *up*, so I wrote a cipher poem in which *the five bends of the lines* signify those streets she walked along as I followed her, unnoticed by her (Vasili Island, 7th line,—Central Avenue—8th—9th lines—Central Avenue—10th line).[12]

If intentions count, the poem is successful: it is completely incomprehensible.

Пять изгибов сокровенных
Добрых линий на земле.
К ним причастные во мгле
Пять стенаний вдохновенных.
Вы, рожденные вдали,
Мне, смятенному, причастны
Краем дальним и прекрасным
Переполненной земли.
Пять изгибов вдохновенных,
Семь и десять по краям,
Восемь, девять, средний храм —
Пять стенаний сокровенных,
Но ужасней — средний храм —
Меж десяткой и девяткой,
С черной, выспренней загадкой,
С воскуреньями богам.

There are five turns concealed
Of benevolent lines on the earth.
Privy to them in the haze
Are five inspired moanings.
You, born far away from me,
Are with me, unsure, communicant
By that far, handsome country
Of the overflowing world.
There are five inspired turns,
Seven and ten along the sides,
Eight, nine, middle temple—
Five concealed moanings,

But more awfully—the middle temple—
Between the tenspot and the nine,
With a black, bombastic riddle,
With burning incense to the gods.

Ignorant of what we are asked to deal with, we turn to Blok's diary for explication—to fact:

In such a mystical condition apropos of Her I met Liubov' Dmitrievna on Vasili Island (where I went to buy a dachshund soon called *Krabb*). She got out of a sleigh on Andreevskaia Square and went along the 6th line, Central Avenue—to the 10th line, I, unnoticed by her, following behind (here—the photographer's window is close to Central Avenue). From this came the "five turns."

and to interpretation:

Her image, presented before me in those surroundings, which I recognized as having a *not coincidental* import, evoked in me, most likely, a feeling not only of *prophetic triumph* but also of human love, which I, perhaps, expressed in some word or glance, evidently, provoking a new manifestation of her sternness.

By such entries the diary seems to make itself suspect: it is not a diary, but memoirs. It sheds no light on the poem. What Blok says was his state of being *before* he wrote the poem is actually what his reading of the poem some seventeen years *afterwards* suggests to him it "probably" was. Blok's notes undercut any organization of the poem except biographical: because we can tie the numbers together only as we are allowed to and because only the notes allow us to, what the notes say is what the poem hangs on. The value of the poem, independent of the poet's biography, is reduced to the meaning, or functions, of a set of peculiar numbers, lines, and religious figures. Or the value of the poem *is* the biography—we have returned to the notes and done away with the poem completely.

If we do so, the manuscript helps us further. In the manuscript,

...the title is in Greek with a translation: Πυθία περιπατέουσα και περπαθέουσα (Pythia Taking a Stroll and Being on Guard [sic] [there are the notes] March 10, ad vesperum ("toward evening") and "Ante Lucem" (Before the Light) and an epigraph from Pushkin:

He had a vision once
Beyond the range of mind.

...the manuscript contains a schematic drawing of these five street turns.[13]

Pythia is the Delphic oracle. The poem is now in pieces. The "metaphysical" system which it relies on or plays with is so personal, so merely arbitrary and so confused that it is hopelessly irrelevant. By following the poem down its comments, notes, and manuscript jottings, as we thought we had to to find meaning, we chased the poem away. We discovered that whatever correlation there may be between a poem and its genesis is carried by the poem—that this poem, which carries nothing, has nothing to carry. The poem was an allegorical invention of experience and, therefore, a failure: what *really* happened, no matter how you take it, is that a lady walked down a street. The biographical approach is become a *reductio ad absurdum.*

Failures of this sort seem to be failures of a habit of mind. Blok was at first satisfied by the pseudo-exotic and exotic language that surrounded adoration of the Beautiful Lady—the obvious postures, the stereotyped language, the allegorical figures and the philosophical enthusiasm that Reality was at hand. He always had a tendency to think morally in terms of black and white; in this book, to perceive aesthetically in black and white. An incomplete poem such as the later one on Kant, "Sizhu za shirmoi" (I'm Sitting Behind the Screen), first entitled "Frightened," becomes clear only if we move in on Blok's reading of Kant and on his correspondence with Belyi, who said that Blok believed that fear of fear was the most actual fear and that he considered Kant afraid in just that way, a man frightened eternally.[14] In this poem it is a moribund morality that, like a photographic negative on a table, seems to be of only one value.

To know the provenience of the Beautiful Lady, however, is not to know her function. If we turn to those poems by Blok explicitly about her, we find that she is supportable only personally, perhaps the way God found himself supported by Anselm. Anselm's proof of God reveals Anselm's conviction, not God's existence. Blok's poems do not force us to accept the Lady as a symbol because of a poetic function; rather, we are asked to accept her beforehand in order to enjoy the poetry. Sometimes the poetry obscures the symbol itself:

Ты — другая, немая, безликая,
Притаилась, колдуешь в тиши.

Ты далека, как прежде, так и ныне,
Мне не найти родные берега.

You are different, wordless, faceless;
Hidden, you bewitch in silence.

You are remote, now as before.
I cannot find the native shore.

The "symbol" is a secret to which neither the cult nor the cultivation of art can assign the satisfactory attributes of mystery.

The beginning of the poem "The Dusk Becoming Evening" (1901) does not declare that faith which otherwise, it seems, the Lady regularly involves:

> Вечереющий сумрак, поверь,
> Мне напомнил неясный ответ.
>
> The dusk becoming evening, believe me,
> Reminded me of an obscure reply.

Reading on in this poem, we find doors and dreams and a white boat, "like a white swan," that follows the Lady. This is an example of a characteristic of Blok's early work: a poem's dependence on the validity of its generating idea. Whereas generally a poet works a poem up from or beyond a first impulse usually given as the opening or closing lines, Blok tends to rest content with explanation of that impulse. In this poem, the impulse stands apart from the body of the analysis, from the poem's involvement in the system of the Lady—as the closing four lines show by their conscious but technical recapitulation and "definition" of the opening theme.

> Вечереющий сумрак, поверь,
> Мне напомнил неясный ответ.
> Жду — внезапно отвóрится дверь,
> Набежит исчезающий свет.
>
> . . .
>
> В этой выси живу я, поверь,
> Смутной памятью сумрачных лет,
> Смутно помню — отвóрится дверь,
> Набежит исчезающий свет.
>
> The dusk becoming evening, believe me,
> Reminded me of an obscure reply.
> I am waiting—suddenly a door will open,
> The vanishing light will fall on me.
>
> . . .
>
> I live in this high realm, believe me,
> With the dim memory of the gloomy years,
> I dimly remember—a door will open,
> The vanishing light will fall on me.

The poem is like a song with a beautiful but too brief melody. The melody sustains itself, but the rest of the poem disappears into adjectives.

Blok's vision, as a habit of mind, encouraged him to believe, out of that intellectual sloth common to everyone, that his poetry was in part divine and, therefore, unalterable for sacred as well as for scientific reasons. For example, he sensed inadequacy in the line

В одних стенах, в одних мечтах

but in revision he could only pick up a word from the preceding stanza and invert the line:

В одних лучах, в одних стенах

(The reference is to "waves of sunlight above on the dark cupolas.") We are taken no closer to that continual play of reality which the poem is about, like the play of "God's light" in the temple dome, and we do see from the rest of the poem—excluding the stanza defining the situation which Blok himself excised—that the basic attitude is romantic: the state of being the poet wants to feel is assigned to his environment (the depth of the dome is "terrible," the reward is facile, "someone" comes and smiles to him) and the private experience is, by figures, given as the universal. The emotion is grandiose and implausible. The line discussed above, revised many years after the poem's first publication, shows us how grand Blok wanted the poem to be, how grandiloquent it actually comes out. Blok sent the poem in a letter to his father in 1902—as if it adequately illustrated his credo and his right to faith in himself—and datelined it *St. Isaac's Cathedral.* Blok located his experience of faith with regard to the institution supporting religious faith, offering it to that official of another institution who had caused him most anguish. In the poem he calls his presence in the cathedral and his vision there his "holiday."

As a result of his belief in the sanctity of his poetry (and of literary composition in general), Blok felt that it was not subject to serious revision or to defense. In a letter to his father in December 1904, he replied to his father's denigration of the little book *Verses about the Beautiful Lady:*

> It strikes me as strange that you find my poems incomprehensible and even accuse me of publicity-seeking and eroticism.... *Almost* everybody accuses me of incomprehensibility, of course, but the other day I was gratified to hear that almost the whole book is understood often to detail and sometimes to tears by completely simple "non-intellectual" people.... Even if I once were to run into "real" criticism, I certainly would accept the most severe attacks with gratitude. Unfortunately, such criticism has so far been only oral—and not much of it. I can't regret that the book has come out, although I don't expect fame.

In the same letter he said that he believed that people would come to believe what he had written about—"this eternal essence"—regardless of how he had written. His effort in his poetry, in his letters, and in his life at that time, as a matter of fact, was to locate the Lady as object and agent of faith very much as Dante located Beatrice—and perhaps as consciously. However, the Lady is private. Beatrice engendered a system; Dante speaks of the privilege of her favor and the encouragement of her love—the freedom of certainty of reality. Blok never was certain. Blok continually hoped for the luck of a vision of the Lady and for the satisfaction of having her love—the freedom of the absence of pain—but he had no method to accomplish what he wanted. He relied on the supplicatory power of verse. His poetry about the Beautiful Lady is not a demonstration of her or of her position; it is prayer for participation, through her offices, in that reality which, he assumes, she *is*. The physics of this poetry runs parallel to the metaphysics: as the science of the verse is the propitiation or invocation of the divine and not the definition, so the experience is the emotion of faith and not the substance.

Many of these poems are a collection of antithetical postures taken pseudo-dramatically from the point of view of an aspect of the author—for example, the poem beginning (and ending):

> Я жду призыва, ищу ответа,
> Немеет небо, земля в молчаньи . . .
>
> I await a call, I seek an answer,
> The sky grows dumb, the earth is silent...

The Lady itself is a figure posited antithetically to the author's persona.

> Вхожу я в темные храмы,
> Совершаю бедный обрад.
> Там жду я Прекрасной Дамы
> В мерцаньи красных лампад.
>
> I go into darkened temples,
> I perform a humble rite.
> There I await the Beautiful Lady
> In the glimmering icon-light.

The Lady is not necessary for satisfaction: anticipation is itself the satisfaction, the emotional crisis of commingled pain and pleasure.

> В тени у высокой колонны
> Дрожу от скрипа дверей.
> А в лицо мне глядит, озаренный,
> Только образ, лишь сон о Ней.

О, я привык к этим ризам
Величавой Вечной Жены!
Высоко бегут по карнизам
Улыбки, сказки и сны.

О, Святая, как ласковы свечи,
Как отрадны Твои черты!
Мне не слышны ни вздохи, ни речи,
Но я верю: Милая — Ты.

In the shadow behind the tall pillar
I shiver at the creak of the doors.
And only a brightly lit image, only a dream
Of Her stares me in the face.

O, I am used to these rizas
Of the majestic Eternal Wife!
High up along the cornices run
Smiles, fairy-tales and dreams.

O, Holy Lady, how the candles are gentle,
How Your features comfort me!
I hear neither sighing nor speaking,
But I believe: the Beloved is Thee.

This poem is interesting for the stage it represents in Blok's technical development. It is one of Blok's first metrically free poems, a definite step in the direction of what Verlaine called "vers libéré," an effort to break up the regularity of stressed-unstressed syllables in the syllabo-tonic scheme. The fact that some of Blok's later poems are in a considerably freer form indicates that Blok only slowly and carefully evolved an accentual verse with which to replace the verse that, despite some experimentation by Tiutchev in the first half of the nineteenth century, had been regarded as uniquely canonical until the Symbolists' experiments. Why Blok and the Symbolists emphasized the new form and the work of the French Symbolists is summed up in a comment by Briusov apropos of Verhaeren. In an article in *The Balance* in March, 1904, Briusov said he deeply admired Verhaeren as "a master of as many rhythms as thoughts." The new ideas required a new music.

The German Romantic and the French Symbolist poetry that may be called the sources for the Russian Symbolist experiments in technique led to slightly different results. Briusov said that the regular *dol'niki*, or accentual verse with a regular pattern of stresses from line to line, proceeded from the German; that the irregular *dol'niki*, or what would ultimately be free verse, proceeded from the French.[15] One finds both in Blok's work. But Blok's "typical" form (indeed, Ushakov's dictionary uses a line from Blok as criterion) may be considered a three-accent line with one or two unstressed syllables between stresses, that is, verse with various unstressed syllables omitted, "pausal verse" (*pauznyi stikh*), derived, Piast said, from the German Romantic accentual verse (and used by Blok in his translations from the German) and, according to Piast, "the most characteristic rhythm of the first volume of Blok's poems."[16]

Actually, Piast is not correct—over four-fifths of the poems in Blok's first book are metrically regular[17]—but it is interesting that Piast was left with that impression. A strictly tonic scheme and a syllabo-tonic scheme cannot be combined in a single principle. In moving from the syllabo-tonic scheme to the tonic and in developing control of the tonic scheme, Blok wrote poems which, although they may technically be of one sort or the other, seem to fall between both. Within a short while, however—by the spring of 1903—he was able to use both kinds of verse without letting them seem commingled and, several years after that, after a period of experimentation, to return to canonical forms of verse with a firm control of the rhythm through metrical variations.

The Beautiful Lady did not survive the period of experimentation. As a symbol she was not adequate to meet the demands Blok increasingly put on his poetry. Blok's ideas frequently stretched out beyond the poems that were to be their embodiment, as in the following poem, written at the end of December 1901:

ДВОЙНИКУ

Ты совершил над нею подвиг трудный,
Но, бедный друг! о, различил ли ты
Ее наряд, и праздничный и чудный,
И странные весенние цветы?...

Я ждал тебя. А тень твоя мелькала
Вдали, в полях, где проходил и я,
Где и она когда-то отдыхала,
Где ты вздыхал о тайнах бытия...

И знал ли ты, что я восторжествую?
Исчезнешь ты, свершив, но не любя?
Что я мечту безумно-молодую
Найду в цветах кровавых без тебя?

Мне ни тебя, ни дел твоих не надо,
Ты мне смешон, ты жалок мне, старик!
Твой подвиг — мой, — и мне твоя награда:
Безумный смех и сумасшедший крик!

TO THE DOUBLE

You performed a difficult deed over her,
But, poor friend, did you discern
Her marvelous, holiday clothing
And strange, spring flowers?...

I waited for you. But your shadow flashed by
In the distance, in the fields I, too, walked through,
Where she, too, once rested,
Where you sighed over the mysteries of life...

And did you know that I would triumph?
Will you vanish, having achieved but without love?
That I will find an insanely young
Dream without you in the bloody flowers?

I need neither you nor your affairs,
To me you are absurd and pitiful, old man!
You deed is mine,—and your reward belongs to me:
Mindless laughter and an insane shout!

In the manuscript, Blok dedicated the poem to "my other 'I.'" On the same day he wrote the poem, before he wrote it and afterwards, he jotted two entries into his diary:[18]

I have split in two. And here I wait, conscious on the edge of a forest, but—as the other—I perform in far-away fields a sacred deed. And—terrible dream!—I, waiting, begin incomprehensibly to grieve for the one performing the deed and the deed performed....

Although [the poem] did not come out, still there is a good idea for a poem: the murderer-double will perform [the deed] and fall away, but the contemplator-double, who took no part in the murder, gets all the reward. The thought is mad, just as the reward itself is madness, which will coagulate in the sweet contemplation of what the other has achieved. Memory of the knife will be ideal, for although the knife was also real, it was in dreams—that is the great mystery.

The poem and the idea behind it show the considerable influence on Blok, especially in this early period, of Dostoevsky's thinking, of a kind of dramatization of antinomies clearly perceived but complex, profound and irresoluble. Blok's poem is narrower than his idea for it. It does not probe that transfer of madness from the self as agent to the self as thinker which, his note says, the thinking requires. The poem may be taken as an allegory of one's violation of one's ideals, of one's potential perfection, but Blok's concern for that perfection and its loss seems to prevent him from analyzing the actual struggle of self with self, the contestants in the real drama, as he later understood it.

In other poems of this period, the drama is between the poet's own emotional potentialities. For example:

Бегут неверные дневные тени.
Высок и внятен колокольный зов.
Озарены церковные ступени,
Их камень жив — и ждет твоих шагов.

Ты здесь пройдешь, холодный камень тронешь,
Одетый страшной святостью веков,
И, может быть, цветок весны уронишь
Здесь, в этой мгле, у строгих образов.

Растут невнятно розовые тени,
Высок и внятен колокольный зов,
Ложится мгла на старые ступени...
Я озарен — я жду твоих шагов.

The day's uncertain shadows run.
The bells' call is high and clear.
The church steps are lit up,
Their stone is alive—and awaits your footsteps.

You will pass by here, you will touch the cold stone
Covered with the fearful sanctity of time,
And, perhaps, you will drop a flower of spring
Here in the mist by the stern images.

The rose-colored shadows grow indistinctly,
The bells' call is high and clear,
The mist lies on the old steps;
I am surrounded with light, I await your footsteps.

The pleasure the lines depict is contemporary with them. The poet's delight is the pain of non-gratification. The "you" in this poem, dedicated to Sergei Solov'ëv, is, like the Lady, irrelevant to the actual condition.

The Lady comes closest to being some*thing* when it becomes one of Blok's two hypostatized, contradictory ultimates, but then, usually, it is so clearly a verbal manufacture, a product of fictive thinking, that it functions not as a symbol but as a trope. In the following stanza, for example, the postures are clear; the vocabulary is typical of Blok's early poetry; and the Lady, identified by a capital letter, a convenience for syntactic organization and declaration of the poet's general attitude:

Я и мир — снега, ручьи,
Солнце, песни, звезды, птицы,
Смутных мыслей вереницы —
Все подвластны, все — Твои!

I and the world—snows, streams,
The sun, songs, stars and birds,
Successions of vague thoughts—
All are subject, all are Yours.

The emotional success of the poet's condition is, like that of a perverse love, self-destruction in self-glorification, of that transcendent and immanent freedom which is because it is approached and which is approached because it is, that ultimate, impossible equilibrium.

Ты свята, но я Тебе не верю,
И давно всё знаю наперед:

. . .

Буду я взывать к Тебе: Осанна!
Сумасшедший, распростертый ниц.

И тогда, поднявшись выше тлена,
Ты откроешь Лучезарный Лик.
И, свободный от земного плена,
Я пролью всю жизнь в последний крик.

You are divine but I do not believe You,
And I have now long known all things to come:

. . .

I will call to You: Hosanna!
Gone mad and prostrate on the floor.

And then, raised above mortality,
You will reveal Your Radiant Face
And, freed from the world's captivity,
I'll pour my life into one last cry.

The artificiality of the position comes through any brilliance of the verse.

The Beautiful Lady is not just a legacy from Solov'ëv or a figure of a literary cult but is chiefly, in Blok's poetry, a product of language (initially supported by a desire for conviction) conceived and used as a sort of nexus in a conglomeration of words which worked better without it. The Lady is, in this aspect, an illustration of certain symbolic words which more nearly successfully achieve their symbolic functions when the illustration is absent. Where the moral is wanting the words come to life; that is, they become their appropriate gesture.

In the two poems "The Dusk Becoming Evening, Believe Me," referred to earlier in this chapter, and "There on the Street There Stood a House," (1902) each a lyric of about twenty lines, some eight words are identical, some dozen very similar, and some three dozen so used that they have analogous connotations in the two poems. The first poem involves a second person directly; no person is specified in the other. Peculiarly, however, the second poem has a greater impact on us—is more nearly successful—because the unwieldy figures are removed and the words made to work out their play. The general tone is colloquial and descriptive, exactly that kind and quality of attitude which Blok could most easily and most meaningfully work from. The poem begins from a specific observation. from some thing perceived; it is present in time, in the sense that it specifies an extended past—that is, a past which covered a considerable amount of time, a "real" past. The first poem moves from comment into speculation, from an instant of the past transformed from activity to accomplishment to an instant of the future considered not as activity but as accomplishment. A characteristic of the first poem is the use of the word "pale" to describe "dreams," "you," and "heights." It is not only used imprecisely and tritely but also confusedly: it is too usual and too unproductive a word to endure standing as attribute to three various nouns or pronouns in the space of thirteen lines. Repetition reduces it to nothing but the conventional signification a dictionary gives. A difficult because commonly used word, it is killed by its use in the poem. It is posture, stuffing, mere ambulant sound.

Both poems are organized pretty much on the same system of syntactic and linear repetitions. In the second poem, however, a more careful specification of activity by the words and the elaboration of a systematic metaphor move us forward.

In the first poem, the metaphor of the swan as the boat on the fiery stream of the poet's songs, all following the Lady, is a parade of theologically related "symbols" the meaning of which is arbitrary. In the second poem, the metaphor of the cornice as the frown disfiguring the face that is the wall carries out as well the metaphor of the window as the eye and the shutter as the eyelid. We have a non-logical imposition of two unrelated conditions, which is, of course, not new but is given as if it were. We may not now think the metaphor unusual or brilliant, but we do, I think, respond to it in terms of the ineffable drama it presents. The motions of the words move us:

Там — в улице стоял какой-то дом,
И лестница крутая в тьму водила.
Там открывалась дверь, звеня стеклом,
Свет выбегал, — и снова тьма бродила.

Там в сумерках белел дверной навес
Под вывеской «Цветы», прикреплен болтом.
Там гул шагов терялся и исчез
На лестнице — при свете лампы жолтом.

Там наверху окно смотрело вниз,
Завешанное неподвижной шторой,
И, словно лоб наморщенный, карниз
Гримасу придавал стене — и взоры...

Там, в сумерках, дрожал в окошках свет,
И было пенье, музыка и танцы.
А с улицы — ни слов, ни звуков нет, —
И только стекол выступали глянцы.

По лестнице над сумрачным двором
Мелькала тень, и лампа чуть светила.
Вдруг открывалась дверь, звеня стеклом,
Свет выбегал, и снова тьма бродила.

There in the street stood a certain house,
And the steep stairway led into the dark.
There a door opened with clanging glass,
The light ran out, and again the darkness roamed.

There in the twilight over the door and under the sign "Flowers"
The awning shone white, affixed with a bolt.
There the sound of footsteps was lost and vanished
On the stairs in the yellow light of a lamp.

There up above a window looked down,
Curtained by a motionless blind,
And, like a frowning forehead, the cornice
Imparted a grimace to the wall, and a stare...

There in the twilight the light trembled in the windows,
And there was singing, music and dancing.
But in the street there was no noise or talking—
Only the shining of the windows was projected.

A shadow flashed along the stairs above
The gloomy yard, and the lamp barely shone.
Suddenly a door opened with clanging glass,
The light ran out, and again the darkness roamed.

Valéry said that the task of the poet is to transfer his own state of consciousness to another. This requires that the poet first have one and that he then manufacture some kind of fluency in which to locate the reader's consciousness. Blok's technique is smooth. He was adroit, resourceful. He had an extraordinary facility. For example, in the 1901 poem "Twilights, Twilights of Spring," the words almost fall apart into the instruments their letters are.

Сумерки, сумерки вешние,
Хладные волны у ног,
В сердце — надежды нездешние,
Волны бегут на песок.

. . .

В сердце — надежды нездешние,
Кто-то навстречу — бегу...
Отблески, сумерки вешние,
Клики на том берегу.

Twilights, twilights of spring,
Cold waves at one's feet,
In the heart—otherworldly hopes,
And the waves run onto the sand.

. . .

In the heart—otherworldly hopes,
Someone to meet me—I run...
Reflections, twilights of spring,
Shouts on the opposite shore.

A kind of incantation catches up the reader beyond the meter or alliteration or the repetition of the consonants (especially of K, T, and D) so that the poem seems to be pure music. The affect of the music, however, is at the expense of meaning. Although the tone of the poem is of the contrast between hope and despair, between misery and ecstasy, between indifference and love—how on this side of the river the poet is waiting for the consummation of love through the invisible "thou" on the other—and although we are moved by the motion of the words, when we analyze the poem we find very little in it. As the poet is cut off from his psyche or Muse or Lady, so we are cut off from the actuality we require. However we may be touched by this poem's partial movement, we desire exactly what it denies: the gesture that would put it, like Humpty-Dumpty, together again.

This poem (and other, later poems) is the sort of poetry that Blok became popular for, a kind of love poetry which, a friend has told me, served young couples in St. Petersburg before the First World War much the way popular songs serve young couples now. I think of other early poems of this sort by Blok, poems such as "I, Very Wise and All Worn Out," "I Loved Tender Words," "You Are Divine, but I Do Not Believe You," or "We Met Each Other at Sunset." These poems are to be sharply differentiated from Blok's successful later work and, perhaps more important for an understanding of Blok, from the more ambitious and complicated poetry of this first book, particularly certain poems in the last section "A Fork in the Road."

A confusion of emotions as given in a confusion of motion in verse debilitates by division some of Blok's poems and, in fact, bewildered him. The poem in this third section—a poem (1903) dedicated to Andrei Belyi—that begins:

Так. Я знал. И ты задул
Яркий факел, изнывая
В дымной мгле.

So. I knew. And you blew out
The blazing torch, perishing
In the smoky haze.

is really two poems which do not fit together except rhetorically:

В бездне — мрак, а в небе — гул.
Милый друг! Звезда иная
Нам открылась на земле.

Неразлучно — будем оба
Клятву Вечности нести.
Поздно встретимся у гроба
На серебряном пути.

. . .

И тогда — в гремящей сфере
Небывалого огня —
Светлый меч нам вскроет двери
Ослепительного Дня.

In the chasm, darkness; in the sky, a hollow roar.
Sweet friend! Another star
Revealed itself to us on earth.

. . .

Inseparably, we two
Will pledge ourselves to Eternity.
We will meet late by the grave
On the silver path.

. . .

And then in the roaring sphere
Of a fantastic fire
A shining sword will unseal for us the doors
Of the Blinding Day.

The manuscript has as epigraph three lines from Belyi's poem "The Image of Eternity,"[19] which is picked up in the eighth line of Blok's poem as it stands—or, we may say, in the second line of the "second" poem. Zhirmunskii has called the first six lines a "metrically independent beginning," noting that it was omitted in the 1912 and 1914 editions.[20] Neither the beginning nor the rest of the poem is successful with, or without, the other, a peculiar difficulty that later clarity of emotion and better metrical control removed in Blok's poetry in general.

That the love poetry as popularly understood was not what Blok regarded as an essential sort of poetry, and that the love poetry which Blok wrote that excited the popular imagination was not what literary people respect him for, is witnessed both by the inadequacies and confusions of the love poetry and by the discoveries and successes of the "other" poetry, of poems such as the following (1903), from the third section, which illustrates Blok's development from classical versification to the establishment of accentual versification as an equally acceptable standard.

По городу бегал черный человек.
Гасил он фонарики, карабкаясь на лестницу.

Медленный, белый подходил рассвет,
Вместе с человеком взбирался на лестницу.

Там, где были тихие, мягкие тени —
Желтые полоски вечерних фонарей —

Утренние сумерки легли на ступени,
Забрались в занавески, в щели дверей.

Ах, какой бледный город на заре!
Черный человечек плачет на дворе.

A black man ran around the town.
He put out the street-lamps, clambering on a ladder.

The slow, white dawn came up,
Together with the man climbed up the ladder.

There where the soft, quiet shadows had been—
The little yellow strips of evening lights—

The morning twilight lay on doorsteps,
Got in the curtains and the cracks of doors.

Ah, how pale the city is at dawn!
The little black guy is weeping in the yard.

There is no regular binary or ternary meter in this poem. Each verse has four stresses. The intervals between stresses vary from one to three (as compared to Blok's "usual" *dol'niki* with three stresses in each line and intervals of one or two unstressed syllables between stresses). Each pair of verses tends to have identical intervals in both lines except as interlocking masculine, feminine, or dactylic rhymes—itself not a usual combination in one poem—tie alternate lines together. Each line is divided and is marked by a definite caesura, a device which acquired great importance in Blok's poetry of this time. In the first quatrain, the rhymes are masculine—dactylic——masculine—dactylic, the masculine being approximate and the dactylic, tautological. In the second quatrain, the rhymes are regular, alternating masculine—feminine a b a b. The final couplet is a paired masculine rhyme. The structure of the poem is clear and definite, determined by the accentual pattern and by the very interesting rhyme scheme. The demands of "free" meter are interestingly met.[21]

The affect in regular verse of the continuous coincidence of the syntactic and rhythmic structures is monotony or bouncing. In "free" verse, it is organic unity and vitality. What happens in this poem is that both the contradictory principles of "regular" rhyme and "irregular" meter are put to work—not to mention certain phonetic devices for determining rhythm, such as alliteration, assonance, consonant frequency, and shifting stress. Shuvalov and Nikitina have pointed out in their book on Blok that

...the celebrated melodiousness of Blok's poetry...[depends] on the fact that a verse or verse-unit (two contiguous lines or stanzas) usually comprise a self-sustained group...; [even when the syntactic unit is not the verse-unit] the syntactic series as usual corresponds to the rhythmic.

The syntactic violations of rhythm occur in such relationship to other syntactic units that they appear as a series of syntactic dependencies stated or understood. The syntactic unit *does* correspond to the rhythmic because rhythmic movement is, in this and in many of Blok's later poems, the basic principle of syntactic organization.

The poem "A Black Man Ran around the Town" is of interest on two counts: it is an experiment in meeting the greater demands of less regularized verse patterns in which an organic principle regulates the movement, and it invokes a transubstantiated world without referring to it. The Beautiful Lady is out of mind. The lamp-lighter and his city are seen by the poet as if from heaven, until the last line, which indicates that the poet has come down close enough to see tears or to hear the man crying. The actual, romanticized experience is given as parallel to that imaginary world which tantalizes the poet. In other words, despite its shortcomings, particularly its declarative rather than implicative tone, the poem is Symbolist. It commingles the worlds of actuality and of mystery in reciprocal terms; it *is* in both. What the poem lacks is that vibrancy or activity of language in which the ideas and the sounds of words are enjoined to be music by the imagination. What the poem contains is understanding of the complex of a moment of life and suggestion of the terms by which that complex is judged.

Only a few years after the poems of this first book Blok perceived that what he had to do was not to celebrate mysticism as a body of myth, his key and keystone for which had been the Lady, but to embody it literally in those figures of activity in which he perceived it and through which he could express its pattern of meaning—to put the real toad in the imaginary garden. As he wrote Belyi in October 1905, experience itself is inadequate to art because the basic experience is experience of ignorance. The poet's work is to make meaning in a game of words:

> I have never (note *never*, even when writing *all the poems* about the Beautiful Lady) been able to express my experiences adequately; in fact, I've never had any; the word desn't mean anything to me. I simply led a dissolute and beautiful life which I've now left off (I both don't want it and don't need it), and, having left off, I still can't understand much. Why do you think me a mystic? I'm not; rather, I think I've always been a rowdy. My place is not so much with you, the Seer, who knows the way, as with M. Gor'kii, who knows nothing, or with the decadents, who also know nothing.
>
> You know why I write like this. But there is a difference between me and the decadents. As a matter of fact, I am disgusted with them more and more. Besides, they don't know, but I "quietly know" (yes, that happens), but "what," not "how." I'll never be able to explain this, and I'm rather inclined to utter words of repudiation if compelled to explain.... There's no end to my lack of discipline in what involves depth—and to "immobility," too, as you call it. But lack of discipline is worse than immobility....
>
> But I don't play with mysticism, I play with words, very tediously and badly. I know that mysticism is *real* and terrible and that it will punish me....

This is the paradoxical position taken in dramatic terms or in intellectually meaningful relation to social behavior, analogous to the Christian position Forese expresses to Dante in *Purgatorio:* "And not once only, while circling this road, is our pain renewed: I say pain and ought to say solace." It is not only an uncomfortable position at best; it is self-consuming unless expressed in a system which violates neither aspect of it. It does not lead to a game between "reality" and the "self," to war between the individual and his environment. It is itself the war—the war of the journey and the pity, as Dante put it in the second canto of the *Inferno.* In art, it is the play itself, the drama in and of the mind.

V

Poems

1904–1908

"...ou bien faut-il aller droit au rhythme et le prendre comme moelle unique de l'idée lyrique."—E. Verhaeren

Blok's poetry did not change unexpectedly after *Verses about the Beautiful Lady* except to those who had presumed that Blok would maintain the cult of the Lady at the expense, if need be, of the requirements of developing his poetry. The general principles of versification accessible to Blok are illustrated in his first book. Blok increased the accuracy of his poetic forms and the scope of achieved content in the poems.

The poems in Blok's second book present a technical development and a continuation of the same essential theme, the theme of love, with increased emphasis on themes drawn from contemporary urban life. Love, as presented in the second book, is not idealized or romantic love, but those affections for self and for an ideal which play against each other in the psyche seeking pleasure, power, and, ultimately, freedom. Treatment of the theme involves the whole complex of self-interest, energy, error, and impossibility—all actual conditions as well as their opposites—which to be understood can be given only in a body of symbols.

Blok's effort was to connect the activities of men with the events of nature—perhaps, even, to reconcile men and nature—by incorporating both into art. He knew the contradictions involved: that the arbitrary character of the sequences of natural events was infrequently meaningful and frequently not beautiful, and that purposive or putatively purposive human actions, always involving not merely sequence but also consequences, were often frightening, horrible, important, and beautiful at once. He saw that the issue was not one of beauty, as he had first understood it through the convention of the Lady, but one of beauty as exemplified in both moral and physical power. The center of exercise of this power had become, he saw, the city, the agent and the repository of culture and of civilization.

He supposed that one might appeal to an ideal or presume an ideal condition, but that what mattered and what obtained in verse followed directly from the power of its music to overcome the actual power conflicts. The pressures of literary fashions, of other poets, and of the verse techniques then generally available limit and in many ways obscure, even to Blok himself who had to expend energy on supporting the fashions, the knowledge he wanted poetry to be.

The poems in the second book, as presently constituted, are chiefly those poems that appeared originally in Blok's second volume of poems *Nechaiannaia Radost'* (An Unexpected Joy) (1906) and in his third, *Zemlia v snegu* (The Earth in Snow) (1908), which also included the poems in the cycle *Sn̆ezhnaia Maska* (The Snow Mask), published separately as a pamphlet in 1907. The text of the present second book is that of the second volume of Blok's *Collected Poems* in the fourth, or 1919, edition. There are seven sections:

1. "Puzyri zemli" (The Bubbles of the Earth), a group of 13 poems written in 1904 and 1905 and serving as an introduction, in terms of theme and imagery, to what Blok himself considered a transitional stage, his poetry of the period 1904–6.
2. "Nochnaia fialka" (The Night Violet), subtitled "A Dream," a rather long, narrative fantasy written in 1905–6, which Blok said was an almost exact description of what he had seen in a dream.
3. "Raznye stikhotvoreniia" (Various Poems), a group of 79 poems written between January 1904 and August 1908 not connected by any thematic thread specifically and containing some difficult poems and poems in a new style (rather extensive technical experiment), and some easy, popular poems, and some poems, such as "A Girl Sang in the Church Choir," which were both "experimental" and "popular."
4. "Gorod" (The City), 45 poems written between February 1904 and February 1908, tied together by images of the city and city-life but also by certain political and psychological complications which Blok associates with the modern city and civilization.
5. "Snezhnaia Maska" (The Snow Mask), 30 poems written, with one exception, in January 1907, dedicated to Natal'ia Volokhova, an actress in Kommissarzhevskaia's theater, divided in two sub-sections: "Snows" (16 poems) and "Masks" (14), and all called by Blok, in manuscript, "a lyric poem." The poems were all written in about two weeks, very much with Volokhova in mind, and are held together, Blok felt, by a consistent lyric intensity.
6. "Faina" (Faina), 31 poems written in the period 1906–8, some for Volokhova, some for Blok's mother, and some for other women but grouped together by the idea of ultimately inaccessible, often gypsy-like, women.
7. "Vol'nye mysli" (Free Thoughts), four rather long lyrics written in June and

July, 1907, conversational in tone, direct in response to ordinary experience, and authoritatively accomplished in terms of technique.

Blok's second book may be considered linked to his first in several ways, beyond the theme of love that runs throughout all Blok's poetry and dramas. The devices and attitude connected in the first volume with the Beautiful Lady are, in the second book, connected with other female figures. In the third section of the first book, in a poem written in 1903, there are the lines:

Или это Ясная мне улыбается?
Или только моё сердце влюбленное?
Или только кажется? Или всё узнается?

Or is this the Clear One smiling to me?
Or is this merely my heart fallen in love?
Or does it merely seem so? Or will all be revealed?

The rhetorical questions are aimed toward a dilemma of perception. The same sort of question is raised in the 1906 poem "Neznakomka" (The Unknown Lady), in the cycle "The City." Although one may observe that both the device and the attitude of which it is partial expression have carried over from the first book to the second, one would add that, in the second example, the question is aimed at the poet himself:

И каждый вечер в час назначенный,
(Иль это только снится мне?)

And every evening at an appointed hour
(Or do I only dream this?)

The "answers" to the "questions" raised by the "real" world are not to be found in the "ideal" world. The poet's difficult task is to work in both at once. The greater precision in the use of the device contributes directly to that sense of dramatic tension between the worlds the poet sees that he wishes to convey to us. The convention of the Beautiful Lady was in part an appeal to a mystic illusion, but it was also a collation of inadequately elaborated and inexpertly exploited figures, images, and poses. Blok's devotion to the Lady followed not from conviction so much as from confusion. When, with maturity and greater confidence of craft, the confusion cleared, the Lady disappeared. The Lady in this sense was compensation for failures of verse and, therefore, dear to its author. When the verse was no longer liable to such failure, the convention became superfluous.

This was not a sudden change. There are poems of the Beautiful Lady "type," but with slightly different images, and, often, very weak poems, written in 1907 or 1908—for example, "She Came from the Sunset," written in November 1907. Conversely, there are in Blok's first book poems that are in form and content connected with the realistic material and technical experiment characteristic of the second book as a whole. It may be true that to turn from the poems about the Beautiful Lady to the poems of 1904–6 is to turn from images of doubles, dwarves, swamp devils, and wizards, to turn from poems about temples, sunsets, and beautiful snow to poems about factories, labor, hunger, and death, but it is also true that this contrast does exist among the poems of the first book itself. The poem to Blok's "other self" has been referred to. Along with poems from the Beautiful Lady cycle proper, poems such as "Snova blizhe vechernie teni" (The Evening Shadows Are Closer Again) (1901) there are poems, particularly in the third section, that lead directly into the poems of the following years presented in the second book. For example, the poem "Fabrika" (The Factory) (1903) is an observation on the unjust exploitation of the poor and the mockery with which their labor is regarded. The poem "Iz gazet" (From the Newspapers) (1903) was written a little over a month after Blok had received Briusov's *Urbi et Orbi*, which he said contained "the subtlest and most poignant inspirations and thoughts in simple and sensitive language." Blok's poem uses a technical scheme with an accentual pattern and includes three approximate rhymes. It approaches the tone of conversational prose:

Встала в сияньи. Крестила детей.
И дети увидели радостный сон.
Положила, до полу клонясь головой,
Последний земной поклон.

Коля проснулся. Радостно вздохнул,
Голубому сну еще рад наяву.
Прокатился и замер стеклянный гул:
Звенящая дверь хлопнула внизу.

Прошли часы. Приходил человек
С оловянной бляхой на теплой шапке.
Стучал и дожидался у двери человек.
Никто не открыл. Играли в прятки.

Были веселые морозные Святки.

Прятали мамин красный платок.
В платке уходила она по утрам.

Сегодня оставила дома платок:
Дети прятали его по углам.

Подкрались сумерки. Детские тени
Запрыгали на стене при свете фонарей.
Кто-то шел по лестнице, считая ступени.
Сосчитал. И заплакал. И постучал у дверей.

Дети прислушались. Отворили двери.
Толстая соседка принесла им щей.
Сказала: — Кушайте. Встала на колени
И, кланяясь, как мама, крестила детей.

Мамочке не больно, розовые детки.
Мамочка сама на рельсы легла.
Доброму человеку, толстой соседке,
Спасибо, спасибо. Мама не могла...

Мамочке хорошо. Мама умерла.

She rose in radiance. Made the sign of the cross over the children.
And the children saw a joyful dream.
She made, bending her head to the floor,
Her last earthly reverence.

Kolia woke up. Sighed joyfully,
Delighted still with the azure dream in mind.
A rumble of glass rolled through the house and died away:
A door, clanging, slammed downstairs.

Hours passed. A man came
In a warm cap with a tin badge on it.
The man knocked on the door and waited.
Nobody answered. They were playing hide-and-seek.

It was the gay, frosty Christmas-tide.

They hid Mama's red kerchief.
She used to go out in the kerchief in the morning.
Today she left the kerchief home:
The children hid it in the corners.

Twilight stole up. The children's shadows
Jumped along the wall in the light from the street.
Someone came up the stairs, counting the steps.
Counted them all. And wept. And knocked on the door.

The children listened. They opened the door.
Their fat neighbor brought them some soup.
She said: "Eat." She knelt down
And, bowing like Mama, made the sign of the cross over the children.

It does not hurt mama, rosy children.
Mama lay down on the track herself.
To the kind woman, the fat neighbor,
Many thanks, many thanks. Mama could no more...

Mama is all right. Mama died.

It is also true, however, that the second book marks a turning point in Blok's development. What actually happened was that Blok gradually gained mastery over poetic forms and gradually said more nearly precisely what he wanted to say. When at a given moment a publisher would prepare a volume of his poetry for publication, Blok would organize or reorganize the poems he had available for it into more or less coherent groups. Blok's development, in this sense, is something like the walk a man takes who goes three steps forward and two back, for Blok insisted on carrying with him to the end all the poetic baggage he ever acquired. In regard to the second book, it is the one step forward that is most interesting.

Mystical devils were not new to literature in Blok's time: Gogol had used them, and they were accessories or symbols in the work of Sologub and Remizov. Blok points to what he wants to be considered his use of them by affixing as epigraph to the first section of this second book, "The Bubbles of the Earth," two lines from *Macbeth*, I, iii:

> The earth hath bubbles, as the water has,
> And these are of them.

The lines come from Macbeth's and Banquo's first meeting with the witches. The old hags deliver their terrible prophecy and vanish. Macbeth cannot reassure himself that they do not mean less than he dreams of. Banquo identifies the terror in the unholy alliance by the lines which characterize the witches as momentary figures of powerful reality. Fulfillment of the prophecy immediately follows the scene.

It might seem that Blok has merely shifted his mystical habitat from an eyrie to a cave, that he has turned to a demi-monde of devils because, being of the earth and closer to us, they appear more real than figures of heaven. The moment in *Macbeth* from which the epigraph comes is a crossroad of politics and mystery. It is a demonic insight anticipating and even requiring the demonic act, yet simultaneously destroying itself by its own corruption. Blok's use of it suggests new awareness on his part of the limits and obligations of poetry.

He again refers to these lines from *Macbeth* in the later poem "Ona prishla s moroza" (She Came In from the Frost) (1908) in which the Paolo and Francesca story is recapitulated and reapplied and the Launcelot story is replaced by a reading of *Macbeth*, the story of the modern cavalier—an imperfection which prevents the lovers in Blok's poem from kissing and lets only the doves kiss, the image Dante uses *for* Paolo and Francesca in Hell. Love in these terms does not desire and is not moving toward its own perfection; it is the clearest, in so far as it is the most personal, form of power. The devils are its agents, and the earth is its home. Blok found in Shakespeare's work understanding of the continual shifting of the balance of this power. In a letter to Ellis in March 1907, he said about Shakespeare: "I deeply admire him; and perhaps most deeply of all—in all the world's literature—*Macbeth*."

Blok's poem "She Came In from the Frost" is in the "Faina" cycle but it may be used here to draw attention to two points: to the use over a period of time of the same thematic material and also to the technical experimentation or freer technique characteristic of this second book. The poem is free verse:

Она пришла с мороза,
Раскрасневшаяся,
Наполнила комнату
Ароматом воздуха и духов,
звонким голосом
И совсем неуважительной к занятиям
Болтовней.

Она немедленно уронила на пол
Толстый том художественного журнала,
И сейчас же стало казаться,
Что в моей большой комнате
Очень мало места.

Всё это было немножко досадно
И довольно нелепо.
Впрочем, она захотела,
Чтобы я читал ей вслух Макбета.
Едва дойдя до пузырей земли,
О которых я не могу говорить без волнения,
Я заметил, что она тоже волнуется
И внимательно смотрит в окно.

Оказалось, что большой пестрый кот
С трудом лепится по краю крыши,
Подстерегая целующихся голубей.

Я рассердился больше всего на то,
Что целовались не мы, а голуби,
И что прошли времена Паоло и Франчески.

She came in from the frost,
Flushed,
Filled the room
With the odor of fresh air and perfume,
A clear voice
And a chatter completely disrespectful
Of work.

She immediately dropped on the floor
A fat volume of a literary magazine,
And it at once began to seem
That in my big room
There was very little space.

All this was a bit annoying
And rather awkward.
Besides, she wanted
Me to read her *Macbeth* aloud.
Having scarecely got to *the bubbles of the earth*,
Which I cannot talk about without emotion,
I noticed that she, too, was agitated
And intently looked out the window.

It turned out that a big striped cat
Was with difficulty clinging to the edge of the roof,
Lying in wait for kissing pigeons.

I got mad chiefly at the fact
That it wasn't we who were kissing, but the pigeons,
And that the time of Paolo and Francesca was gone.

To return to the first section of the second book: the poems in "The Bubbles of the Earth" are lightly haunted by words like "swamp," "spring," "imp," and the continual use of "face," "wings," "water," "key," "gold," "strength," "sky," "sick," "quiet," "crown," "die," "eye," "earth"—a vocabulary very much like that of the first book. Unlike the poems of the first book, however, a poem of the second book may be a game or a joke, as the dedication of the poem "Starushka i cherteniata" (The Old Woman and the Little Devils), to "Grigorii E." suggests: Grigorii E. was a hedgehog (ëzh) that lived at Shakhmatovo, Blok's mother's place, in the summer of 1905 when this poem was written. Blok plays off explicitly mystical references—for example, "Holy Places"—against "the field Christ," this natural bundle of portable thorns.

The first poem in "The Bubbles of the Earth" is not an aspect or series of aspects of Blok. Rather, the poet takes himself as an aspect of the poem. He appears in it as a scarecrow, the residual pose of the natural movements of spring which the poem by invocation has created. He stands to his poem as the scarecrow stands to spring: deformed, artificial, unchanging, frightening or powerful, and illuminated by it. If one can imagine for a moment Shakespeare on the side of the witches in *Macbeth*, the analogy to Shakespeare Blok wanted to suggest would be complete.

The poem is also apt introduction to the differences between Blok's second book and his first: it is written in a free ternary rhythm, predominantly anapestic, without rhyme. The syntactic units are the rhythmic, held together by various repetitions of words and phrases. What *is* is not what Blok *sees;* what he sees is the matter of the poem. In this poem he has expunged his personality to an extent that makes the poem itself the "blank measure" of organic, aesthetic understanding:

На перекрестке,
Где даль поставила,
В печальном веселья встречаю весну.

На земле еще жесткой
Пробивается первая травка.
И в кружеве березки —
Далеко — глубоко —
Лиловые скаты оврага.

. . .

И жалкие крылья мои —
Крылья вороньего пугала —
Пламенеют, как солнечный шлем,
Отблеском вечера...
Отблеском счастия...

И кресты — и далекие окна —
И вершины зубчатого леса —
Всё дышит ленивым
И белым размером
Весны.

At the crossroads,
Where distance has set me down,
In sad gaiety I meet the spring.

The first grass breaks through
The still stiff earth.

In the lace of the birch—
Far off—deep—
Are the lilac slopes of the ravine.

. . .

And my pitiful wings—
The wings of a scarecrow—
Are aglow like the helmet-sun
With a reflection of the evening...
A reflection of happiness...

And the crosses and the far-away windows
And the tops of the serrated forest—
Everything breathes in the lazy
And blank measure
Of spring.

Blok's first long poem is "The Night Violet," begun November 18, 1905, and finished May 6, 1906, and subtitled "A Dream." Blok said in a letter to E. P. Ivanov on December 3, 1905, that:

> This poem is almost an exact description of a dream I had.... On November 16 I dreamed what I have since lived on. Such amazing dreams happen once a year—once every couple of years.

The poem begins with the announcement that memory will relate what happened, and what happened is presented as a real journey of the imagination and its guide through the country of the mind. The dream landscape with its inaccessibly nonrational sequences ("What is more pleasant in the world than the loss of closest friends?") is cut out against a kind of didactic catalogue of modern, "social" sequences ("The hour of factory whistles and the working-day, the hour of forgetting evil and good, ...and the depravedly long conversation, About the bad condition of the stomach"). The physical analogy to the journey of the mind is a walk through a swamp, like the Slough of Despond, analogous actually to the life in restaurants at night and suggestive of the possibility of each person's becoming, by a mask, his own king.

What Blok took from folklore he did not try to reproduce in imitation of folklore, as Lermontov or other poets had. He used the dwarves and devils for his own ends; he altered the general forms for his own story. "The Night Violet" has nothing in common with the verse principles of folk narrative poetry, but it does use the traditional plot structure to bind together its dream and actuality.

The poem has a formal introduction and a formal conclusion—the hero prepares himself and his equipment for an adventure, he enters the royal chamber—"But only kings assembled in the hut."—he successfully meets an opponent, and the exploit is defined and celebrated. Instead of a horse, there is a friend; instead of royal benediction, there is the realization of essentially royal personality; instead of an agon, there is a drinking bout; instead of a martial victory, there is the accession of the mind to a superior consciousness. The old figures are there: the king (the prince), the queen (princess)—as ever, spinning—and the *druzhina.* The epithets are those we find in Blok's poetry generally. The poem is about an adventure of a "youth, the brave hero," the creature, as Blok says, "of the Scandinavian sagas."

In July 1905 Blok wrote three poems included in the section "Various Poems," and which in manuscript he grouped under the heading "Skazki" (Fairy Tales). In the 1912 edition of his second volume of collected poems, Blok himself pointed out that "the development of this theme [of these poems] is to be found in the lyric drama... [The Puppet Show]; the same motifs are also in *Verses about the Beautiful Lady.*"

The third of the three poems is perhaps farthest from the play. It contains images of the sea and ships—and of the lighthouse—which may be found in quite a few of Blok's poems of this, and a somewhat later, period. In the second poem of the series, "The Poet," the instruments of style set up a pattern and work toward obviating the plausibility of pattern. The specifics of verse are not only themselves the idea and its vehicle but also the only possible realization of that idea by organized violation of it. The poem is written from the point of view of a child and in language accessible to a child. It mocks itself formally. It carefully moves toward prose yet preserves its poetry through a form of drama—the bemused self acting out the emotional history of a moment:

ПОЭТ

Сидят у окошка с папой.
Над берегом вьются галки.
— Дождик, дождик! Скорей закапай!
У меня есть зонтик на палке!
— Там весна. А ты — зимняя пленница,
Бедная девочка в розовом капоре...
Видишь, море за окнами пенится?
Полетим с тобой, девочка, зá море.
— А за морем есть мама?
— Нет.
— А где мама?
— Умерла.
— Что это значит?

— Это значит: вон идет глупый поэт:
Он вечно о чем-то плачет.
— О чем?
                    — О розовом капоре.
— Так у него нет мамы?
— Есть. Только ему нипочем:
Ему хочется зá море,
Где живет Прекрасная Дама.
— А эта Дама —добрая?
                                        — Да.
— Так зачем же она не приходит?
— Она не придет никогда:
Она не ездит на пароходе.
Подошла ночка,
Кончился разговор папы с дочкой.

THE POET

They sit at the window with Daddy.
The daws gyre over the beach.
"Drizzle, drizzle! Start dripping quick!
I've got an umbrella on a stick!"
"There's the spring. But you're winter's prisoner,
Poor little girl in a pink hood...
See, the sea foams beyond the windows?
Let's us fly, child, beyond the sea."
"But is Mummy beyond the sea?"
                                        "No."
"Then where's Mummy?"
                                        "She's dead."
                                                    "What's that mean?"
"It means: look, there goes the silly poet:
He's always crying about something."
"What about?"
                    "About a pink hood."
"Cause he has no Mummy?"
"He has one. Only he doesn't care:
He'd like to go beyond the sea"
Were the Beautiful Lady lives.
"And this Lady—is she kind?"
                                        "Yes."
"Then why doesn't she come here?"
"She'll never come.
She never takes a ship."
The night came up.
Daddy's chat with daughter ended.

The poem is a dialogue organized by rhyme—a, b, a, b—and by the dependency of the answers on the questions. The scheme of questions and the kind of answers reveal the characters in the dialogue. It is commentary on what Blok considers his relation to the outside world and his own internal concepts. It is an effort by Blok to involve his whole poetic attitude in actual life, between the simplistic but penetrating intuitions of a child and the rational understanding of the mature intellect, both of which are delimited by what inevitably happens (nightfall). It is a poet's effort to get beyond himself. Because he knows he cannot, the tone is light. It is propaedeutic to that more complex rhythmic iconoclasm which Blok associated with the spirit of music. As V. M. Zhirmunskii said in his book on Blok:

A word is not so much a bit of valid material for poetic craftsmanship as it is rather an obstacle for the poet, who would wish to "express himself without words." This dynamism, in terms of an artistic and actual effort, breaking down the established limits of art and of culture... the poet himself liked to call "the spirit of music."

The first poem in this series of three is called "Balaganchik" (The Puppet Show), and it was this poem which was the source for Blok's drama *The Puppet Show*, finished at the end of January 1906, published in *Fakely* (Torches) in April. The poem was written in July 1905. Toward the end of that year, as Orlov notes,[1] those who attended Viacheslav Ivanov's "Wednesdays," especially Chulkov, decided to try to organize a new, Symbolist theater, "Fakely." Chulkov suggested to Blok that he work the ideas and theme of the poem "The Puppet Show" into a play for this theater. The theater was never established, but the play was written and first performed in Kommissarshevskaia's Theater December 30, 1906.

The poem is a description of a puppet show and a play on the reality of make-believe. The resolution of the puppet show in the poem and some of the lines (such as the ones about the cranberry juice and the cardboard helmet) coincide with the ending of the play. The play has more characters and is more complicated. The poet who, in this instance, wrote the poem introduces himself as a character in his own play.

Вот открыт балаганчик
Для веселых и славных детей,
Смотрят девочка и мальчик
На дам, королей и чертей.
И звучит эта адская музыка,
Завывает унылый смычок.

Страшный чорт ухватил карапузика,
И стекает клюквенный сок.

Малрчик

Он спасется от черного гнева
Мановением белой руки.
Посмотри: огоньки
Приближаются слева...
Видишь факелы? видишь дымки?
Это, верно, сама королева...

Дебочка

Ах, нет, зачем ты дразнишь меня?
Это — адская свита...
Королева — та ходит средь белого дня,
Вся гирляндами роз перевита,
И шлейф ее носит, мечами звеня,
Вздыхающих рыцарей свита.

Вдруг паяц перегнулся за рампу
И кричит: — Помогите!
Истекаю я клюквенным соком!
Забинтован тряпицей!
На голове моей — картонный шлем!
А в руке — деревянный меч!

Заплакали девочка и мальчик,
И закрылся веселый балаганчик.

The puppet show is open
For gay and wonderful children.
A girl and boy are looking
At the ladies, kings, and devils.
And there's that infernal music,
The mournful bow is moaning.
A terrible devil has caught a tot,
And cranberry juice is running.

The Boy

He will be saved from the black anger
By a sign of a white hand.
See: the flames
Approach from the left...
Do you see the torches? you see the traces of smoke?
It must be the queen herself...

The Girl

Ah, no, why do you tease me?
It's the infernal retinue...
The queen—she goes in broad daylight
All wrapped in rose garlands,
And a retinue of sighing knights,
Their swords clanging, carries her train.

Suddenly a clown bends over the footlights
And shouts: Help!
The cranberry juice is flowing out of me!
I'm swathed in rags!
On my head is a cardboard helmet!
And in my hand a wooden sword!

The girl and boy began crying,
And the gay puppet show closed.

The poem foreshortens both the drama between the children and the puppets and the drama in the children's minds. The play expands both clearly.

Blok was very much aware of what Ibsen, Strindberg, Chekhov, Verhaeren, and especially Maeterlinck were trying to do in the theater and, though he seems still to have escaped from one aspect of himself to another through his dramas, he learned something from them all. In the first draft of *The Puppet Show* he compares his heroes with the heroes of Maeterlinck and Verhaeren:

We can recognize these people sitting in a room with dark corners, under the electric lamp around the table. Their faces are all importance, not one of them is ingenuous. They talk excitedly and nervously, as if every second getting close to something remote, sensing the quiet flight of what they can't yet put into words. These people, whom Maeterlinck likes to seat together in a hall and peer at how they become afraid, Verhaeren puts alone behind closed shutters to listen to footsteps on the street, to think on them, to fathom them, to turn their lives into convulsion, to fill them up with clattering and splashing on their own past as long as all ways out are not closed and a dark, terrible hysteria has taken over the soul. In a word, these people—"maniacs," people with a "shattered equilibrium," whether all together or each by himself in his corner—think the same thought about drawing near and about the person who is drawing near them.[2]

In the preface to the 1908 edition of his plays, Blok himself insisted that they were "lyric dramas," that is, in their proper function they presented

...in elegant and divers forms... all the richness of the refined and fragmentary experience [of the soul]: ...the ideal lyric poet is a complex agent who recreates with equanimity mutually contradictory experiences.

"The single basic [character] type and its desires," on which, Blok says each play hangs is the mask of the poet himself. He announces that Pierrot in *The Puppet Show*, like the Poet in *The King in the Square* and in *The Unknown Lady*, seeks "a beautiful, free and brilliant life" as given in the images of the "Eternal Woman": Columbine (in draft called Masha), and, in the other plays, the Architect's Daughter and the Unknown Lady. What holds all the plays together is that "'transcendental irony' which the Romantics talked about" and which we know is an aspect of the author's function, the residue of the mimesis through which he moves his mask. He actualizes his personality by masking it in a bitter, conventional mimicry. By playing dramatic extensions of aspects of himself against each other, he illuminates the audience as a street light illuminates a street.

That the play was put on at all shows in what high regard Blok was held as an innovator and poet. Kommissarzhevskaia wanted to make her theater the "theater of the free actor, the theater of the psyche, in which the external would follow from the internal."[3] Meierhold's bold, imaginative staging had already won him celebrity. The performance raised a furor:

...*The Puppet Show* provoked a real uproar.... Some, enraged, whistled and hissed; others applauded wildly.... Passions were enflamed, and this kept up at every performance when "those who protested even came armed...." Meierhold's name was famous throughout theatrical Petersburg and became the butt of joke and parodies[4]

In *The Puppet Show* Blok exploits and defines a series of actualities through the masks of art. The title means both a show-booth, as for a Punch-and-Judy show, and the show itself. The personae in the farce are the oldest fools of all: the trinity Columbine-Pierrot-Harlequin. We are offered a set of fashionable men and women (mystics), three pairs of lovers, a clown, and, epitome of the joke, the author himself.

The stage directions specify that the play opens with the mystics seated at a table and, a little apart from them, a Pierrot "like all Pierrots," white, sad, thoughtful. The mystics' first conversation refers to an "approaching event" of which "the wind gave the sign." Pierrot appeals to Columbine. The poetry is tight, deliberately artificial and yet inflated—rather an exposition of feeling than a play of emotion itself. The author enters, speaks prose: to deny responsibility for Pierrot, who, he says, is mocking him—"I didn't write my play for a show-booth, I assure you"—and, suddenly embarrassed to be on stage, disappears.

In these first few minutes we have been made to see a series of levels of "reality" all of which are given simultaneously in the momentary actuality of the theater: the mystics' intuition, Pierrot's historical convention and eternal sadness, and the author's duality—his prior existence and his physical presence—none of which is referable to another. They are merely coincident. The failure of the play to become the intended satire is the failure of these aspects to impinge on each other. They remain, like somewhat inappropriate jokes, reciprocally embarrassing.

The attempt to connect Pierrot and the mystics by analogous visions—of Columbine and of "a maid from a far-away land"—does not lead to an adequate definition of either point of view. What they see may seem silly. Left there, we must take what they see as the substance of the play. A girl in white appears: Pierrot calls her his fiancée Columbine; the mystics, Death. They begin to argue about who is correct. Harlequin enters, persuades Columbine to leave with him, Pierrot scoots off, and the author appears, like a priest, in front of the curtain:

> I wrote a really real play...: it's all about mutual love between two young souls! A third person bars their path, but the bars finally fall, and the lovers are united eternally in wedlock!

The clowning and the costumes, the author says, are the actors' own irresponsible juggling, just as are the history and the allegory. But there is no end to the declaiming (although the lady in one of the pairs of lovers is assigned the device of repeating, as her speeches, merely the last word of her lover's) and no repair. We do not know what "real" is; as the clown who is beat over the head shouts, "Help! All the cranberry juice is running out of me!"

In the ensuing confusion, the author reappears, the masks and scenery are suddenly removed, the author flees, and Pierrot sings his last, sad song: "I'm very sad. You think it funny?" All the possibilities have been made available to the audience except one, which is, unfortunately, outside the play: the possibility of mimetic response.

It is characteristic of Blok that he used certain central, "simple" themes, but what he understood to be involved in them may not be satisfactorily simplified. Like most poets, he transposed and stole from himself—for example, the "O liubvi, poezii u gosudarstvennoi sluzhbe (Dialog)" (Dialogue on Love, Poetry, and Government Service) (1906) was originally a dialogue among the Poet, the Fool, and the Courtier in *The King in the Square* (1906). Unlike most poets, Blok kept working over an idea: he tried to expand a concept to his satisfaction without violating it, without allowing it to become *another* concept due to the exigencies of another expression.

In November 1906, about a month before the première of *The Puppet Show*, Blok wrote another poem with very much the same title ("Balagan") and on very much the same theme, but directed not so much to the theme or ideas as to their exemplification. Blok seems to have wanted his play to be as dynamic as Shakespeare's, for he chose as epigraph to this poem a quote from Dumas's play about Kean: "Well, old nag, let's have a go at our Shakespeare!" Aware that he, Blok, had described a series of postures, rather than of gestures, he required the actual presence of the actors—real people—to animate his "moral" into being:

Лицо дневное Арлекина
Еще бледней, чем лик Пьеро.
И в угол прячет Коломбина
Лохмотья, сшитые пестро...

Тащитесь, траурные клячи!
Актеры, правьте ремесло,
Чтобы от истины ходячей
Всем стало больно и светло!

В тайник души проникла плесень,
Но надо плакать, петь, идти,
Чтоб в рай моих заморских песен
Открылись торные пути.

Harlequin's daytime face
Is even paler than Pierrot's countenance.
And Columbine puts his rags away
In a corner, all colors sewn together...

On with you, mournful nags!
Actors, true up your craft
So that a platitude
Becomes painful and bright!

Mold has gotten into my inmost soul,
But I must weep, sing, move,
So that the beaten paths open up
Into the heaven of my foreign songs.

Except for use of such words as "rags." "countenance," "way," or "inmost soul"—words Blok uses again and again—the poem offers nothing that may be put against the earlier poem or the play, yet the "theme" is the same.

One finds the same sort of "variations" in the poems on *Peer Gynt* or, more interesting from the viewpoint of Blok's later work, in the poems on the Christ-theme, which runs through Blok's work explicitly from 1905 on. The first poem on this theme—"Vot on—Khristos—v tsepiakh i rozakh" (There He Is—Christ—in Chains and Roses)—is interesting particularly because in *The Twelve* (1918) Blok again picks up the idea that follows from Dürer's Veronica, that the portrait of Christ is a self-portrait:

В простом окладе синего неба
Его икона смотрит в окно.
Убогий художник создал небо.
Но Лик и синее небо — одно.

. . .

И не постигнешь синего Ока,
Пока не станешь сам, как стезя...

Пока такой же нищий не будешь,
Не ляжешь, истоптан, в глухой овраг,
Обо всем не забудешь, и всего не разлюбишь,
И не поблекнешь, как мертвый злак.

In the simple setting of the dark blue sky
His image looks in the window.
A destitute artist invented the sky.
But the Face and the dark blue sky are one.

. . .

And you will not comprehend the blue Eye,
Until you yourself become the way...

Until you will be such a beggar,
And, trodden down, lie in the ditch,
And forget everything and cease to love all,
And wither like dead grain.

These poems point up a "problem" of Symbolist poetry. They controvert reading a word into a symbol from its occurence in several poems: they illustrate the absence of necessary correspondence among its uses from poem to poem. In the absence of a coherent system to which all uses can be applied, each use stands or falls alone. If a word accumulates for us a meaning greater than the meaning it has in any one context, that is the accidence of our reading and of the poet's habit of mind, that accidence which fits adjectives to their nouns.

Concerning Blok's work, I would make one general exception to that statement and then would reassert it through still another illustration. The exception is the use of the "mother" image. The "mother" occurs not so much as a figure *in* the poems as a figure *behind* the poet and his poetry to whom the work is addressed, the poet's patron. Biographically speaking, this was pretty much the way Blok looked on his mother, but the attitude is in all the poems dedicated to her or in which a mother and son are figures, as in the poem "Syn i mat'" (Son and Mother) (1906). In that poem, the son, perhaps too obviously, is the poet who moves from his romantic dreams into disillusion through adventure, suffers, and returns to his mother to die, that is, to find peace and release. The poem is an example of a romantic's failure to dramatize away from himself his discontent with his own propensity for dream. In a more interesting poem on the same subject, "Moei materi" (To My Mother), written in the summer of 1905, Blok shows greater consciousness of what the individual owes himself and not the mother, and is more deft at inventing, through the use of the weathervane symbol, an analogy to himself in terms of his understanding of his relation to his mother. Blok has invented a sort of dramatic parallel to put himself at a remove from his own biography and his poem closer to his reader:

Тихо. И будет все тише.
Флаг бесполезный опущен.
Только флюгарка на крыше
Сладко поет о грядущем.

Ветром в полнебе раскинут,
Дымом и солнцем взволнован,
Бедный петух очарован,
В синюю глубь опрокинут.

В круге окна слухового
Лик мой, как нимбом, украшен.
Профиль лица воскового
Правилен, прост и нестрашен.

Смолы пахучие жарки,
Дали извечно туманны...
Сладки мне песни флюгарки:
Пой, петушок оловянный!

It's quiet. It'll be quieter still.
The useless flag has been lowered.
Only the weathervane on the roof
Sings sweetly about what is to come.

Stretched by the wind against half the sky,
Agitated by smoke and sun,
The poor cock is enchanted,
Tossed into the blue depths.

In the circle of the skylight
My face is beatified as if by a halo.
The profile of the waxen face
Is straight, simple, and calm.

The fragrant resin is hot,
The distance is forever in haze...
The songs of the vane sound sweet to me:
Sing, little tin rooster!

The Beautiful Lady disappeared when she was no longer necessary to prevent certain failures of verse. In the following poem, the female figure is actual and is herself looking forward to the bright equilibrium of a world to come. The poem is a meeting-place of that sweet sentiment for which Blok was widely popular and of that new, accentual versification for which he was respected:

Девушка пела в церковном хоре
О всех усталых в чужом краю,
О всех кораблях, ушедших в море,
О всех, забывших радость свою.

Так пел ее голос, летящий в купол,
И луч сиял на белом плече,
И каждый из мрака смотрел и слушал,
Как белое платье пело в луче.

И всем казалось, что радость будет,
Что в тихой заводи все корабли,
Что на чужбине усталые люди
Светлую жизнь себе обрели.

И голос был сладок, и луч был тонок,
И только высоко, у Царских Врат,
Причастный Тайнам, — плакал ребенок
О том, что никто не придет назад.

A girl in the choir in church was singing
Of all those worn out in an alien land,
Of all the ships set out on the ocean,
Of all who forgot the joy at hand.

So sang her voice, up to the spire,
And a ray of the sun made her shoulder white;
Each in the darkness looked and listened
How the white dress sang in that light.

It seemed to them all that joy was coming,
That all ships lay in a quiet creek,
That the people worn out in the foreign country
Had found themselves a bright, new life.

The voice was sweet, and the light was subtle,
And only on high at Heaven's Gates,
Knowing the Secrets, a child was weeping
That nobody will ever come back.

The poem is an example of four-stress accentual verse with a caesura between the second and third stresses and with either one or two unstressed syllables between stresses. The rhyme scheme is regular a b a b, F M F M (two rhymes of the eight are approximate). The "free" rhythm, which perhaps carried the original idea for the poem, is given firm shape by the rhyme; the poem moves easily. It helps one see how Blok's virtuosity and technique displaced one sort of strictness by another and moved both closer to that vitality which it is the function of form to follow.

The immediate musical effect of Blok's verse was considerable. Kornei Chukovskii remembers that

At that time long ago when we were young, Blok's poetry affected us as the moon affects lunatics. The mellifluence of his lyricism was often excessive, and it seemed to us then that... he did not so much possess his own sounds as he was possessed by them, that he was not the high-priest of his own art so much as its victim.... It seemed that a verse flowed by itself, as if independently of its author's will, through a series of frequently repetitive sounds:

И приняла, и обласкала,
И обняла,
И в вешних далях им качала
Колокола.[5]

V. M. Zhirmunskii said, from a different point of view:[6]

The victory of the principle of purely tonic verse patterns over Lomonosov's foot-patterns has come about in our time, in the Neo-Romantic period, and this seems to us just as important a revolution in the history of Russian versification as the introduction of the syllabo-tonic system itself by Trediakovskii and his followers. There can be no doubt that the work of Aleksandr Blok was largely responsible for this revolution.

In this sense, all the latest Russian poets learned from Blok and not from his predecessors, as Derzhavin, Batiushkov, and Pushkin learned Russian versification from Lomonosov and not from Trediakovskii.

His [Blok's] work has a similar importance in terms of the decanonization of exact rhyme, a decanonization completed in Russian poetry in the last few years.

The poems in the fourth section of the second book, "The City," cover roughly the same period as those in the previous section, but they are united by common reference to aspects of city life, and they also look ahead, in their political understanding and imagery, to Blok's later poems such as *The Twelve* and *Retribution*—extensive, dramatic attempts to understand an age.

The following poem, written in 1904, came *before* some of the Beautiful Lady poems, only emphasizing again the fact that Blok's thematic material changed gradually—that he did not so much substitute later material for earlier but rather saw the earlier material as involving a greater circle of references and requiring a more objective and actualized (more dramatic) treatment. The three friends' walking together, their attitudes to themselves, and the way they are responded to in the following poem anticipate *The Twelve*. In manuscript, Blok called the poem a sonnet, and there are fourteen lines rhymed a b a b, a b a b, c d d c, e e:

Я жалобной рукой сжимаю свой костыль.
Мой друг — влюблен в луну — живет ее обманом.
Вот — третий на пути. О, милый друг мой ты ль
В измятом картузе над взором оловянным?

И — трое мы бредем. Лежит пластами пыль.
Всё пусто — здесь и там — под зноем неустанным.
Заборы, как гроба. В канавах преет гниль.
Всё, всё погребено в безлюдьи окаянном.

Стучим. Печаль в домах. Покойники в гробах.
Мы робко шепчем в дверь: «Не умер — спит ваш близкий»...
Но старая, в чепце, наморщив лоб свой низкий,
Кричит: «Ступайте прочь! Не оскорбляйте прах!»

И дальше мы бредем. И видим в щели зданий
Старинную игру вечерних содроганий.

I press my crutch with a plaintive hand.
My friend, in love with the moon, lives by its deception.
Here's a third on the road. O, my sweet friend, is it you
In the rumpled cap with the leaden stare?

And the three together stroll pensively along. The dust's in layers.
All's empty—here and there—in the never ending heat.
The fences are like graves. Stuff's rotting in the gutters.
All, all's buried in this cursed desolation.

We knock. Sadness in the houses. The deceased in coffins.
We whisper meekly through the door: "He isn't dead—your dear one sleeps..."

But an old woman in a cap wrinkling her low brow,
Shouts: "Get away from here! Don't insult his ashes!"

And we wander on thoughtfully. And we see through the cracks of buildings
The age-old game of evening shudders.

In August 1904 he wrote a poem called "Gimn" (Hymn), with which he was at first very pleased. It is in irregular accentual pattern, with shifting patterns of interlocking rhymes. It is, literally, a hymn to the sun; it is also a playing with rhetoric, an effort to turn poetry into the immediacy of declamation (not into pomposity), coming down to—or building up to—the last word, the last line, "Praise!" The experiment and the technical skill are all the more impressive if one remembers that Blok was not quite twenty-four and that his first book had not yet been published (it appeared in October, the month he finished his university thesis; he was twenty-four in November). This is the same kind of manipulation of rhetoric that in many of the other poems of this period, particularly in the Beautiful Lady poems, was unsuccessful and that in later poems, particularly *The Twelve*, is successful. One of Blok's continual difficulties, as it was one of Baudelaire's, was to work together into a poem rhetoric and antirhetoric.

In March 1904 Blok wrote a poem called "Obman" (Fraud), a kind of dramatic parable of a street incident involving beauty (a girl), violence (soldiers), and corruption (a dwarf), which may be read as anticipation of *The Twelve* and in which the same *kind* of figures, thought, and metaphor occur but in a more carefully and consciously organized dramatic plan. The violence of indifference parallels the violence of passion and is horrible. In this poem, both the world of the whore and the dwarf and the soldiers and the world of the "anagoges" come alive by being yoked together.

В пустом переулке весенние воды
Бегут, бормочут, а девушка хохочет.
Пьяный красный карлик не дает проходу,
Пляшет, брызжет воду, платье мочит.

. . .

Утро. Тучки. Дымы. Опрокнутые кадки.
В светлых струйках весело пляшет синева.
По улицам ставят красные рогатки.
Шлепают солдатики: раз! два! раз! два!

. . .

Пронеслись, — и струйки шепчут невнятно.
Девушка медленно очнулась от сна:
В глазах ее красно-голубые пятна.
Блестки солнца. Струйки. Брызги. Весна.

The waters of spring, mumbling, run by
In the empty alley, and a girl laughs.
Drunk, a red midget won't let her by,
Dancing, splashing, wetting her dress.

. . .

Morning. Puffs of cloud. Smoke. Upside-down vats.
Dark blue dances gaily in the limpid little streams.
They put red turnstiles up in the streets.
The soldier boys slap along: one! two! one! two!

. . .

They rushed on—the little streams whispered vaguely.
Slowly the girl came to from her dream.
Her eyes saw red and light blue spots.
Spangles of sunlight. Water. Splashing. Spring.

The connections among the girl, the dwarf, and the soldiers are made consistent with the tone of the poem by the language: the Russian for "they put [red] turnstiles up" is much like the Russian for "to cuckold." The absurdity, the impotency, the violation and the violence are all brought together by the intensions and extensions of the words. In this poem, as in Blok's later dramatic poems, verbal repetition is a method of building meaning. The last line, a catalogue of impressions leading the poem back to its context "spring," is unusually successful.

Even those poems in this book that are not successful seem still to be part of a transitional stage and to belong to it more than to the first book or to the third, with various poems with which they may be contemporary. Even as Blok was trying to work out a scheme for the Beautiful Lady, for example, he was working against the necessity for using such a figure. Even where the experimentation—and Blok's period of greatest experimentation is represented by the poems of this book, of which about one-fourth are not in syllabo-tonic verse—is unsuccessful, that is, where Blok has failed to create a *poem*, as in the following example of a ternary beat, it does establish an atmosphere and it helps define the limits to which experimentation may go:

Улица, улица...
Тени беззвучно спешащих
Тело продать,
И забвенье купить,
И опять погрузиться
В сонное озеро города — зимнего холода...

A street, a street...
The shadows of people hurrying silently

To sell their bodies,
And to buy oblivion,
And to sink again
Into the dreamy lake of the city—of the winter cold...

Blok himself was not certain of the limits to which he could push his poetry and of the permanent value of those "extremes" which he felt he had reached. As he wrote Sergei Solov'ëv in March 1904, just a few days after he had written "Fraud":

I write long poems, often indecent, but these satisfy me more than what I've done before and seem more powerful. Don't scold me for indecency; behind it there's *just the same* in me as in my former "diffused" self, but now in the forms of cries, madness, and frequently tormenting dissonances.

In Blok's well-known poem "The Unknown Lady," (1906), the obverse and reverse are pressed together. Blok himself, in a footnote in the 1912 edition of his *Collected Poems*, said that the poem is tied in thematically with a series of other poems and with the play *The Unknown Lady*. In the preface to the 1908 edition of *Lyric Dramas*, he outlines what it is he is moving from and toward. The central idea is, he says, a quest

...for a beautiful, free and brilliant *life* which alone can dump from the weak shoulders [of the heroes of the plays] the unbearable burden of *lyric* doubts and contradictions and dispell importunate and illusory doubles.

This is the transition from illusion to disillusion, from romantic conviction to skeptical mastery. Even the implausible and unappealing "Dialogue on Love, Poetry, and Government Service," which takes Blok's earlier poetry as given data, follows from ironic, or dramatic, treatment of his own previously celebrated mantic attitude.

The play *The Unknown Lady*, finished in November 1906, seven months after the poem of the same title and very clearly connected to it (in earlier editions than the definitive one), bore three epigraphs, one of them a quatrain from the poem. The two epigraphs that remain in the definitive edition come from Dostoevsky's *The Idiot* and refer to Nastasia Filipovna. The Unknown Lady, however, is not Nastasia Filipovna. Definitions from which characters "start" and functions by which they become "alive" are dissimilar quantities. What Dostoevsky dramatizes in his novel Blok, in his play, requires us to believe. No one is moved, I suspect, by what the character The Poet reads from his notebook about the life and eyes he has observed or by what the characters Verlaine, Hauptmann, Drinking

Companion, Seminarist, The Man in the Overcoat, or The Blue Man offer as comment. Worse still, what The Poet *says* is, at times, effrontery:

> I understand your grief.
> Just like you, I'm all alone.
> I guess that, like me, you're a poet.

Although at the end of this play between "dreams" and "reality" one is expected to respond psychically, I do not think one cares *which* "Mary" all the characters may be said to be looking for. Rather, one must be interested in this play for innovations in style and language which it incorporates—for example, the use of inexact hyperdactyllic rhymes and trochaic tetrameter in dramatic dialogue:

> Голубой
>
> В блеске зимней ночи тающая,
> Обрати ко мне свой лик.
> Ты, снегами тихо веющая,
> Подари мне легкий снег.
>
> Незнакомка
>
> Очи — звёзды умирающие,
> Уклонившись от пути.
> О тебе, мой легковеющий,
> Я грустила в высоте.
>
> *The Blue Man*
>
> Pining away in the luster of the winter night,
> Turn your face toward me.
> You, quietly covered in an aura of snows,
> Give me a light snow.
>
> *The Unknown Lady*
>
> Eyes are dying stars
> Falling from the way.
> I longed for you, my
> Light auraed one, up high.

Although Blok felt as early as January 1900, not long after he had entered the university, that drama was more real than poetry,[7] not his plays but his poetry contains life-like figures. In the lyric poem "The Unknown Lady," what is secret or transcendental is the meaning of actuality indiscernible in ordinary confusions and only temporarily seized by moving into the impermanent state of drunkenness, that other actuality. The poem indicates Blok's awareness of the relativity of a point of view, as if, could he do it, he would get behind his own metaphors as they, in turn, get behind actuality. That he must end with—and end the poem on—convention was, most likely, less satisfactory to him than to us.

НЕЗНАКОМКА

По вечерам над ресторанами
Горячий воздух дик и глух,
И правит окриками пьяными
Весенний и тлетворный дух.

Вдали, над пылью переулочной,
Над скукой загородных дач,
Чуть золотится крендель булочной,
И раздается детский плач.

И каждый вечер, за шлагбаумами,
Заламывая котелки,
Среди канав гуляют с дамами
Испытанные остряки.

Над озером скрипят уключины,
И раздается женский визг,
А в небе, ко всему приученный,
Бессмысленно кривится диск.

И каждый вечер друг единственный
В моем стакане отражен
И влагой терпкой и таинственной,
Как я, смирен и оглушен.

А рядом у соседних столиков
Лакеи сонные торчат,
И пьяницы с глазами кроликов
«In vino veritas!» кричат.

И каждый вечер, в час назначенный,
(Иль это только снится мне?)
Девичий стан, шелками схваченный,
В туманном движется окне.

И медленно, пройдя меж пьяными,
Всегда без спутников, одна,
Дыша духами и туманами,
Она садится у окна.

И веют древними поверьями
Ее упругие шелка,
И шляпа с траурными перьями,
И в кольцах узкая рука.

И странной близостью закованный,
Смотрю за темную вуаль,
И вижу берег очарованный
И очарованную даль.

Глухие тайны мне поручены,
Мне чье-то солнце вручено,
И все души моей излучины
Пронзило терпкое вино.

И перья страуса склоненные
В моем качаются мозгу,
И очи синие бездонные
Цветут на дальнем берегу.

В моей душе лежит сокровище,
И ключ поручен только мне!
Ты право, пьяное чудовище!
Я знаю: истина в вине.

THE UNKNOWN LADY

In the evening above the restaurants
The burning air is wild and hollow;
A spring-time, putrefying spirit
Directs the drunken shouting.

Far off, above the alley's dust,
Above the tedium of suburban houses,
The baker's pretzel sign has a gold tinge,
And children's crying resounds.

And every evening behind the railroad barriers,
Cocking their derbies,
The confirmed wits take the ladies
For a walk between the gutters.

The oarlocks creak above the lake,
A woman's squeal is heard,
And in the sky, schooled to everything,
The disk squints foolishly.

And every evening my only friend
Is reflected in my glass,
Stilled and deafened, as I am,
By the tart and mysterious moisture.

By the little table next to me
The sleepy waiters hang about,
And drunkards with rabbit eyes
Cry, "In vino veritas!"

And every evening at an appointed hour
(Or do I only dream it?)
A girl's figure tightly held in silk
Moves in the misted window.

Slowly having passed among the drunks,
Always without followers, alone,
Breathing mists and perfumes,
She sits down at the window.

A fragrance of ancient superstitions
Comes from her resilient silks,
Her hat with mourning feathers,
And the rings on her narrow hand.

I, chained by the strange nearness,
Look behind the dark veil
And see an enchanted shore
And an enchanted distance.

Obscure mysteries are entrusted to me,
Someone's sun is presented to me,
And the bitter wine runs through
All the windings of my soul.

And the drooping ostrich feathers
Are swinging in my brain,
And the unfathomable blue eyes
Blossom on the distant shore.

A treasure lies inside my soul
And the key is given to me alone!
You're right, drunken monster!
I know: truth is in the wine.[8]

The world of euphony and the world of pain are significantly indistinguishable, as, Blok remembers, Dante showed:

[The countryside is] green boredom. And the city is gray boredom.
There is no pain in the first circle of Dante's Hell, only *longing*. This is considered the "mercy of heaven." But we seek pain in order to avoid ennui.[9]

"The Unknown Lady" moves toward the meaning of the Latin phrase (it ends with a recast form of the phrase) and toward the experience of the noxious smell. It is a real landscape because we are made to perceive the painfulness of the stereotypes it uses—the drunks, the whores, the smart-alecks, the dreams and the disillusions—by the cacophony which animates them. The central symbolic and female figure, here changed into the opposite of what it was in some of the earlier poems, at least in terms of verbal function, is animated successfully. What seems characteristic of Blok's better poems is a commingling of intellectualism and sensuousness in which the character as a mask or definition is occluded by its actions in a dramatic sequence. In this poem the drinking, like the drama, is a colloquial attempt at escaping into one's actual personality for which the dream of one's potential comes alive.

One never knows where one's personality *is*. The moment of the ecstasy is also the moment of disillusion, just as then the wine-induced illusion fades. The wonderful and the monstrous cohabit the world. The effort of Blok's inventiveness is to build a real tension so that the whore may be, as he sees her, both beautiful and deformed at the same time. The coincidence is his invention.

The dictionary says that the grotesque is, among other things, the distortion of aesthetic relations analogous to the comic distortions in the mental world. As comedy complements reason, so the grotesque completes the beautiful. The animal mask among the flowers—the hideous face of the innocent whore—is the obverse of the decoration among the ruins—of the figure of the Beautiful Lady itself. Zhirmunskii argues that the kind of "game" Hoffmann played is carried on in that mystic attitude which sees the real world as "...illusory, unreal: romantic irony distorts this reality into a hideous grotesque."[10] In "The Unknown Lady," Blok argues that regardless of moral judgment, because aesthetic consciousness alone makes experience available to the intellect, both elements of a contradiction do really obtain: ultimately, there is grace in perversion. The poem itself is the only plausible meetingplace of all its elements, of the poet and the whore, of the illusion and the reality. What ever is known is known only *in* the poem. One does not escape from "reality" to "illusion," or vice versa; one simultaneously enjoys both.

This is not to say that Blok did not respond to the political corruption around him, as he understood it, with a more nearly political poetry.[11] He hated the sham world of the bourgeoisie, the "confirmed wits" walking with their ladies. He associated this world with ruin. His political consciousness and activity, such as it was, moved against it. He was in a profound but politically unimportant sense subversive of the then existent social order. Although he never got into serious political trouble with that order, it is interesting that his poem "Guardian Angel," written in August 1906,[12] a rather poor coupling of an image of political freedom to an image of absolute freedom—"We are free souls! We are foul slaves!"—was considered by the censor to be dangerous material of "a revolutionary inclination." One line in the poem was even read as "incitement to heinous and criminal acts." Blok wrote the poem on his third wedding anniversary and, although he did not dedicate it, directed it to his wife. The magazine in which it first appeared in 1907 was confiscated and the editor prosecuted by the government.[13] Orlov points out the correspondence between this poem and Nekrasov's poem "For That I Deeply Scorn Myself," which deals with the same sort of political self-consciousness in a similar sort of metrical scheme and which further shows the direct influence on Blok of Nekrasov's social consciousness and technique.

Use of the city in Blok's poetry is more or less coincident with his entrance into its life, that is, from about 1903 on, but it is clearest in the group of poems called "The City." It is also coincident with the influence on him of contemporary literature, particularly the work of Briusov and, among foreigners, of Verhaeren. Blok himself pointed out in a note in the 1911 edition of his second book that the first poem in this section, a poem called "Poslednii den'"(The Last Day) and written in February 1904, had been written under the influence of Briusov's poem "Kon' bled" (The Pale Horse). Verhaeren's work was much admired by the Russian Symbolists in general, and some of it was even printed in its original French in Russian magazines. How Blok found it illustrative of what he thought a poem should involve is indicated in the following stanza from Verhaeren's "L'Effort" (Hard Work), with its antithetical constructions and appellative language, its praise of what is actual and its suggestion of a transformation through a spiritual or ideal understanding.

O ce travail farouche, âpre, tenace, austère,
Sur les plaines, parmi les mers, au cœur des monts,
Serrant ses noeuds partout et rivant ses chaînons
De l'un à l'autre bout des pays de la terre!
O ces gestes hardis, dans l'ombre ou la clarté,
Ces bras toujours ardents et ces mains jamais lasses,
Ces bras, ces mains unis à travers les espaces
Pour imprimer quand même à l'univers dompté
La marque de l'étreinte et de la force humaines
Et recréer les monts et les mers et les plaines,
D'après une autre volonté.

O this savage labor, austere, dogged and rough,
In the middle of mountains, on the seas and plains,
Tightening its bonds and riveting its chains
From one end to the other of the lands of the earth!
O these fearless gestures in shade or light,

These always ardent arms and never tired hands,
These arms, these hands united across vast lands
To imprint on a subdued universe still
The trademark of embrace and of power of men
And to recreate the plains and the seas and mountains
Following another will.

Blok did write poems that were intended to move us politically as well as aesthetically. In a letter to his father on December 30, 1905, he explained that

I'll never become a revolutionary or a "builder of life," not because I don't see any sense in one or the other, but simply because of my nature, faculties, and the content of my spiritual experiences.... The one obstacle to earning money (by writing) is revolution, but in this sense I'm not (perhaps from frivolity) afraid of it.

On October 18, 1905, the day after the tsar's manifesto of the establishment of a constitution of sorts, Blok wrote two poems both included in this section, "The City." The first poem was overtly political. Because of it, the issue of the paper *Our Life* in which it appeared was confiscated by the police.

Вися над городом всемирным,
В пыли прошедшей заточен,
Еще монарха в утре лирном
Самодержавный клонит сон.

И предок царственно-чугунный
Всё так же бредит на змее,
И голос черни многострунный
Еще не властен на Неве.

Уже на до́мах веют флаги,
Готовы новые птенцы,
Но тихи струи невской влаги,
И слепы темные дворцы,

И, если лик свободы явлен,
То прежде явлен лик змеи,
И ни один сустав не сдавлен
Сверкнувших колец чешуи.

Hanging above the universal city,
Imprisoned in the dust of the past,
Autocratic sleep still lingers
Over the monarch in the lyric dawn.

The royally cast-iron ancestor
Still rages astride the snake;
The many-stringed voice of the rabble
Is still impotent along the Neva.

Flags flutter from the houses,
New fledglings are prepared,
But the streams of the Neva are quiet,
And the dark palaces are blind.

If freedom's face is evident,
The serpent's face is clearer still,
And not one joint of the flashing
Rings of the scaley skin is squeezed.

The "ancestor" is a reference to the statue of Peter the Great and, through it, to Pushkin's "The Bronze Horseman." The reference occurs again in the same language in *Retribution*. In this poem, however, the reference is limited to political use. Both the contemporary experience and the historical tradition which it fuses are expressly political. In the last stanza, the political oppositions are given as personifications, much as in a morality play. The poet judges not the relative values of the conflict but the dangerous allure or predominance of what he presents as the evil, or wrong, side. The allegory does not successfully animate those political principles in terms of which it moves.

In the other poem, politics is appropriated by art to more than political ends:

Еще прекрасно серое небо,
Еще безнадежна серая даль.
Еще несчастных, просящих хлеба,
Никому не жаль, никому не жаль!

И над заливами голос черни
Пропал, развеялся в невском сне,
И дикие вопли: Свергни! О, свергни!
Не будят жалости в сонной волне...

И в небе сером холодные светы
Одели Зимний Дворец царя.
И латник в черном не даст ответа,
Пока не застигнет его заря.

Тогда, алея над водной бездной,
Пусть он угрюмей опустит меч,
Чтоб с дикой чернью в борьбе бесполезной
За древнюю сказку мертвым лечь...

The grey sky is still beautiful,
The grey distance, still without hope.
There still are lines of paupers begging bread
For whom nobody's sorry, nobody's sorry!

And over the bays the voice of the rabble
Has been lost, scattered in the Neva's sleep.
The wild howls—"Dethrone! O, dethrone!"—
Don't arouse pity in the dreamy wave...

The cold lights in the grey sky
Clothed the tsar's Winter Palace.
The cuirassier in black will not reply
Until the dawn has reached him.

Then flushing scarlet above the watery abyss,
Let him more sullenly set down his sword,
So that in the useless struggle with the wild rabble
For the ancient legend he fall like the dead...

Both poems describe a grey, foggy, autumn day. Both poems use certain words: "sleep," "Neva," "palace," and Pushkin's phrase "the voice of the rabble." This poem, however, immediately moves away from its political starting point to a dramatization in miniature of the values and principles which are involved in political conflict. Although neither poem states what happened on October 17, this poem indicates that at some moment previous to itself there was an actual effort at political change: at relieving the grey sky (which is *still* beautiful), at giving perspective meaning (which *still* offers no hope), at alleviating the suffering of the poor (who *still* beg, who are *still* miserable and unpitied and unsurprised). The repetition of the phrase "For whom nobody's sorry" gives the poem the impetus of dramatic irony. The phrase like a symbol tends to take on meaning and cuts back against the attitude first suggested to give the poem the scope of several "contradictory" aspects of the social condition. The line is made to bear on more than it syntactically refers to. The present moment is the homologue of history. It is also the point which by its reality and immediacy makes anagogical interpretation plausible.

The poem divides into two parts; each of those parts, into two. There are four stanzas, each of which is "complete" in itself and each of which advances an "argument." There is a gradual transition from the "actual" to the "literary." The first stanza gives the setting and the time at which the action takes place. The second stanza gives the practical conflict leading into the whole political dilemma: the war of the rich and the poor, of which there is, as Blok suggests, no resolution: "The wild howls...don't arouse pity in the dreamy wave." This is the allegorical extension of the physically descriptive fourth line of the first stanza. In the third stanza, moving by extension of the dream-in-wave image to the grey sky on a transcendent level, the poem turns to a literary actuality—to a description of a statue of a cuirassier on the roof of the Winter Palace, as Blok pointed out in a footnote, who "will not reply until the dawn has reached him." This is also a description of the opening scene of Aeschylus' *Agamemnon*, in which the herald on the palace roof announces simultaneously the sunrise and the receipt, by beacon system, of the news of the Argive success. The miseries of the war and the failures of the government in Agamemnon's absence move the herald, who warns us not so much about good news as about the bad he has collected. "I sing," he says, "only to weep again the pity of this house." Who knows the play knows the catastrophe—the king's death—and the irony involved in that death, knows also that the bad news of the past repeatedly and relentlessly runs over into the future. This is what Blok has perceived and what torments him.

Blok's articles and poetry are filled with images or suggestions of impending personal and societal doom: "Isn't one of us doomed irrevocably to perish?" "We are hurling ourselves directly under a mad *troika* to certain death." "I think that people of recent generations have in their hearts a persistent sense of catastrophe." "Destruction is inevitable." Like Dostoevsky, he identified the devil with the bourgeois, the polluter of life who will perish by his pollution: says Blok,

> Go away from me, Satan, go away from me, bourgeois, just so we don't touch each other, see each other, hear each other; whether I'm better or much worse than him, I feel defiled, I feel nauseous; go away from me, Satan.

The corruption is pervasive, almost invisible and horrible, rolling like an epidemic toward a terrible end. It is like the false and foul things which Baudelaire identified as the work of Satan, omnipresent throughout nature, and from which he prayed for deliverance, as in this excerpt from a letter to his mother:

> Souls of those I have loved, souls of those I have sung, strengthen me, support me, put off from me the lie and the corrupting vapors of the world; and you, my God, grant me the grace of producing a few beautiful verses to prove to myself that I am not the last among men, that I am not inferior to those I scorn!

For Blok the moment of drama is the essence of the historical moment.

In the fourth stanza he identifies the herald with Agamemnon—dramatically quite possible, in the sense that, as Dostoevsky presented it, the catastrophe and the prevision of it are identical, that what we call the catastrophe is only the end-product or expression of a process which has already taken on independent life and become historically necessary. Blok assigns his cuirassier (going by syntax, for the moment) Agamemnon's condition: "flushing scarlet above the watery abyss." Agamemnon had come home across the ocean to die in his own blood-bath, stabbed three times with a sword. Clytemnestra announced that he was reduced to his transgression, that righteousness had triumphed and that the cycle of purification had come full swing. We know that she does not know enough. Blok tells us that, specifically, we know the legend of the curse of the house of Atreus *after* its original resolution, that we know it as continually operative, and that we know the imperative of interrupting the *historical* process by yielding to the *drama*, by taking our revenge on ourselves. The notion is not so much that whoever stands as king will be overthrown by the mob as that the position itself is untenable and unendurable; that both the mob and its victim are separately wrong, that important activity must be in the name of that organizing, aesthetic consciousness which takes "the ancient legend" as paragon and as instance. This is the fourth moment of the poem: the activity summed up, by description, analysis, and literary analogy, into its dramatic essence or symbolic meaning. We have no paraphrase for it: all the gestures of Agamemnon and the tsar are frozen in and re-animated by the statue and the terrible, Cassandra-like cries of the poor.

At the same time that he was caught up in the political whirlpool that followed the year 1905, Blok was trying to define by poetry what he regarded as the essence of lyricism. In January 1907 he wrote the 30 poems in "The Snow Mask" cycle. In a letter to Briusov on March 24, 1907, Blok explained his intentions and what he considered his accomplishment:

> Slowly coming to understand dramatic form but still having very poorly mastered the language of prose, I try more and more to put into verse what belongs to it particularly—song and lyricism—and to express in drama and in prose what previously willy-nilly was expressed only in verse.
>
> However, *An Unexpected Joy* is still far from embodying this principle of uniform distribution of material, and, I, therefore, of course, didn't succeed in adequately putting my experiences into words. My next little book (which is still held up at the printer's) [*The Snow Mask*] will be, I think, more of a unit, and digressions from lyricism in lyricism, as have happened in my work before, are fewer.

Once the booklet was out, however, Blok felt its limitations. He felt that the principle which he had asserted in it was self-defeating, precisely the direction he did not wish to move in:

The little book is subjective to the last degree, accessible to the narrowest circle of readers. I'm growing out of that little book already, although it's the latest. *An Unexpected Joy* still is better.[14]

The poems in "The Snow Mask" section move with a lyric excitement or surcharge of energy close to delight. They are exhibits of technique. They try for response without commitment. They represent the closest Blok came to the structure of music in the structure of poetry. The poem called "Snow Cursive" is a sort of pyrotechnics of rhythm and rhyme. Lines vary in length from one syllable to eleven; some are in pairs connected by interlacing rhymes, some are in quatrains with alternating rhymes or with paired rhymes. Some rhymes are exact, some at least canonical, and some lines are broken so that the rhyme, although there, is screened by the syncopation. The poem moves from

Снежная мгла взвилась.
Легли сугробы кругом.

Да. Я с тобой незнаком.
Ты — стихов моих пленная вязь.

The snowy haze soared up.
Snow-drifts lay around.

Yes. We haven't met.
You're the captured cursive of my verse.

to

О, стихи зимы среброснежной!
Я читаю вас наизусть.

O silver-snow verses of winter!
I read you by heart.

It is a poem of love to a lady and to the poetry itself—to the "Muse," because the lady is considered the catalyst of the poetry. The poem is not really "about" anything; it leads to an ecstasy, which in fact, it has produced. Unlike the earlier poems which chiefly described a spring landscape, this poem is devoted to winter in the sense that the snow here moves through various moments and forms to become the poetry itself.

Zhirmunskii has pointed out that "...the basic metaphor in a poem like

'Under the Masks' becomes the immediate object of a metaphorical process for one or more derivative metaphors of the second degree, as it were, moving off in several directions."[15] "Under the Masks" is a complex of non-rational metaphors. The method is, of course, basically romantic—obviously so in lines like

> Ночь сходила на чертоги,
> Замедляя шаг.
>
> Night descended on the chambers,
> Slowing down its step.

This is extension of a private impression by a process of metaphoric realization of an image into a poetic "theme."

The uncertainty of conviction yet the certainty of attitude, the skeptical game of language, and the control of convention are apparent in the 1907 poem "Vtoroe kreshchen'e" (The Second Baptism):

> Открыли дверь мою метели,
> Застыла горница моя,
> И в новой снеговой купели
> Крещен вторым крещеньем я.
>
> И в новый мир вступая, знаю,
> Что люди есть, и есть дела.
> Что путь открыт наверно к раю
> Всем, кто идет путями зла.
>
> . . .
>
> Ты мне сулишь еще мгновенья?
> Пророчишь, что весна придет?
>
> Но посмотри, как сердце радо!
> Заграждена снегами твердь.
> Весны не будет, и не надо:
> Крещеньем третьим будет — Смерть.
>
> Snowstorms opened up my door,
> My chamber froze with cold,
> And in the new snow-font
> I was given a second baptism.
>
> Entering the new world, I know
> That there are men and things to do,
> That the way to heaven is open for sure
> To all who follow the paths of evil.
>
> . . .
>
> You promise me other moments?
> You prophesy that spring will come?

But look how happy my heart is!
The sky is stopped with snow.
There will be no spring, and there is no need for one.
The third baptism will be Death.

One may also note the transformative use of natural phenomena, consistent with those aesthetic principles and obligations which Blok insisted on in his 1906 article "Colors and Words." The effort of style is to allow a free play of convention, in colors and words, according to whatever pattern seems significant of the phenomena perceived. The emphasis is on actuality, that is, on the applicability of the images and symbols.

The "freer" the technical form is the greater is the reliance on the juxtaposition of images and symbols to specify some concept of rhythm. Only very rarely, however, does Blok abandon rhyme. In the poem, "Nastignutyi metel'iu" (Overtaken by the Snow-storm) (1907), the lines vary in length from three to fifteen syllables and, more important, have from one to four stresses. There is, however, a pattern of alternating rhymes—assonances—running throughout the poem:

Вьюга пела.
И кололи снежные иглы.
И душа леденела.
Ты меня настигла.

Ты запрокинула голову в высь.
Ты сказала: — Глядись, глядись,
Пока не забудешь
Того, что любишь.

И указала на дальние города линии,
На поля снеговые и синие,
На бесцельный холод.

The blizzard sang.
The snow needles jabbed.
The soul congealed.
You overtook me.

You threw your head back to the sky.
You said: "Look, look,
Before you forget
What you love."

And pointed out the distant lines of the city,
The snowy and deep-blue fields,
The aimless cold.

One researcher, trying to illustrate the connection between French Symbolist discoveries and Russian symbolist practice, said that the poem "Na zov metelei" (The Call of the Snow-storms) is "the nearest the *dol'niki* came to the French *vers libre*," and cited the lines:

> Белые встали сугробы,
> И мраки открылись.
> Выплыл серебряный серп.
> И мы уносились,
> Обреченные оба
> На ущерб.

> The white snow-drifts rose,
> The darkness opened.
> The silver crescent emerged,
> And we rushed away,
> Both predestined
> To suffer loss.

This is not so. The poem is rhymed (assonance), in this stanza—a b c b a c—and only slightly differently in the others. The lines vary in length from one to three stresses. A definite rhythmic pattern is established, throughout the poem as in this stanza, by the rhyme. The rhythmic function of rhyme is evident. This, precisely, was one of Blok's major contributions to problems of versification. As Nikitina and Shuvalov put it, "Blok rightfully has come to be regarded as the canonizer of non-canonical forms of verse."

Intellectually, the "idea" behind these poems may be said to derive in part from Schopenhauer's notion of the spirit of music and from Nietszche's concept of the contrasting principles of Apollonianism and Dionysianism, a principle that in Russia was advanced particularly by Viacheslav Ivanov. In 1906 Blok had planned a play on this general theme—"Hyperborean Dionysos"—and in his notebooks had referred to "the fresh cycle" into which he would enter under the aegis of Dionysos.

In October 1907, Blok wrote Belyi that:

> ...I write, or try to write, *as a man* with a desire for health and simplicity. For example, "On Lyricism": I believe in the correctness of the point of departure: I know that in lyricism there is the danger of *decay* and I persecute it. *I* beat *myself:* such is the import of my articles in general, quite apart from literary evaluations, which one may disagree with as one pleases (even I admit the incorrectness of a number of things). Whipping myself for lyric poisons, which threaten me, too, with destruction, I try to warn others, also.

In the October of the year before, he had written the poem "V Oktiabre"

(In October), included in the cycle "The City." Incidentally descriptive of the ordinary events of city life and facetious in tone, it is about himself, filled with sympathy for the suffering—and for himself:

Открыл окно. Какая хмурая
  Столица в октябре!
Забитая лошадка бурая
  Гуляет на дворе.

. . .

Всё, всё по старому, бывалому,
  И будет, как всегда:
Лошадке и мальчишке малому
  Не сладки холода.

Да и меня без всяких поводов
  Загнали на чердак.
Никто моих не слушал доводов,
  И вышел мой табак.

I opened the window. What a frowning
  Capital in October!
A beaten brown horse
  Circles in the yard.

. . .

Everything's the way it was, long ago,
  And will be, forever:
The cold weather is not sweet
  For the horse and the little boy.

Yes, and without any cause at all
  They have driven me up to the attic.
Nobody listened to my arguments,
  And my tobacco is all gone.

Three weeks after the October 1, 1907, letter to Belyi, Blok wrote the first part of the long lyric "Zakliatie ognëm i mrakom" (An Incantation by Fire and Darkness) included in the "Faina" cycle of this second book. It is not only an attempt to transcend the injustices the other poem takes notice of, but also a definite and successful effort of the intellect to describe a musical sensuousness powerful and complete in itself:

О, весна без конца и без краю —
Без конца и без краю мечта!
Узнаю тебя, жизнь! Принимаю!
И приветствую звоном щита!

O spring without end, without boundary—
Without end, without boundary—dream!
I know you, life! I accept you!
And I hail you with thundering shield!

From the viewpoint of one's own emotions, eroticism alone may seem real—a solipsistic delight in imaginary and complete gratification on a sexual level, as suggested by poems like "Pesnia Fainy" (Faina's Song) (December 1907) or, in the final section of this book, the poem "V diunakh" (On the Dunes) (July 1907). "On the Dunes" is remarkable for its inversion: the passion that conveyed the image of the Beautiful Lady is expended on an accessible woman who finally runs away. The poem works from the words to the emotion, not, as before, from the emotion to its words:

Я не люблю пустого словаря
Любовных слов и жалких выражений:

I don't like the empty dictionary
Of love words and sorry phrases:

The words are taken for real, as we say, from the start. The consummation asked for is equally real:

И пусть она мне крикнет:
«Твоя! Твоя!»

And let her shout to me:
"I'm yours! Yours!"

To be worthwhile the drama of a poem must be accomplished. The present success must be both meaningful and verifiable, in the sense that it can be repeated or legislated. Oddly, the talent which does verify it is, for Blok, no guarantee:

The lyric poet gives people nothing. But people *come* and *take* it.
Poets are interesting in so far as they differ.... Consequently, the center of gravity of every poet is his own personality.[16]

What the poet must "get over" in order to be successful is what most impells him to poetry. Eroticism is the failure of the sensual intellect to sustain its play, the difference between the musical sensuousness of that quatrain beginning "O spring without end, without boundary" and the physical surexcitation of:

Я гнал её далёко. Исцарапал
Лицо о хвои, окровавил руки
И платье изорвал. Кричал и гнал
Её, как зверя, вновь кричал и звал....

I chased her far. I scratched my face
Against the pine-needles, bloodied my hands
And tore my clothes. I shouted and I chased
Her like a beast, shouted again and called....

The erotism of a strong impulse or craving is readily translated into eroticism. The generic desire or activity occupies itself with enumeration of specific satisfactions real or imagined. It is a nonpoetic impulse to poetry which can be adequately satisfied only poetically. Discussion of transcendent love seems to involve a kind of amatory apophasis: the ecstasy inspired by the Beautiful Lady appears as an experience much like the ecstasy purchased from a whore. In either instance, if the report in poetry of the ecstasy is limited to classification of moments of violence, chiefly, and bewildered power, the poem remains only a kind of mirror-catalogue of the poet's remembered responses. The bad poems about the Lady and the bad erotica both err in the direction of inadequate self-celebration.

The movement in subsequent poems is away from both the allegorical Lady and the artificial whore to an understanding of their essential properties—what Blok calls the musical essence of the world. The understanding is offered alone in three of the four poems that comprise the sequence "Free Thoughts," a title that comes, Bonneau has suggested in her book on Blok, from Apollon Grigor'ev's poem "The Question," in which there are two lines about "new thoughts read in a novel by Sand, free, terrible thoughts." The poems are socially conscious poems that refer to a free consciousness beyond the restrictions of political and social activity. The three poems[17] contrast strikingly with those in "The Snow Mask," which had appeared not long before these were written. The poems are emotionally subdued. They are metaphoric understatement. In moments, these poems, which are long narratives with lyric passages, are quietly beautiful, such as the following excerpt from the poem "Nad ozerom" (Above the Lake) (1907). Blok says that he is talking with the lake, but,

> Оно меня не видит — и не надо.
> Как женщина усталая, оно
> Раскинулось внизу и смотрит в небо,
> Туманится, и даль поит туманом,
> И отняло у неба весь закат.

> It doesn't see me—and it needn't.
> Like a tired woman it lies
> Sprawled out looking at the sky;
> Becoming misty, misting the distance,
> It has severed the whole sunset from the sky.

This is a lyric of description, like the setting for a play. The following lines from the poem "O smerti" (On Death) are the setting for the episode of a workman's death, which follows them:

Однажды брел по набережной я.
Рабочие возили с барок в тачках
Дрова, кирпич и уголь. И река
Была еще синей от белой пены.
В отстегнутые вороты рубах
Глядели загорелые тела.
И светлые глаза привольной Руси
Блестели строго с почерневших лиц.

Once I wandered along the shore.
Workmen were wheeling firewood, bricks
And coal in barrows from the barges. The river
Was bluer still for all the whitecaps.
The unbuttoned collars of their shirts
Showed shining sunburnt bodies,
And the radiant eyes of unfettered *Rus'*
Shone sharply on their darkened faces.

It is a quietly ironic poetry that exposes false values to ridicule by confronting one absurdity with another—or with itself, as in "V severnom more" (On the North Sea):

Прочтя все надписи: «Навек с тобой.»
«Здесь были Коля с Катей.» «Диодор
«Иеромонах и послушник Исидор
«Здесь были. Дивны божии дела». —
Прочтя все надписи, выходим в море
В пузатой и смешной моторной лодке.

Reading all the inscriptions: "Forever yours."
"Kolia and Katia were here." "Diodor
The monk and the novice Isidor
Were here. God moves in mysterious ways."—
Reading all the inscriptions, we set out to sea
In a paunchy and silly motor boat.

The poems are modern poetry—conversational, lyric, ironic, shaped by the aptness and surprise of metaphors taken from everyday life. Chukovskii, who knew Blok's St. Petersburg, says in his memoirs that especially "The Unknown Lady," "Above the Lake," and "On the North Sea" seem to him pictures in his own memory, descriptions of what was really happening:

In short, many of Blok's poems are for me, as an old *Peterburzhets*, connected with such concrete, genre, everyday, actual images that these poems, which seem so hazily enigmatic, strike me frequently as being just as accurate a reproduction of actuality as, say, the poems of Nekrasov.

The idea of freedom of which the Beautiful Lady and the whore were unsatisfactory symbols is here given, natural to the poetry, as images antithetical to but following from the images of actuality:

...Мы глядим
С молитвенной и полною душою
На тихо уходящий силует
Красавицы под всеми парусами...
На драгоценный камень фероньеры,
Горящий в смуглых сумерках чела.

...We look
With full and prayerful soul
On the quietly receding silhouette
Of the sea queen under sail...
On the gem of the precious diadem
Burning in the swarthy dusk of heaven.

It is a symbolism built by analogy to a perceived system of actual correspondences—that absurd motorboat and the beautiful yacht—which says what it needs to and means much more. All of Blok's metaphorical extensions or thematic developments preceed accurately and reliably in literary terms—the syntax and the connection are always there—but the elaboration of meaning involves an intensity of response or a metaphysic to which we readers are seldom inclined.

The two worlds that seem to be brought against each other are not exactly the antinomies they may at first appear. The metaphors that carry them are drawn from what we ordinarily term the real world. Metaphor, as Wallace Stevens remarked, "creates a new reality from which the original appears to be unreal." Blok considered himself as vascillating perpetually between these "realities," and pictured this in figures contrasting, typically, "above" and "below."

The poems in "Free Thoughts" are indications of mature talent, of craftsmanship, and of the transition in poetry from the use of images to enucleate ideas to the use of images as ideas. After this point, Blok tried to make his style precise in order to expand his meaning—to define the complex of social relations by a coherent, dramatic understanding.

Blok was aware of the difficulties of writing successful poetry. He was aware of the necessity of constructing figures in his poems so that they would light up actual behavior and urban life. In the city, he said, "in a magic vortex and magic light the terrible and beautiful visions of life occur."

It would not have been difficult for Blok to have repudiated his early work. Mere stubbornness is not satisfactory explanation for the tenacity with which he insisted on supporting it, as he insisted in his letter to Belyi on August 6, 1907, and as he insisted to the end of his life. He is right in saying that his work is all of a piece. This may not be usual, but, for Blok, it is correct. From the start, he saw in definable terms all he ever came to see. It is the increasing accuracy or sharpening of vision that allowed him to discard nonfunctioning devices, to alter his imagery and to expand his technique. Like Baudelaire, he saw the content and figures of actuality as dreams and saw dreams as the substance of actuality. The work of the symbols was to contain that otherwise inexpressible, intolerable complexity.

What had been prayer and invocation to the Beautiful Lady became discourse (as in the following poem, "Kogda vy stoite na moëm puti" [When You Stand on My Way, 1908]) as the lady became more obviously real. The perfume that he, the poet, takes from the living flower by impressing it into poetry he would have the lady restore—vindicate—by the vitality of her love and beauty:

Сколько ни говорите о печальном,
Сколько ни размышляйте о концах и началах,
Всё же я смею думать,

Что вам только пятнадцать лет.
И потому я хотел бы,
Чтобы вы влюбились в простого человека,

Который любит землю и небо
Больше, чем рифмованные и нерифмованные
Речи о земле и о небе.

Право, я буду рад за вас,
Так как — только влюбленный
Имеет право на звание человека.

No matter how much you talk about sad things,
No matter how much you think about ends and beginnings,
Still, I dare think,

You are only fifteen.
And therefore I would wish
That you would fall in love with a simple man,

Who loves the earth and sky
More than rhymed and unrhymed
Speeches about the earth and sky.

Indeed, I will be happy for you,
Since only a lover
Has the right to be called a man.

VI

Poems

1907–1916

Donner la vie idéale à celui qui n'a pas la vie réelle.—Leconte de Lisle

In 1907 Symbolism was becoming accepted in Russia, as it had earlier in France. Its tastes and innovations were becoming literary canons—even as it was dissolving as a movement. Belyi and Ivanov moved beyond their differences to emphasize the evangelical aspect of art; the literary gatherings at Ivanov's apartment on Wednesdays ended; Blok and Belyi split for several years over literary disagreements and private jealousy; Briusov moved ubiquitously among all groups trying to revitalize what, more than ten years before, he had bravely and sensationally introduced; a number of second-rate imitators were crowding the "little magazines"; and under the umbrella of Symbolism new talents were developing who would extend what the Symbolists had discovered. Despite the changes, Blok insisted on the integrity of his convictions, so that, except in the beginning, he never moved with the school, never moved deliberately against it, and kept working toward the sort of poetry the French pre-Symbolists and Symbolists had had in mind, the kind of poetry Briusov had urged on Russia with his first little anthology in 1894.

During the period between the 1905 Revolution and the World War Blok came to maturity as a poet. His most beautiful, most powerful lyrics were written in these years. Work on his long, brilliant poem *Retribution* was all but completed before the end of the war. Despite the pressures of literary factions around him, he repeatedly stood alone, eschewing theory, explaining his judgments with tact and conviction, and writing poetry.[1] It is these lyrics of Blok's maturity which best exemplify the potentialities of poetry that the theories of the Symbolists had defined.

Zhirmunskii said that Blok's "third book" of poems guarantees his position among the best Russian lyricists—Derzhavin, Pushkin, Baratynskii,

Tiutchev, and Lermontov. Blok's third book includes all of his shorter lyrics written between 1907 and 1916 as grouped by him in the fourth, or 1921, edition of the third volume of his *Collected Poems.* The book is divided into ten sections, each section presenting a certain (some, a definite) thematic unity. Within each section, the poems, with some exceptions, are presented in chronological order. The sections are as follows:

1. "Strashnyi mir" (The Terrible World), 48 poems written between February 1909 and July 1916, many of which are ironic treatments of the diabolic aspects of life.
2. "Vozmezdie" (Retribution), 17 poems written between July 1908 and December 1913 on the general theme of the loss that follows from deception in love, as given particularly in the poem on the Don Giovanni theme "Shagi komandora" (The Steps of the Commander).
3. "Iamby" (Iambs), 12 poems, dedicated to his half-sister, Angelina, written between June 1907 and February 1914 and published first as a pamphlet in Petersburg in 1919. Quite a few of the poems, especially in their first versions, were originally intended as parts of Blok's long poem *Retribution.*
4. "Ital'ianskie stikhi" (Italian Verses), 24 poems, among them the most exquisite and moving lyrics Blok wrote, composed chiefly during Blok's trip to Italy in May and June 1909, but subsequently revised.
5. "Raznye stikhotvoreniia" (Various Poems), 25 poems written between the summer of 1908 and the summer of 1916 and dealing mostly with the poet's self-consciousness.
6. "Arfy i skripki" (Harps and Violins), 72 poems written over much the same period—March 1908 to February 1916—and held together loosely by what might be called an ideal, even romantic, sense of music.
7. "Karmen" (Carmen), 10 poems written in March 1914 for the opera singer Liubov' Del'mas, known for her performance of the title role in Bizet's opera.
8. "Solov'inyi sad" (The Nightingale Garden), a lyric in seven sections published as a pamphlet in 1918 but finished in October 1915, a kind of "story in verse" descriptive of the little village of Guéthary on the Bay of Biscay, where Blok had lived for a while in the summer of 1913.
9. "Rodina" (The Native Land), 26 poems written between May 1907 and March 1916 on the theme of Russian history as seen from the viewpoint of conditions in Russia in Blok's time.
10. "O chëm poët veter" (What the Wind Sings About), six poems, originally dedicated to his wife, written in October 1913 and published in *Russkaia mysl'* (Russian Thought) in 1915, songs of emptiness but suggesting redemption.

The third book returns to the specifics and intensity of vision of Blok's first book. In August 1907, Blok wrote Belyi that

...all the things I have written *so far* which I consider successful (and they are few) are *symbolist* and *romantic*.... I stand on a solid course, and... everything I have written is organic continuation of the first *Verses about the Beautiful Lady.*[2]

Taken literally, Blok's statement does not make sense, because almost all his poems written between 1902 and 1907—that is, between the Beautiful Lady poems and this letter—are obviously not continuation of the Lady at all. What it means is suggested by Leconte de Lisle's phrase that the task of poetry was "to give the ideal life to the man who has no real life."[3] The Beautiful Lady poems were, Blok thought, a picture of the ideal life, but only the later poems, by depicting equally the absence of any "real" life, offer the reader the vision of reality which Blok believed the task of poetry to be. In this sense, the progression from the early fantasies to the later dramatic visions does represent an organic continuation. The poems about the Lady may be said to be the original vision, which seemed —especially in retrospect—to have been effortless. The other poems represent the hard work of bringing the vision to life. This is part of what Blok meant when he said to his mother as he lay dying that only his first book, about the Beautiful Lady, was real and that all the rest was literary contrivance. The statement also indicates Blok's awareness of the great difficulty of making things real, of giving his figures a realness which depends, like texture, on its contrary—the imaginary garden, or, for Blok, the contrivance of the Lady. In Blok's later poems, the Lady's place is taken by other and more nearly concrete images of absolute freedom. In the August 6, 1907, letter to Belyi, Blok says he does not understand Belyi's view that the later poems are not connected with those about the Beautiful Lady and other early work. The Lady, perfected, disappeared, but the effort at perfection was a development of the initial vision. Blok could not work toward such perfection within the framework of any cult or any coterie. As he said in the same letter to Belyi, he had not, in the period since 1902, subverted their old beliefs, but he did wish to avoid literary impediments, believing himself, he emphasized, "*sufficiently strong to stand alone.*"

In his late twenties and early thirties, when he wrote most of the poems in this third book, Blok no longer took the poet's intoxication as itself transcendent. Rather, he considered it the instrument for cutting through the limits and illusions of ordinary consciousness to reveal that other, real world.

For Blok, as for Baudelaire, this involves a sense of religious sin expressed in images of the confusion and complexity of life and of suffering. The poet's desire or aim has been constant and constantly refined. The possibilities of expression and, in moral terms, of resolution, that once were perceptibly restricted or even, as in Blok's first book, excessively vague, are no more extensive. However, they successfully cut through psychological complexities and are adequate to the conditions of a given poem. The vision of the Lady developed into the dream-vision of a symbolic whore and then became an image of fear and trembling. The Lady was not carried over, but the kind of thinking of which she was once the example was. An excessive emotional ecstasy, heightened by anticipated loss, gives Blok's poetry of this period, Zhirmunskii said,

...an audacity and irrationality of construction previously unknown in Russian poetry—sort of a sense of the presence of a prehistoric chaos, of free cosmic forces, out of a dark "terrible world."

Blok knew that his chief problem was the control of ideas by the specifics of versification. He was aware of the wild ambivalence in his mind between power and impotency and of the necessary balance that the figures of his poetry had to impose. This is what he had in mind when he jotted down in his notebook "...form in art is an organizing spirit, a creative order.... There is no such thing as formless art." Emotions cannot be formed into meaning by the consistency of conscience. They must be overcome; that is, they must be transformed into patterns, which are their meaning, as Blok said in his letter of September 3, 1909, to E. P. Ivanov:

Following him [Pushkin] our literature somehow ceased to be *art*, and all that we valued and value (ending with Tolstoy and Dostoevsky) is a magnificent mess. This won't and mustn't go on.... Art is only the cosmos—the creative spirit shaping chaos (the spiritual and corporeal world). That the world of corporeal and spiritual appearances is *only* chaos there's no point arguing further: this must be clear to the artist (as it was clear to Aeschylus, Dante, Pushkin, Bellini, Leonardo, Michelangelo and will be to future artists). Our great writers (I think chiefly of Tolstoy and Dostoevsky) built everything *on chaos* (they "valued" it) and thereby a ten-fold chaos developed, that is, they were bad artists. Cosmos can be built only *out of* chaos.

Blok valued Poe's work—which he called "an underground current in Russia"—precisely for its expert craftsmanship:

Poe's works seem written in our time, and their scope is so wide that you can hardly consider him an ancestor of so-called "symbolism...." Of course, the "Symbolists" are indebted to Poe more than to anyone else.... Former followers of the principle of "art for art's sake" cannot deny Poe, going on to the next stage by having become "Symbolists" in the more strict sense of the word as opposed to the narrow sense of "decadence."[4]

Blok himself commented that he felt Poe's influence on his early poem

"Noch' grozoi bushevala" (The Night Roared with Thunder) (1900). His 1912 poem "Osennii vecher byl" (It Was an Autumn Evening) in "The Terrible World" section of the third book, is a commentary on Poe's "The Raven." The poem's epigraph is two lines from "The Raven" in Briusov's translation. Blok's poem is a commentary on Poe's in the sense that it is a redramatization of what Blok takes Pce's influence to be. It is a translation of a state of mind and, consequently, an analogy to Poe's poem. "That gentleman" and a "shaggy dog" replace the raven, whom Poe identifies with the devil as prophet. The gentleman comes from *The Brothers Karamazov* and is the one whom Ivan told: "Sometimes I don't see you and even don't hear your voice, like last time, don't always get what you're mumbling because *it's I, I myself am speaking, and not you!*" The devil replies to Ivan, "I'm pleased that we began to thee and thou each other at once." "'You idiot,' Ivan laughed."

Blok's poem is filled with this deep and bitter irony, which is not in Poe's. Although the values which the symbols in Blok's poems have do not necessarily carry over from poem to poem and must in each instance be derived from the particular context (there being no over-all system to which they may be referred), the dog in this poem is much like the dog in *The Twelve*—a solid and pejorative figure of middle-class people and manners. The gentleman in Blok's poem tells the persona, the "I," that

> «Она — всё та ж: Линор безумного Эдгара.
> «Возврата нет. — Еще? Теперь я всё сказал».
>
> She's still the same: *mad Edgar's Lenore*.
> There's no way back. More? I've said it all.

Poe's formal "order" is here applied to the "chaos" of the Dostoevskian material. The gentleman, and the dog who "seems to say: *It's time to give in, sir*," announce the necessity of adjusting in a practical way to one's deepest losses—one's own past (Lenore is dead) and the future which one's lost ideals once promised. This is compunded with and complicated by Blok's feeling that an understanding of the world, as aesthetic perception, is and must be organic: "In poetic apperception of the world there is no split between the personal and the general. The more sensitive a poet is the more he senses 'his own' and 'not his own' together."

Illustration in Blok's poetry of the development of this concept is the changing figure of the protagonist. The protagonist of the first book is a hero in the conventional sense: a lyric "I," a young man, a native son, a handsome swain, a promising "intellectual," or even the conventional clown Harlequin. In the second book, the protagonist is a roué, an habitual drinker and café-dweller, a slightly aged young man, possessor of a literary legacy corrupted by the disuse imposed by irony. The protagonist in the third book typically is a victim of his own emotions, as in the following poem (1910) from "The Terrible World" section:

Там человек сгорел.-Фет

Как тяжело ходить среди людей
И притворяться непогибшим,
И об игре трагической страстей
Повествовать еще нежившим.

И, вглядываясь в свой ночной кошмар,
Строй находить в нестройном вихре чувства,
Чтобы по бледным заревам искусства
Узнали жизни гибельной пожар!

There a man burned up.-Fet

How difficult it is to move in the crowd,
Pretending that oneself has not yet perished,
Narrating to those who've not yet lived
About the tragic play of passions,

Or, peering into one's own nightmare,
To find a scheme in the vertigo of feeling,
That others may discover through art's pale reflections
The fire of this disastrous life.

He is both the agent and the sacrifice of a moment of history, taking on in his own person present responsibility for the oppression of the past and the promise of the future, as the poem that opens the section suggests:

К МУЗЕ

Есть в напевах твоих сокровенных
Роковая о гибели весть.
Есть проклятье заветов священных,
Поругание счастия есть.

И такая влекущая с сила,
Что готов я твердить за молвой,
Будто ангелов ты низводила,
Соблазняя своей красотой...

. . .

Я хотел, чтоб мы были врагами,
Так за что ж подарила мне ты
Луг с цветами и твердь со звездами —
Всё проклятье своей красоты?

И коварнее северной ночи,
И хмельней золотого Аи,
И любови цыганской короче
Были страшные ласки твои...

И была роковая отрада
В попираньи заветных святынь,
И безумная сердцу услада —
Эта горькая страсть, как полынь!

TO THE MUSE

There is in your secret melodies
The fatal news of loss;
There is the curse of sacred legacies,
The profanation of happiness,

And a force of such attraction
That I'm prepared to repeat the rumor
That you brought angels down
Seducing them by your beauty.

. . .

I wished we had been enemies,
So why did you then give me
A meadow with flowers and a starry heaven—
The whole curse of your beauty?

More perfidious than a Northern night,
More intoxicating than golden Ay,
And briefer than a gypsy love
Were your terrible caresses...

There was a fatal delight
In trampling cherished sacred things,
A mad, sweet delight to the heart—
This passion bitter as wormwood!

The agent and the object of the poetry have merged into one concept. The Lady and the Muse represent the same vision. The greater passion of mature sensibility involves also greater destruction, a dichotomy which, although more nearly precise and more nearly actual than disgust or delight, requires that poetry, like the poet's passion, move always against existing corruption toward the promise of real freedom and toward its own purification, as Baudelaire knew: "Myself, I say: the unique and supreme voluptuousness of love lies in the certainty of doing *evil*."

Baudelaire saw the temptations of love as themselves the only and necessary method of purification of beauty. The changes in the original version and the final version of the last stanza of Baudelaire's poem "Hymne" reveal the disinterestedness associated with the mask of beauty as beauty's source:

A la très-Bonne, à la très-Belle,
Qui m'a versé joie et santé,
Salut en la Vie Éternelle,
En l'Éternelle Volupté!

A la très-bonne, à la très-belle
Qui fait ma joie et ma santé,
A l'ange, à l'idole imortelle,
Salut en l'immortalité![5]

It is a spiritualized love which, prompted by some perception, actually grows on its own talent and conscience—on the excellence of its own morality. Basically it is an effort to escape an oppressive sense of guilt through realization of freedom (the crime of real rebellion). It is presented as a drama between emotion which exceeds itself, which confounds the criminal with the victim, and the artist who is never excessive, who succeeds precisely by means of limitations.

Perhaps one aspect of the difference between the poems in Blok's second book and the poems in his third is given by the differences between the two earlier poems on the "double" theme—"To My Double" (1901) and "The Double" (1903)—and the third, 1909 poem called "Dvoinik" (The Double). The first poem talks about the commitment of one half of one's self to the violence the other half does to a girl. The second poem is about the love triangle of one's two selves, given as Harlequin and an old man (a Harlequin Junior and Senior, just as Dostoevsky had a Goliadkin Junior and Senior in his long story *The Double*), and a girl, given as Columbine, to whom the poem is addressed. In the third poem, the two halves are not so readily separated. The poet does not know whether he is what he dreams or whether he is what he has done. He says that he was walking along one foggy October evening, remembering a tune, when a forgotten melody occurred to him, and he began to think of his youth:

Вдруг вижу, — Из ночи туманной,
Шатаясь, подходит ко мне
Стареющий юноша (странно,
Не снился ли мне он во сне?)
Выходит из ночи туманной
И прямо подходит ко мне.

И шепчет: «Устал я шататься,
Промозглым туманом дышать,
В чужих зеркалах отражаться
И женщин чужих целовать...»
И стало мне странным казаться,
Что я его встречу опять...

Вдруг — он улыбнулся нахально, —
И нет близ меня никого...
Знаком этот образ печальный,
И где-то я видел его...
Быть может, себя самого
Я встретил на глади зеркальной?

Suddenly I see: out of the foggy night,
An aging youth comes stumbling
Up to me (strange,
Haven't I seen him before in a dream?),
Comes out of the foggy night
And comes directly up to me.

He whispers: "I'm tired of stumbling,
Of breathing the dank fog,
Of being reflected in other people's mirrors,
And of kissing the women of others..."
And I felt it a strange thing
That I would meet him again...

Suddenly—he smiled impudently—
And there's nobody beside me...
This sad figure is familiar,
I have seen it somewhere before...
Perhaps it was my very self
I met on the mirror's smooth surface?

The quest for life brings one to oneself, not without hope but in despair of ever defining oneself. The unraveling of the future seems only confirmation of the impossibility. Zhirmunskii said about Blok's attitude:

Disgust with the past and despair for the future and in the present that inconsolable sorrow and boredom, that *acedia* which the old religious writers wrote about, or, to use newer and less weighted analogies, "Weltschmerz" or Baudelaire's "spleen"—gradually took possession of the poet.

A poem like "Pesn' ada" (The Song of Hell) (1909), written in terza rima and containing specific references to Dante's *Inferno*, reaffirms this general position (tying it to Dostoevsky's psychology), that is, altering Hell from an imagined physical condition of moral equilibrium enveloping an individual to an actual mental context of aesthetic equilibrium (balance of power) within an individual psyche. In the 1912, or first, edition of the third book, Blok added the following note to the poem:

"The Song of Hell" is an attempt to express the "infernality" (the term is Dostoevsky's), the "vampirism," of our time in the style of the *Inferno*, which is clear from the first words: "The day was departing" ("Lo giorno se n'andava," as the second canto of Hell begins).—"Where is my fellow-traveller? Where art thou, Beatrice?—I go alone...." The world today not only has no heavenly companion, no divine Wisdom, but also not even the earthly wisdom of the pagan Virgil who accompanied Dante through Hell and at the gates of heaven relinquished him to Beatrice (*Inferno*, i, 112–114).

The effort to make the poem representative of its time, that is, to offer it as an understanding of its time, requires a nonlyric organization, although at the same time alienation—here, the absence of Virgil—demands a lyric attitude. The individual's isolation and impotency in social activity impose self-examination and self-elaboration on him; he himself is the beginning and the end. The impotency that demands a lyric attitude also demands a nonlyric organization of expression to overcome the isolation and to make itself credible—to be communicative on the level of the most accessible conversation and to convince the reader (by a seemingly permanent system of values in which the alienated self is at least seemingly adequately located). The office of symbols is to work both ways at once. It is significant that Blok, who was quite conscious of *The New Life* when he was working on *Verses about the Beautiful Lady* and of his relation to it, should have followed Dante as far as he did. Blok's poetry, of course, has no theological "superstructure," but Blok left his poetry as open as possible to poetically anagogical interpretation. "The Song of Hell" catches up a sense of that tradition and that life of symbols which Blok insisted was all that had real value.

Many of Blok's poems of the period 1909–12 seem to have been written on two levels, like the earlier play *The Unknown Lady* (November 1906) or like the 1910 poem "V restorane" (In the Restaurant), which begins:

Никогда не забуду (он был, или не был,
Этот вечер): пожаром зари
Сожжено и раздвинуто бледное небо,
И на желтой заре — фонари.

I'll never forget (that evening—
Was it or wasn't it): the pale sky
Was burned up and split by the sunset,
And street-lamps stood out against the yellow sunset.

The entire poem is overcast, like a vaguely remembered dream, by the intentionally ambivalent parenthetical comment. It is the same as saying that maybe both the fact and the substance of the dream are real and that maybe neither is. Whether or not is irrelevant to the recollection, an analogy to what was. The detail that immediately follows suggests tangible actuality, which is almost immediately controverted:

> Я послал тебе черную розу в бокале
> Золотого, как небо, Аи.
>
> I sent you a black rose in a goblet
> Of champagne as gold as the sky.

This conventional, "refined," and "aesthetic" fancy is followed by an account of a conventional assignation, sharply modified by the poet's pity. The whore appears, as in many of Blok's poems on this theme, against the backdrop of the yellow sunset.

> Ты рванулась движеньем испуганной птицы,
> Ты прошла, словно сон мой легка...
> И вздохнули духи, задремали ресницы,
> Зашептались тревожно шелка.
>
> Но из глуби зеркал ты мне взоры бросала
> И, бросая, кричала: — Лови!...
> А монисто бренчало, цыганка плясала
> И визжала заре о любви.
>
> You shuddered like a frightened bird.
> You passed by, light as my dream...
> And there was a sigh of perfume, eyelashes dozed,
> And the silk excitedly whispered.
>
> From the depths of the mirrors you threw me glances
> And, throwing them, shouted: "Catch!..."
> And her necklace jingling, a gypsy danced
> And screeched at the dawn about love.

The poem ends with unresolved temptation. One cannot "make" anything out of it: it comes to a gesture, which carries and consumes all the emotional energy involved.

The attractiveness of the contrast and the contradiction in the temptation is the impetus behind the second of two poems both called "Demon" (The Demon), the first written in 1910 and the second in 1916. Both are evocative of Lermontov's Demon. The first poem was written under the affect of the death of Vrubel, a painter, in 1910, a death Blok considered a "symbolic" event, as he stated in the introduction to *Retribution.* The Demon in Vrubel's painting, Blok said, "...is a messenger, reporting that in the dark blue-lilac world-night, there is sprinkled the gold of an ancient evening. His Demon and Lermontov's Demon are symbols of our time." He added that if he possessed Vrubel's means he would create a Demon. Blok's first "The Demon" is a close description of Vrubel's paintings, is Lermontov-"influenced," and has a clearly Caucasian note evocative of the locale of Lermontov's poem. The second poem may be considered a version of the "fallen angel" theme as it occurs in Lermontov's poem "The Demon" or, as a general example, in *Faust.* It is a Romantic theme, reaffirming the individuality of the psyche and its efforts to control its experiences. Romanticism is a vindication of man's essential loneliness and vitality. The admission that there exists a sphere of activity on which the ego can exert no appreciable influence and which influences the ego prevents celebration of individual power. The struggle between a man and what is outside him emphasizes the scope of the power involved and the meaningfulness of both sides, in all aspects, independently of each other. Because he cannot hope to understand the world in the sense Faust did, he must make what he does a game. He must encompass both the delight of being free, or transcendent, and the terrible pain of being alienated from his best self in the actual world.

Да, я возьму тебя с собою
И вознесу тебя туда,
Где кажется земля звездою,
Землею кажется звезда.

И онемев от удивленья,
Ты ýзришь новые миры —
Невероятные виденья,
Создания моей игры...

Yes, I'll take you with me,
And carry you up there
Where the earth looks like a star
And a star looks like the earth.

You, struck dumb with surprise,
Will perceive new worlds—
Incredible visions,
The creations of my game...

The Romantic maintained that the ego, with the Devil's support, had all the world before it—and, ultimately, often the Devil too. Blok said that he simultaneously was the Devil and was attracted by the Devil both as real force and as concept. It is in the game of verse that the beauty and the madness lie.

It is very difficult for a man to know which half is which, whether, as Blok put it, one's mirror-image or oneself is real. In the five poems grouped under the title "Pliaski smerti" (Dances of Death), written in 1912 and 1914 and included in this first section, "The Terrible World," the shades of the medieval fable are taken as if alive, that is, as death-in-life. The contrary paradox—life-in-death—seems rationally plausible but actually inaccessible. Death, the essence of life, is self-enforcing as a fact and as an institution. The original sense of the Dance of Death involved an idea of spiritual purgation between death and salvation for a period of several years, at the end of which the cleansed soul offered itself in all humility to God, ready to accept His grace. The flesh had rotted away; only the heart remained among the bones. As the bones were moved from the cemetery to another field, so the heart was moved from the earth to heaven. In the first poem of Blok's series, the intricate distinctions between spiritual and physical life and death are given paradoxically: those who are alive dance the dance of death—as if they had never lived. The poet, or lyric protagonist, who is most conscious and most responsive, is a corpse. There are two dances: the physical dance of those who have never lived and the spiritual dance of the poet who wants to transcend the limitations and horrors of actuality by using its mask but has come to understand that there is no transcendence.

The poem begins very much like the poem "How Difficult It Is to Move in Crowds," written in 1910. However, in this poem the poet does not seem so much a victim of his own emotions (although he partly is) as a victim to that senseless, ritualistic indifference with which the dead call the living the dead and themselves the living. The individual is a double victim: by failing to conform, he is socially irrelevant; by choosing not to conform, he is dependent wholly on himself. Even if this seem preferable to that alienation which conformity and most kinds of socially useful labor impose, it *is* a kind of rebellion difficult to account for from day to day and ultimately, perhaps, absurd, because of the immovable, impersonal social institutions which it is impotently directed against. Ultimately, according to this poem, it is nothing more than a rattling of bones.

Как тяжко мертвецу среди людей
Живым и страстным притворяться!

Но надо, надо в общество втираться,
Скрывая для карьеры лязг костей...

Живые спят. Мертвец встает из гроба,
И в банк идет, и в суд идет, в сенат...
Чем ночь белее, тем чернее злоба,
И перья торжествующе скрипят.

. . .

Уж вечер. Мелкий дождь зашлепал грязью
Прохожих, и дома, и прочий вздор...
А мертвеца — к другому безобразью
Скрежещущий несет таксомотор.

. . .

Он шепчет ей незначащие речи,
Пленительные для живых слова,
И смотрит он, как розовеют плечи,
Как на плечо склонилась голова...

И острый яд привычно-светской злости
С нездешней злостью расточает он...
— Как он умен! Как он в меня влюблен!
В ее ушах — нездешний, странный звон:
  То кости лязгают о кости.

How difficult for a dead man to pretend
To be alive and full of passion among people!
But one must, one must worm one's way ahead into society
Concealing, for one's career, the clanking of the bones...

The living sleep. The dead man rises from the grave,
And goes to his bank, and goes to court, then to the Senate...
The whiter the night is, the blacker the malice of the day,
And the triumphant pens keep squeaking.

. . .

Evening. A gentle rain spatters mud
On passersby, on houses and other rubbish...
A taxicab with its gears grinding carries
The dead man on to still other ugliness.

. . .

He whispers to her tender nothings,
Words captivating for the living,
And watches how her shoulders blush,
And how her head leans sideways...

He squanders the bitter poison of ordinary gall
With supernatural malice...
"How clever! How much he loves me!"
And in her ears a supernatural, strange ringing:
  Bones clanking against bones.

The understanding of the world which this poem expresses is complex. To simplify it by saying that under the veil of entertainment is the reality of tragedy—that death lurks behind the mask of life—is to obscure the various social pressures on the individual which the poem identifies. Both the living and the dead are real. The poet does not choose either. He dramatizes a "moment" when the two are interdependent and difficult to distinguish from each other, confusing dialogue with reflection, hope with fear, and the meaning of life with its negation.[6]

In the second poem of the series, the attitude of despair is given in its simplicity and intensity wholly as a mood, as a place defined by its time:

Ночь, улица, фонарь, аптека,
Бессмысленный и тусклый свет.
Живи еще хоть четверть века —
Всё будет так. Исхода нет.

Умрешь — начнешь опять сначала,
И повторится всё, как встарь:
Ночь, ледяная рябь Канала,
Аптека, упича, фонарь.

Night, a street, a lamp, a drugstore,
A senseless, wan light.
Live another quarter of a century—
All will be the same. There's no way out.

You die—you begin from the beginning,
And everything comes round again:
The night, the icy ripple on the canal,
The drugstore, the street, the lamp.

The end and the beginning are one. The past and the future are identical moments contained in the essence of the present.

Both these poems are also interesting for the occurrence in them of the two most important devices of versification canonized by Blok: assonantal rhyme and various kinds of repetition.[7] It is especially interesting because, as Nikitina and Shuvalov have pointed out, over five-sixths of the poems in the third book are in regular, classical syllabo-tonic metrics, marking a return by Blok to a more usual versification scheme after the "experimental" period characterized by the poems of the second book.[8] We may say, then, that for Blok the period 1900–4 is characterized by conventional versification; 1904–8, by what Zhirmunskii has called "revolutionary innovations"; and 1908–16, by a return to the more conventional specifics with the inclusion of the achievements of the experimental period as a definite part of poetic technique. Devices of repetition—of the beginning of the poem at the end, for example (*kol'tso* [ring])—had, of course, been used in "romances" or "songs" by nineteenth-century Russian poets such as Fet, Grigor'ev, Polonskii and, in other forms, by the Romantics generally. It was also used by the French Symbolists and, some say,[9] was taken from them by the Russian Symbolists as a genuine device. It occurs widely throughout Blok's first book, and other kinds of repetitive devices occur throughout his poetry.

But Blok's most important contribution to versification was assigning to approximate rhymes a status equal to that of conventional rhymes. For example, in the first stanza of "In the Restaurant" the regular, masculine (iambic) rhyme *zarí—fonarí* occurs with the approximate, feminine (trochaic) rhyme in alternating lines *né byl—nébo*, in which the rhyme is a syllable and the initial consonant of the following syllable, other following vowels and consonants being disregarded. In the poem "To the Muse" there is the rhyme *rassvéte—zamétil* in which the final consonant is disregarded (the final "e" in *rassvete* is phonetically indistinguishable from the "i" in *zametil*). The same kind of rhyme occurs in the fourth and fifth poems in the series called "Zhizn' moego priiatelia" (My Friend's Life): *výshel—s krýshi, znakómyi—v ómut*. In the same poems, in which, as usually in Blok's poetry, the masculine rhymes are regular, there occurs such a rhyme as *iunyi pýl—nastupíl*, in which the stress emphasizes the difference between the "hard" and "soft" forms of the one vowel. In the poem "Hours, Days, and Years Go By,"[10] the "hard"—"soft" difference occurs in a feminine rhyme, in which the final syllables are identical: *Chto zh býlo—ukhodílo;* and in the same poem there is an example of a very tricky device, used also in the poem "The Annunciation," of including a foreign phrase as an integral element of a poem by rhyming it regularly with a Russian word:

> И вдруг (как памятно, знакóмо!)
> Отчетливо, издалека
> Раздался голос: Ecce hómo!

By these various combinations of approximate and exact rhymes, Blok more than any other poet made the apocryphal canonical. By interrupting an expected identity, approximate rhyme emphasizes the *meaning* of the rhymed words and of the verse in general.

In the poem "Night, a Street, a Lamp, a Drugstore," the device of repeating the beginning at the end is more than a kind of coda terminating the musical movement of a song. The repetition corresponds precisely to what the poem says. Everything merely repeats itself, and the poem repeats itself, but not merely. The difference is the success, the aptness, of the device.

Although Blok's third book represents a return to more extensive use of standard metrics, not all the poems are standard metrics—even if their parts are. An example is the 1909 poem, included in "The Terrible World," "Pozdnei osen'iu iz gavani" (Late in Autumn from the Harbor), a poem Blok rather liked. Most lines contain three stresses, but the number varies from two to four. The rhymes are either masculine or dactyllic, and throughout the poem there is a regular alternation of dactyllic and masculine line endings. The odd lines, those with dactyllic endings, are trochaic tetrameter, with some irregularities in the last stanza. The even lines, those with masculine endings, are, except for initial irregularities, regular iambic tetrameter with one or two variations. This trochaic-iambic alternation, particularly the shift from the dactyllic endings of the odd lines to the even lines' iambics, produces the discord that is part of the basic rhythm of the poem and that reinforces the poem's sense of loss and sense of pathos:

Поздней осенью из гавани a
От заметенной снегом земли b
В предназначенное плаванье a
Идут тяжелые корабли. b

В черном небе означается c
Над водой подъемный кран, d
И один фонарь качается c
На оснежённом берегу. e

И матрос, на борт не принятый, f
Идет, шатаясь, сквозь буран. d
Всё потеряно, всё выпито! f
Довольно — больше не могу... e

А берег опустелой гавани a
Уж первый легкий снег занес... g
В самом чистом, в самом нежном саване a
Сладко ли спать тебе, матрос? g

Late in autumn from the harbor,
From the earth swept over by snow,
Heavy ships go fore-appointed
Slowly out to sea.

Against the black sky over the water
There stands a lifting crane;
A lonely street lamp bobbles
On the snowed-in shore.

A sailor, not signed on,
Staggers through the snowstorm,
All's lost, all drunken!
Enough—I can't any more...

The shore of the vacated harbor
Was covered by the first light snow...
In the cleanest, softest cerement,
Sailor, do you sleep lightly now?

The poem moves from the harbor and the ships that are gone to the sailor, from a description to a rhetorical question that cuts back on the poem.

Although most of Blok's work is characterized by a distinctive, lyric bias, the lyric characteristics of his poetry are not adequate criteria for its development, as one may see from these poems, nor do they point to its most important accomplishments. It is inadequate and incorrect to say that Blok proceeded from Romanticism to neo-Romanticism, or to say that his

> ...extreme boundaries are the religious lyricism of the *Verses about the Beautiful Lady* and the gypsy motifs of his later years, Vl. Solovëv as his first teacher and Apollon Grigor'ev as a travelling companion and friend at the end of his life's road.[11]

Perhaps a "confrontation" of two poems written ten years apart will help illustrate Blok's development. In the early poem, "Ty strastno zhdësh'. Tebia zovut" (You Passionately Wait. They Call You) (1901), from the Beautiful Lady section of the first book, the poet says that the "you" is at one with nature, is "at home" on the steppe, but that he is restive and sad and does not recognize the voices that call the other person:

О, жалок я перед тобой!
Всё обнимаю, всем владею,
Хочу владеть тобой одной,
Но не могу и не умею!

O, I am wretched before you!
I embrace all, I own all,
I want to own only you,
But cannot, and don't know how!

Ten years later Blok wrote a poem called "Unizhenie" (Humiliation), part of the section "The Terrible World." The obverse of the early, implausible idealism, it shows a fascination with one's own guilt and with personal and social discord, with lust and degradation. The setting is a whorehouse. The poem turns on judgment of the false activity of irrelevant, meretricious love. The opening stanza describes a sunset seen through the window of the whorehouse drawing-room where all the customers are sprawled over the furniture, mixed together in that room as they would never allow themselves to mix any place else, and associates their desire with a desire for death by associating this sunset with the sunset men are hanged against. The poem then describes the narrator's relations with one of the women from his—and her—points of view. The narrator ends the poem:

Ты смела́! Так еще будь бесстрашней!
Я — не муж, не жених твой, не друг!
Так вонзай же, мой ангел вчерашний,
В сердце — острый французский каблук!

You're bold! Be still more intrepid!
I'm not your husband, your man, nor your friend!
So, my yesterday's angel, plunge
Your pointed French heel in my heart!

The poem is sensual, especially the last line. Its power and success is that it dramatizes, even through conventional figures, an emotional surexcitation, that it reinforces the sense of guilt and its judgment of that guilt by a final gesture which returns the emotion generated back on itself. The poem is a dramatization of a lust that requires its own destruction by violence. Blok's early visions of "disinterested passion" have moved to the essence of loving: satisfaction in power, self-consummation and simultaneous harmonization. The suggested masochism is as real as the necessarily imperfect, earlier narcissistic impulse.

The disillusion which Blok experienced occasioned in his poetry a bitterness and irony directed, in love poems, against himself, but frequently in other poems against the world in general, as if the conventions of the world were against Blok. The poet's responsibility to himself is suggested in the poem "Hours, Days, and Years Go By," in which, clearly in the last stanza, the Tristan myth as given in Wagner's *Tristan und Isolde* is "applied" to the poet himself:[12]

Идут часы, и дни, и годы.
Хочу стряхнуть какой-то сон,
Взглянуть в лицо людей природы,
Рассеять сумерки времен...

Там кто-то машет, дразнит светом
(Так зимней ночью, на крыльцо
Тень чья-то глянет силуэтом,
И быстро спрячется лицо).

Вот меч. Он — был. Но он — не нужен.
Кто обессилил руку мне? —
Я помню: мелкий ряд жемчужин
Однажды ночью, при луне,

Больная, жалобная стужа,
И моря снеговая гладь...
Из-под ресниц сверкнувший ужас —
Старинный ужас (дай понять)...

Слова? — Их не было. — Что ж было? —
Ни сон, ни явь. Вдали, вдали
Звенело, гасло, уходило
И отделялось от земли...

И умерло. А губы пели.
Прошли часы, или года...
(Лишь телеграфные звенели
На черном небе провода...)

И вдруг (как памятно, знакомо!)
Отчетливо, издалека
Раздался голос: Ecce homo!
Меч выпал. Дрогнула рука...

И перевязан шелком душным
(Чтоб кровь не шла из черных жил)
Я был веселым и послушным,
Обезоруженный — служил.

Но час настал. Припоминая,
Я вспомнил: нет, я не слуга.
Так падай, перевязь цветная!
Хлынь, кровь, и обагри снега!

Hours, days, and years go by.
I want to shake off some sort of dream,
To look people and nature in the face,
To clear away the twilights of the ages...

There someone is waving, teasing with the light
(As on a winter night on a porch
Someone's shadow, like a silhouette, will glance
And the face quickly will hide).

That's the sword. It—was. But it is not needed.
Who has enfeebled my hand?
I remember: a fine string of pearls
Once at night in the moonlight.

A diseased, mournful frost,
And the smooth, snowy surface of the sea...
A flash of horror from under the eyelashes—
An ancient horror (give me to understand)...

Words? There were none. What was there?
Neither dream nor waking. Far away, far away
It rang out, faded, went away
And separated from the earth...

And died. But the lips sang.
Hours passed, or years...
(Only the telegraph wires
Hummed in the black sky...)

Suddenly (how memorably, how familiarly!)
Distinctly, from a distance
A voice resounded: Ecce homo!
The sword fell. The hand shook...

With my arm bound in a sling of stifling silk
(So the blood would not leave the black veins)
I was gay and obedient,
Disarmed I was in service.

But the hour struck. Thinking back,
I remembered: *no, I am not a servant.*
Fall off, colored sling!
Spout, blood, and stain the snow!

The poem is obscure (it is about shaking off a dream), symbolist, and genuinely dramatic. The *amour courtois* tradition given in the images of the cavalier in service to the sensual and beautiful, semi-mystical lady seems to be confounded with the wound inflicted on the protagonist—the poet—by himself through the relation to the lady. He cannot say whether the love and the service were real or not, but the wound (like the sword, the blood, the sling, the telegraph wires and the shadow on the porch) is real. This is all part of the "I." He would assert himself as a man against his dream and against the requirements of duty by emphasizing the suffering and the loss, by pouring his blood on the snow. Although if by his love he must lose himself, he would have the loss be real; that is, he would find himself—he would be certain of his reality—through his loss. He would cut back through the convention to which he became bound in order to secure the lady's affection by an iconoclastic self-sacrifice.

What from an original point of view is seen as sacrifice of oneself is, from a subsequent point of view, social catastrophe. The conventions cannot account for the basic impulse—the "life force"—that mysteriously and really lurks behind what people do, the "unseen eyes," as Blok puts it in the poem "Est' igra: ostorozhno voiti" (There Is a Game: You Enter Carefully), which are terrible precisely because you cannot catch them. You enter carefully, the poem says, to hypnotize people's attention and, unnoticed, follow your prey with your eyes. No matter whether a person be refined or coarse, he must respond, and his anxiety must increase. He feels the eyes upon him, but he cannot understand whose they are. It does not involve self-interest, love, or revenge. It is "just a game, like a game among children," played out in all gatherings of people, where there are "these hidden detectives." You yourself cannot understand why sometimes you want to see people but, having seen them, leave feeling not quite your same self. "There is a good and there is an evil eye," only it would be better not to discover whose, because "each of us" has in himself too many "unknown, playing forces." A thousand years from now, the poem continues, we will not be able to measure the soul, we will hear the flight of all the planets, but:

А пока — в неизвестном живем
И не ведаем сил мы своих,
И, как дети, играя с огнем,
Обжигаем себя и других...

Meanwhile, we live in an unknown
And do not know our own strength,
And, like children playing with fire,
We burn ourselves and others...

The uncommitted and uncontrolled force in, or behind, ourselves, leads to an accidental and universal destruction, the immolation that follows regularly but without reason from indifferent power.

The sixth poem in the series "My Friend's Life," first written in 1909 at the same time as a light poem directly stating the "theme" of both,[13] ties the "game" to the reader through a cataloguing of the events of a day looked at through the prism of Blok's consciousness. The poem's rhythm is not reducible to any particular meter. It is basically a ternary pattern with a variable number of feet and a variable anacrusis, similar to the pattern of "The Night Violet" and, like it, unrhymed. Two-thirds of the way through, the beat becomes irregular (there occur one-syllable intervals between stresses). The effect, reinforced by the absence of rhyme, is one of rhythmic prose, very much in keeping with the colloquial language and emphasizing the strongly ironic tone (made clear by the use of ironic italics). The poem begins:

День проходил, как всегда:
В сумасшествии тихом.
Все говорили кругом
О болезнях, врачах и лекарствах.
О службе рассказывал друг,
Другой — о Христе,
О газете — четвертый.
Два стихотворца (поклонники Пушкина)[14]
Книжки прислали
С множеством рифм и размеров.
Курсистка прислала
Рукопись с тучей эпиграфов
(Из Надсона и символистов).
После — под звон телефона —
Посыльный конверт подавал,
Надушенный чужими духами.
Розы поставьте на стол,
Написано было в записке,
И приходилось их ставить на стол...
После — собрат по перу,
До глаз в бороде утонувший,
О причитаньях у южных хорватов
Рассказывал долго.
Критик, громя футуризм,
Символизмом шпынял,
Заключив реализмом.
В кинематографе вечером
Знатный барон целовался под пальмой
С барышней низкого званья,
Ее до себя возвышая...
Всё было в отменном порядке.

The day passed like always:
In quiet madness.
Everybody around me was talking
About illnesses, doctors, and medicines.
A friend told about his job,
Another talked of Christ,

A fourth—about the news.
Two versifiers (*worshippers of Pushkin*)
Sent me volumes
With a lot of rhymes and meters.
A girl student sent
A manuscript with a swarm of epigraphs
(*From Nadson and the Symbolists*).
Later—as the phone was ringing—
A messenger handed me an envelope
Scented with unfamiliar perfume.
Put the roses on the table,
It said in the note,
And you had to put them on the table...
Later—a fellow writer,
Drowned in his beard up to his eyes,
Expounded on
Southern Croatian keens.
A critic, railing at *Futurism*,
Used *Symbolism* for nagging,
Winding up with *Realism.*
In the evening in the movie-theater
A noble baron necked under a potted palm
With a young lady of low calling,
Raising her up to his level...
Everything was in excellent order.

and ends:

Буйно забьются в мозгу
Слишком светлые мысли...
И, укрощая их буйство,
Словно пугаясь чего-то, — не лучше ль,
Думаешь ты, чтоб и новый
День проходил, как всегда:
В сумасшествии тихом?

Thoughts that are too lucid
Wildly throb in the brain...
And curbing their uproar,
As if afraid of something,—*wouldn't you rather,*
You think, *that the next*
Day passed like always:
In quiet madness?

The conversational, ironic tone reinforces the actuality of the poses and of conventional phrases like "vague memory" or "hidden feeling," undercutting their apparent, and previously accepted, mystical significance, although such phrases, even in this poem (as in Sterne's work or in Gogol's), are themselves used seriously, that is, as reality contrary to and contradictory of actual events. There being nothing to the day, it does seem better that the day be nothing. However, as the irony makes clear, this is not a point of view one could or would enact.

The final poem in the section, "Golos iz khora" (A Voice from the Choir), looks beyond the players and the game with real despair and a consciousness of cosmic doom. It is a tragic vision of life given in a series of apocalyptic prophecies contrasted to the sharp, jig-like rhythm of the verse: a little *danse macabre* itself. There is a poignant irony in the apostrophes to the "children" and in the lines that say that one should be satisfied with one's life "quieter than water, lower than grass," which is a Russian saying signifying humility. The poem, revised February 27, 1914, was first written June 6, 1910. Showing again, perhaps, how a poem is generated, the first two lines in that first version contain the germ of the poem and were revised into a more dramatic form to become the last two lines of the final version:[15]

Как часто плачем — вы и я —
Над жалкой жизнию своей!
О, еслиб знали вы, друзья,
Холод и мрак грядущих дней!

Теперь ты милой руку жмешь,
Играешь с нею, шутя,
И плачешь ты, заметив ложь,
Или в руке любимой нож,
    Дитя, дитя!

. . .

Весны, дитя, ты будешь ждать —
    Весна обманет.
Ты будешь солнце на небо звать —
    Солнце не встанет.
И крик, когда ты начнешь кричать,
    Как камень, канет...

Будьте ж довольны жизнью своей,
    Тише воды, ниже травы!
О, еслиб знали, дети, вы,
    Холод и мрак грядущих дней!

How often we weep, you and I,
Over our pitiful life!
O, if only you knew, friends,
The cold and the darkness of coming days!

Now you squeeze your darling's hand,
Joking, play with her,
And you weep, seeing a lie
Or a knife in the hand you love,
Child, child!

. . .

Child, you will wait for Spring—
Spring will fool you.
You will summon the sun into the sky—
The sun won't get up.
And your shout, when you'll begin to shout,
Will vanish like a stone in water...

Be satisfied then with your life,
Quieter than water, lower than grass!
O, if only you knew, children,
The cold and the darkness of coming days!

This is the end of "the terrible world": disillusion and the paralytic fear of impotency.

The next section in the third volume, "Retribution" (not to be confused with the long poem of the same title), begins with a very popular poem which illustrates an aspect of the confluence in the post-1907 poems of standard metrics and Blok's experimentation and which lightly sets the theme of the section. Although the poem is in regular iambic pentameter with alternating feminine-masculine rhymes (in the third line of the first stanza, for example, all five stresses are there, which is not usual, and the metric scheme is fully "realized"), in several lines, such as the first, the introduction of two pyrrhic feet interrupts the scheme: that is, ◡′ ◡◡ ◡′ ◡◡ ◡′◡ instead of ◡′ ◡′ ◡′ ◡′ ◡′◡. Ever since the eighteenth century, of course, Russian versification has admitted pyrrhic feet in trochaic and iambic meter; this occurs readily, since long words and certain proclitics and enclitics do not admit secondary stress. What is interesting, however, is that the pyrrhic alternations emphasize the meaning of the words. The three stresses in the first line fall on each of the three nouns, drawing attention to them, and giving the *impression* of three-beat accentual verse. This is an example, typical for Blok's third book, of modified standard metrics, except that in this example the modification is more a semblance than an actual modification. The last stanza repeats the first by contrast.

Like other poems in this section, the poem is about losses in love. The poet's revenge on the lady who has left him and left her picture behind—his revenge on himself, actually—is to discard the picture that makes the memory possible:

О доблестях, о подвигах, о славе
Я забывал на горестной земле,
Когда твое лицо в простой оправе
Передо мной сияло на столе.

Но час настал, и ты ушла из дому.
Я бросил в ночь заветное кольцо.
Ты отдала свою судьбу другому,
И я забыл прекрасное лицо.

. . .

Уж не мечтать о нежности, о славе,
Всё миновалось, молодость прошла!
Твое лицо в его простой оправе
Своей рукой убрал я со стола.

I would forget about valor, deeds,
And glory on this mournful earth,
When your face in its simple frame
Would shine before me on the table.

But the hour came, and you left the house.
I threw the sacred ring into the night.
You gave your fate up to another,
And I forgot your beautiful face.

. . .

One can't now dream of tenderness, of glory,
Everything has passed, youth has gone!
With my own hand I have taken your face
In its simple frame off the table.

The poems that begins:

Ночь, как ночь, и улица пустынна.
  Так всегда!

A night like any other night, and the street's deserted.
  So it is always!

makes a wry face at the platitude of death:

День, как день: ведь решена задача:
  Все умрут.

A day like any other day: the job's laid out:
  Everybody dies.

In some of the poems, Blok mocks himself—for example, "I Don't Remember Today What There Was Yesterday" (1909) or "The Circle of Being Is Tight" (1909). Some of the poems, such as "On the Death of a Baby," (1909) written about a month after his wife's only child, Dmitrii, had died, eight days old, are serious, simple responses to tragic loss. "On the Death of a Baby" is more or less in the form of a dialogue between the poet and his grief. The poet asserts in the face of the ceremony of death and the ritual of bereavement his own quiet determination to keep his loss to himself—to grieve without God—the child whom he wanted to love being gone.

In the poem "The Steps of the Commander" (1910–12) the Don Juan legend is taken up as a symbol of retaliation in which each act is considered part of a sequence leading to one fatal end, stressed by repetitions in the verse. It is a poem about lust and cruelty in love, the simultaneous sublimation and destruction of personality in an ultimate, intimate experience:

Холодно и пусто в пышной спальне,
    Слуги спят и ночь глуха.
Из страны блаженной, незнакомой, дальней
    Слышно пенье петуха.

Чтó изменнику блаженства звуки?
    Миги жизни сочтены.
Донна Анна спит, скрестив на сердце руки,
    Донна Анна видит сны...

. . .

Жизнь пуста, безумна и бездонна!
    Выходи на битву, старый рок!
И в ответ — победно и влюбленно —
    В снежной мгле поет рожок...

Пролетает, брызнув в ночь огнями,
    Черный, тихий, как сова, мотор,
Тихими, тяжелыми шагами
    В дом вступает Командор...

. . .

На вопрос жестокий нет ответа,
    Нет ответа — тишина.
В пышной спальне страшно в час рассвета,
    Слуги спят, и ночь бледна.

В час рассвета холодно и странно,
    В час рассвета — ночь мутна.
Дева Света! Где ты, донна Анна?
    Анна! Анна! — Тишина.

Только в грозном утреннем тумане
Бьют часы в последний раз:
Донна Анна в смертный час твой встанет.
Анна встанет в смертный час.

It's cold and empty in the luxurious bedroom,
The servants sleep, the night is still.
From a blissful, unknown, distant country
Comes the sound of a cock's crowing.

What are the sounds of bliss to the traitor?
The moments of life are numbered.
Donna Anna sleeps, hands folded on her heart,
Donna Anna dreams...

. . .

Life is empty, mad and fathomless!
Come out and fight, old fate!
And as an answer—triumphant and enamored—
A horn sings out in the snowy haze...

A black motorcar as quiet as an owl
Flies through the night, splashing it with light.
With a quiet, ponderous tread
The Commander walks into the house...

. . .

There is no answer to the cruel question,
No answer, just the silence.
It's terrible in the luxurious bedroom at the hour of dawn,
The servants sleep, the night is pale.

It's cold and strange at the hour of dawn,
At the hour of dawn the night is turbid.
Maid of Light! Where are you, Donna Anna?
Anna! Anna! Just the silence.

Only the clock in the threatening morning
Fog strikes for the last time:
Donna Anna will arise in your hour of death.
Anna will arise at the death-hour.

The automobile has replaced the owl as agent and symbol of wisdom and doom, has very much become an agent and symbol of corruption itself (here, of adultery, as in Eliot's *The Wasteland* and elsewhere).[16]

Because no adequate intellectual analysis of the existing social condition is possible, there being no common system but only a "common" heritage, thought is replaced by drama, even if the drama is necessarily incomplete.

The dramatic conflict of the opposing contraries and their symbolization affords insight, Blok suggests, however intolerable, into the moves and motives of men. The poem is a play of images catching up the sequences and consequences of a "moment" of civilization (as distinguished from culture, which Anna represents) that must recur. The scheme of symbols presents the poem as an ineffable composite of meaning and experiences of which the poem is not itself a part but which it seeks to transcend by its final symbol—or epiphany. This is what I mean by saying that the poem comes to judgment, although there is no criterion external to itself to which it may apply. It is an example of poetry in which what is arbitrary is eliminated and what is absolute is revealed, the meaning evoked by a game of things. The evocation is as subtle, as difficult, and as essential as Baudelaire imaged; the excellence, that with which he made a play of things; the mystique, the same; and the performance, substantially of the same sort. Burenin's parody of the poem seems only to emphasize its modernity and acuity.[17]

The third section of the book, "Iambs," is a series of poems, most of which were taken from early versions of the long poem *Retribution* and established as a series by extrapolation of the values behind that poem. *Retribution*, in its early drafts, was dedicated to Blok's half-sister, Angelina. In its final form, this series is dedicated to her memory (she died in 1918). The epigraph to the section is from Juvenal's *Satires:* "Facit indignatio versum." And the righteous anger at social injustice, the indignation at the discrepancy between human potentiality and what actually obtains, is given in the poem "Yes. So Inspiration Dictates" (1911–14), originally (in a slightly longer form) part of the third chapter of *Retribution:*

> Да. Так диктует вдохновенье:
> Моя свободная мечта
> Всё льнет туда, где униженье,
> Где грязь, и мрак, и нищета.
> Туда, туда, смиренней, ниже, —
> Оттуда зримей мир иной...
> Ты видел ли детей в Париже,
> Иль нищих на мосту зимой?
>
> Yes. So inspiration dictates:
> My free dream
> Always clings to where there is humiliation,
> Filth, darkness, and poverty.
> There, there, more humbly, lower,
> From where another world is more easily seen...

Have you seen the children of Paris,
Or the beggars on the bridge in winter?

A kind of ironic despair is given in the first six lines of a poem (1910–14) also originally part of the same chapter of *Retribution* but later taken out and reworked:

В огне и холоде тревог —
Так жизнь пройдет. Запомним оба,
Что встретиться судил нам бог
В час искупительный — у гроба.

Я верю: новый век взойдет
Средь всех несчастных поколений.

In the fire and ice of anxiety
Life will be gone. Let us both remember
That God ordained us to meet,
In the hour of expiation, at the grave.

I believe: a new age will rise
Among all unhappy generations.

The poems are not only explicit statements of Blok's politics and political sympathies, but also, and more important, they label the source of poetry itself. Precisely the perception of the contradiction between what is and what ought to be gives rise to genuine artistic images. Where the "chaos" of suffering is most apparent the "cosmos" of freedom is most significantly made. The "ideal life" must seem all the more inevitable to those who do not have even a substitute for a "real" one. This real failure, as Blok sees it, is the condition of all time. This is what he would catch up in the "iamb," which, he says in the introduction to *Retribution*, he considers the essential expression of his era.

Failure sometimes engenders its negation. The violations of historical tradition are also the impetus to its transformation. The loss may be called successful that also presents, by symbols, a discovery of freedom.

A sense of such a loss, personal and involving tragedy, a change in the life of the community, and the alteration of tradition, runs through the cycle of brilliant poems called "Italian Verses," the fourth section of the third book. Blok and his wife spent April, May, and June 1909 in Italy. Blok was overcome, annoyed, enchanted, disappointed, angry, and disconsolate about what he saw there. His letters home to his mother report his enthusiasms and his complaints. In other letters he thanks Briusov again for having urged him to make the trip to Ravenna and offers offhand opinions. His notebooks of the trip contain jottings, lists of pictures, galleries and such. Only the series of prose sketches *Molnii iskusstva* (The Lightning Flashes of Art), subtitled "An Unfinished Book of 'Impressions of Italy,'" hints at the brilliance and broad understanding in the poems, which, like the sketches, were written or at least started during the trip. But the articles are sketches, comments, impressions—vivid pictures and thoughts by a traveler. The poems are concentrated. Some have a metaphysical quality, a dramatic compactness in which the world of the future is seen as pressed down on and bound by the history of the past. The point of departure is the present, the cities of Italy and Italian art. The poet turns from that perfection through his poems to perfection to come.

In the third poem in the three-poem series on Venice, Blok focusses on the real and ever-perishing moment in which, he believes, all things actual and transcendent have their being and in which, as the moment becomes other moments, they are reborn. The metaphors of poetry are photographs of these divers, transient, and still future particularities:

Слабеет жизни гул упорный.
Уходит вспять прилив забот.
И некий ветер сквозь бархат черный
О жизни будущей поет.

Очнусь ли я в другой отчизне,
Не в этой сумрачной стране?
И памятью об этой жизни
Вздохну ль когда-нибудь во сне?

Кто даст мне жизнь? Потомок дожа,
Купец, рыбак, иль иерей
В грядущем мраке делит ложе
С грядущей матерью моей?

Быть может, венецейской девы
Канцоной нежной слух пленя,
Отец грядущий сквозь напевы
Уже предчувствует меня?

И неужель в грядущем веке
Младенцу мне — велит судьба
Впервые дрогнувшие веки
Открыть у львиного столба?

Мать, что́ поют глухие струны?
Уж ты мечтаешь, может быть,
Меня от ветра, от лагуны
Священной шалью оградить?

Нет! Всё, что есть, что было — живо!
Мечты, виденья, думы — прочь!
Волна возвратного прилива
Бросает в бархатную ночь![18]

The persistent rumble of life grows fainter.
The flood of worries ebbs.
An unknown wind is singing through black velvet
About the future life.

Will I wake up in another homeland,
And not in this gloomy country?
And sometime in a dream will I sigh
Remembering this life?

Who will give me life? Will a descendant of a doge,
A merchant, a fisherman, or a priest
In the coming darkness share the bed
Of my future mother?

Captivating the ear of a Venetian maid
By a tender canzone, my future father has,
Perhaps, already had, through the tune,
A foreboding of me?

And is it really fated that in the age
To come I, a young child,
Should first open
My trembling eyelids by the lion's column?

Mother, what do the toneless strings sing?
Do you already dream, perhaps,
Of shielding me from the wind
And the lagoon by your sacred shawl?

No! All that is, that was—still lives!
Dreams, visions, thoughts—away with you!
The wave of the recurrent tide
Plunges into the velvet night.

The beginning of the poem very much suggests the mood of Tiutchev's poetry. The individual feels himself on the edge of an infinity into which actuality fades away, like the tide and the hollow rumble of the sea, and out of which the song of the future life becomes audible, like a rising wind. The poet wonders not only if he will be actually reincarnated (or if, as he is, consequently, he is not a reincarnation), but also if he will not recreate himself in his dreams, that is, if the contrary of dreams is not the fact of metempsychosis. If there be such life, the question then is: from what does it proceed? (This is, so to speak, arguing history backwards, before it has occurred.) The individual—the poet, the "I" of the poem—has no way of knowing, since he cannot distinguish what of the contemporary is significant. In this sense, he does not know where he is. What would seem most significant would be prostration of himself, reduced to his essential vitality and naiveté—himself as a child—before the lion's column, before the symbol of that power which has preserved culture and civilization through the ages. Should he not begin there to study and to be the future, although his mother may be prepared to shroud him in his own innocence? No, because what remains of the past is the present, and that is what is alive, whatever it may subsequently be. Wherever one may be said to have been or to be going to be, one is here, now, on the edge of that velvet night into which the tide, like time, ebbs.

The symbols in the poem are not only metaphors—the hollow sound of the sea is life—but also links connecting this poem, more than almost all of Blok's other poems, to that idea of historical development outlined in "The General Plan of the *Historical Scenes*." It is one of the few examples in Blok's work in which the poetry coincides with an external scheme designed to correlate events in a systematic and extrapoetic way. One may say that the poem's power is the result of this coincidence, or one may say that at the time of writing the poem Blok felt the scheme to be so immediate he was able to translate it directly into vivid metaphor.

Most of the poems in the third volume are centered chiefly on the disparities in city life and on the machinations of civilization. There are descriptions of trolleys and buildings, street-lamps, shops, the sky and sunsets, snow; the harsh sounds of entertainment, of whores and gypsy music; the kinds of people moving wildly in the great confusion (students, sailors, drunks, merchants, shopkeepers, officers, gamblers); and over them, all, the great, grey, beautiful, throbbing, corrupt, foul, indifferent city. The poems of the Italian cycle differ in raw content and in treatment. As their "city"-titles suggest, these poems are about isolated impressions of time and culture as perceived together in examples of the Western heritage. The power and elegance of these poems follow from Blok's sense of experiencing history directly in the still living remains of preceding culture.

The monumentality of the tradition is contrasted to the vitality which it still preserves. The city that is dead is also a sleeping child—the past and the future together:

Всё, что минутно, всё, что бренно,
Похоронила ты в веках.
Ты, как младенец, спишь, Равенна,
У сонной вечности в руках.

. . .

А виноградные пустыни,
Дома и люди — всё гроба.

. . .

Лишь по ночам, склонясь к долинам,
Ведя векам грядущим счет,
Тень Данта с профилем орлиным
О Новой Жизни мне поет.[19]

Everything transient, everything mortal
You have interred in the ages.
You sleep like a child, Ravenna,
In the arms of drowsy eternity.

. . .

The empty expanses of vineyards,
The houses, the people—are tombs.

. . .

Only at night, bending into the valleys,
Keeping count of the ages to come,
The shadow of Dante with its eagle profile
Sings to me about the New Life.

Although the life of the town has necessarily left its real culture behind, as the Adriatic has moved away from Classe, the culture still remains, like Galla Placidia, Theodoric, and Dante, to haunt the serious mind. In this sense, the "new life" is always at hand.

What is described, like the Umbrian hills in the beginning of the poem on Perugia, engenders an emotion suited to the idea behind the poem, given in the epigraph to the poem in Blok's journal: "Carita, justicia, fide [*sic*] (the words of a girl)."

День полувеселый, полустрадный,
Голубая гарь от Умбрских гор.
Вдруг — минутный ливень, ветр прохладный,
За окном открытым — громкий хор.

Там — в окне, под фреской Перуджино,
Черный глаз смеется, дышит грудь:
Кто-то смуглою рукой корзину
Хочет и не смеет дотянуть...

На корзине — белая записка:
«Questa sera... монастырь Франциска...»

A day half happy, half harrowing,
A light-blue mist coming from the Umbrian hills.
Suddenly—a moment's downpour, a cool wind,
And, inside the open window, a loud choir.

There in the window under Perugino's fresco,
A black eye laughs, a breast sighs:
Someone reaches toward the basket
With a swarthy hand but dares not pull it up...

There is a white note on the basket:
"Questa sera... At the St. Francis monastery..."

The assignation is located in the worlds of lovemaking and of monastic vows. The play on kinds of morality, as given in the deleted epigraph, depends on the antitheses among the words.

The same sort of play between actual denotation and moral judgment is found in the seventh poem in the series "Florence," a poem in which the historical brilliance of the town and its contemporary meretriciousness are contrasted bitterly in one figure:

Голубоватым дымом
Вечерний зной возносится,
Долин тосканских царь...

Он мимо, мимо, мимо
Летучей мышью бросится
Под уличный фонарь...

. . .

Дымится пыльный ирис,
И легкой пеной пенится
Бокал Христовых Слез...

In light-blue smoke
The evening heat rises,
King of the Tuscan valleys...

Like a bat flittering by,
Flittering by,
It will dash under the street-lamp...

. . .

Smoke rises from a dusty iris,
And the goblet of Christ's Tears
Is covered with light froth...

"Lacrimae Christi" is a brand of Italian wine.

The labor of a poem itself—the working out of the "idea"—can be (theoretically) made to photograph, like a movie and like memory, what the poet really saw—the delightful image:

Искусство — ноша на плечах,
Зато, как мы, поэты, ценим
Жизнь в мимолетных мелочах!
Как радостно предаться лени,
Почувствовать, как в жилах кровь
Переливается певуче,

. . .

И грезить, будто жизнь сама
Встает во всем шампанском блеске,
В мурлыкающем нежно треске
Мигающего Cinéma!
А через год — в чужой стране:
Усталость, город неизвестный,
Толпа, — и вновь на полотне
Черты француженки прелестной!...

Art is a load on one's shoulders;
But how we, being poets, value
Life in all its fleeting details!
How sweet to yield to laziness,
To feel one's blood flow
Melodiously from vein to vein,

. . .

And day-dream, as if life itself
Rises up in all its champagne glitter,
In the gently purring crackle
Of the blinking Cinéma!
A year later, in a foreign country:
Fatigue, an unknown city,
A crowd—and once more on the canvas
The features of a charming French girl!...

In Blok's notebook, "Perugia" is connected with "Blagoveshchenie" (The Annunciation), having been originally the beginning of the latter. "The Annunciation" is difficult and, it seems to me, one of the most successful and most beautiful of modern lyrics. As Orlov points out, the early manuscript draft varies only insignificantly from the published text. S. M. Solov'ëv saw in several of the Italian poems, particularly in the last four stanzas of "The Annunciation," a reflection of the themes of Pushkin's "Gavriliada."[20] Blok did not deny Solov'ëv's observation, but he did not admit it as being seriously informative, his design being substantially different. In a note on the poem in the third volume of the 1912 edition of his *Collected Poems*, he said:

Under his [Giannicola Manni's] "Annunciation" and other New Testament frescoes [in the Collegio del Cambio in Perugia] is inscribed: ite procul moneo, sacer est locus, ite profani. As if having protected himself by this adjuration with its suggestion of the personal (moneo) from the profane spectator inclined to suspect blasphemy, the artist allows himself, with a kind of intimacy (the eternal companion of demonism) to portray scenes of everyday life.... The demons of art dictated "Leda and the Swan" to the man who had conceived the "Annunziazione" and the one who conceived the "Gavriliada"—the author of the poem "Among Many Pictures" [Pushkin].

From the note one concludes that Blok's poem is intended to encompass both the Russian and Italian traditions, just as it uses both the Russian and Latin languages. Pressing the note on the poem, one observes that Blok described a moral condition in Russia and modern society in general by describing the epitome of the emotional dilemma of a Catholic lady long ago. Gabriel's announcement to her is a free translation of the Latin "Ave, Maria, gratiae plena!" (in Russian, following Church Slavonic, "Raduisia, Maria, blagodatnaia") Blok has made the girl who was "blessed among women" unique in the world for beauty. Even his Latin (this place of love is sacred) is a modification of the other Latin inscription from a warning in the direction of a judgment and, therefore, of a revived and sharper emotional expression (Blok added the *amor*).

С детских лет — видения и грезы,
Умбрии ласкающая мгла.
На оградах вспыхивают розы,
Тонкие поют колокола.

Слишком резвы милые подруги,
Слишком дерзок их открытый взор.
Лишь она одна в предвечном круге
Ткет и ткет свой шелковый узор.

Робкие томят ее надежды,
Грезятся несбыточные сны.
И внезапно — красные одежды
Дрогнули на золоте стены.

Всем лицом склонилась над шелками,
Но везде — сквозь золото ресниц —
Вихрь ли с многоцветными крылами,
Или ангел, распростертый ниц...

Темноликий ангел с дерзкой ветвью
Молвит: Здравствуй! Ты полна красы!
И она дрожит пред страстной вестью,
С плеч упали тяжких две косы...

Он поет и шепчет — ближе, ближе,
Уж над ней — шумящих крыл шатер...
И она без сил склоняет ниже
Потемневший, помутневший взор...

Трепеща, не верит: «Я ли, я ли?»
И рукою закрывает грудь...
Но чернеют пламенные дали —
Не уйти, не встать и не вздохнуть...

И тогда — незнаемою болью
Озарился светлый круг лица...
А над ними — символ своеволья —
Перуджийский гриф когтит тельца.

Лишь художник, занавесью скрытый, —
Он провидит страстной муки крест
И твердит: — Profani, procul ite,
Hic amoris locus sacer est.

From childhood on—reveries and visions,
The caressing haze of Umbria.
Roses blush like flames along the fences,
The fragile bells sing across the air.

The gentle friends are much too playful,
Far too impudent their open glance:
Only she alone in the everlasting circle
Weaves and weaves her own silk design.

Her modest hopes have wearied,
Fantastic dreams occur.
Suddenly—vermillion clothing
Shuddered on the gilded wall.

She bent her face down over her silk weaving,
But everywhere, through her eyelashes of gold
She saw—was it a whirlwind with wings of many colors
Or an angel prostrate at her feet...

The dark-faced angel with the impertinent branch
Speaks: Greetings! Thou art full of beauty!
She trembles at the passionate news,
Two heavy braids fell off her shoulders...

He sings and whispers—closer, closer,
Now over her—a tent of rustling wings...
She limply drops lower and lower
Her darkened, bedimmed eyes...

Quivering in disbelief: "Is it I? Is it I?"
And puts her hand across her breast...
But the fiery background blackens—
She cannot leave, or rise, or breathe...

And then the bright circle of her face
Is lit up by an unknown pain...
And over them, symbol of self-will,
Perugia's griffin claws a calf.

Only the artist, hidden by a curtain,
Foresees the passion of the crucifix
And reiterates: Profani, procul ite,
Hic amoris locus sacer est.

Blok's note on the poem, the subject of the poem, and its achieved content suggest a series of analogies basically dramatic in nature. The griffin with its prey is analogous to the pregnant Virgin. The griffin, Blok reminds us, has been a political symbol of Perugia since pagan times; the Virgin, the symbol of the Church. Artistically analogous and socially confluent, they are met here in this poem by their own consequences: the sacred passion of the child-victim, Christ, and the glorification of all the experiences in the art of the fourteenth and fifteenth centuries and the art of this poem. The event is a parallel to the pre-Christian story of Leda and Zeus, given as essential, aesthetic experience of power, beauty, violence, and violation in, for example, Yeats's poem. Blok presents it as a little play, emphasizing the seemingly arbitrary nature of what happened and the sensuality that must pervade it, as sensuality pervades usual, similar human experiences. The sanctity of Mary's virginity is seen in two phases: that of a girl, ripe for marriage, among other girls who know her desirability and, after God has chosen Mary, as that of the pure-in-heart whose purity has been fulfilled by what seems to be violation. What before the fact seems casual or accidental, after the fact seems all the more clearly to have been preordained. Blok emphasizes this by emphasizing the facts of sensuality, of power, of normalcy, and of wonder. God's appearance through an angel as if out of a whirlwind, as in *Job*, supports the sense of personality involved, quite contrary to fourteenth or fifteenth century representations of the scene in which the gestures and responses have been transmuted into gold.

Blok plays off the artistic representation of the event against the plausible occurrence. What the lady feels—what *happens* to her and to us—is the subject of this poem, brought out all the more clearly by being put against the artistic dogmatism or conventionality that transcribed it in gold leaf as appropriate, stylized gesture. One cannot too much emphasize Blok's sense of meaningful experience. The essence of the complex of actions is available only to the artist who, by organizing it, can connect and identify desires and their results, especially in so far as identification of one thing with another occurs in simultaneous moments. It is at this ultimate, mysterious point that the Latin meets the Russian. To what love the place is sacred we do not know, any more than we can ever understand, Blok suggests, the love for which Christ offered himself as sacrifice. That is beyond understanding, like the essential mystery of this poem or of all beautiful things.

Blok uses the word that means "holy" and "passionate," as in "Passion Week," in both meanings twice in the poem. He uses "impudent" or "impertinent" twice to refer to the ladies around Mary, the central virgin, and to Gabriel, the disfigurer of the virgin. There are two webs of meaning, in both of which the symbols work: the religious web based on the canonical story and Christian morality and the aesthetic web based on immediate experience and sensuality or power. The poem is as sacred to love as the poet can make it, binding the experience and the religion of love together in one set of symbols. The figure of the Virgin in this poem is the same sort of ultimate figure as the Beautiful Lady in the earlier poems, only she is "real." In this poem she is a figure that generates meaning, a figure to which meanings attach themselves except as transcended by the whole meaning of love, which the poem is about.

A kind of suppleness and gracefulness, without power, is evident in the five poems called "Poslaniia" (Epistles) in the fifth section of Blok's third book. Each of the five poems derives its impulse and style from the work of the poet to whom it is addressed. Like the poem "Khudozhnik" (The Artist), they are uses of poetry for self-definition on a greater than personal scale. They are "definitions" of ability, not of value, of the antagonism between the usual world—what a man's eyes see—and the creative world—what the mind's eye sees:

Длятся часы, мировое несущие.
Ширятся звуки, движенье и свет.
Прошлое страстно глядится в грядущее.
Нет настоящего. Жалкого — нет.

The hours stretch out, carrying the universal.
Sounds, motion, and light expand.
The past passionately peers into what's to come.
There is no present. Nothing is sad.

The poet, who has made a "cold, steel cage" for his "bird of freedom" and who now hears it on the window-sill sing back the songs he made, is "tormented" and "waiting for something new"—and is bored. There being no particular activity by which to specify the present moment, the present seems merely an invisible bridge between the past and the future. This is the obverse of that experience, as given in the Venice poem, which maintains that only the present is real.

The seeming contradiction was supported by a dichotomy in Blok himself, which becomes apparent in the "typical" hero of his later poems, a man who is tired and suffering and sophisticatedly disillusioned. The dichotomy originates in Blok's perception of the irreconcilability of performance and reality. The later poems generally develop a sense of loss of youth and of ideals, a sense of bewilderment and of a confused ambivalence ("love"—"hate") toward the world, expressed in the inaccessibility of happiness, the domination by external events, a sense of sinfulness or guilt and the remorse of conscience, and ultimate failure and loss, or general ruin.

Habitual disappointment with performance leads to disillusionment, to righteous anger—that *indignatio* Blok referred to—and to imprecation, as in the poem, "Ty tverdish', chto ia kholoden," first called "To a Friend," written during the World War, in which Blok turns the accusations against him—"You assert that I am cold, reserved and dry"—back against the "whole world" that "has become barbaric":

Не стучись же напрасно у плотных дверей,
Тщетным стоном себя не томи:
Ты не встретишь участья у бедных зверей,
Называвшихся прежде людьми.

Ты — железною маской лицо закрывай,
Поклоняясь священным гробам,
Охраняя железом до времени рай,
Недоступный безумным рабам,

Don't knock vainly on thick doors,
Don't tire yourself with useless moaning:
You'll find no sympathy among the poor beasts
That once upon a time were people.

Cover your face with an iron mask,
Worshiping sacred graves,
Protecting with iron, until the day come, the heaven
Inaccessible to mad slaves.

This is not an ironic poem; it is plain bitter.

Yet, even in this poem, Blok suggests that there is always really some place else to be. There is another, maybe ultimate, experience to enfold, beyond death, as he said in the earlier (1910) poem on Vera Kommissarzhevskaia's death, included in the next section, "Harps and Violins":

Смотри сквозь тучи: там она —
Развернутое ветром знамя,
Обетованная весна.

Look through the clouds: there she is—
A banner unrolled on the wind,
The promised spring.

The equilibrium between liberation and freedom was symbolized for Blok by aviation. He wrote his mother in April 1910, "In people's flying, even their unsuccessful trips, there is something time-honored and required of mankind, something consequently on a grand scale." Adequately expressed, the limit of equilibrium is approached and apprehended by a successful change of technique corresponding to actual failure, as in the last line of the following poem (1910):

В неуверенном, зыбком полете
Ты над бездной взвился и повис.
Что-то древнее есть в повороте
Мертвых крыльев, подогнутых вниз.

Как ты можешь летать и кружиться
Без любви, без души, без лица?
О, стальная, бесстрастная птица,
Чем ты можешь прославить творца?

В серых сферах летай и скитайся,
Пусть оркестр на трибуне гремит,
Но под легкую музыку вальса
Остановится сердце — и винт.

You spun up above nothing and hung there
In uncertain and unstable flight.
There is something ancient in the turning
Of dead wings tucked down and bent out.

How can you fly and spiral
Without love or a soul or a face?
O steel, passionless bird,
What can you offer your maker in praise?

Fly up and wander about in grey spheres,
Let the orchestra roar in the grandstand,
But while the light tune of a waltz goes round
The heart—and the propeller—stop.

Blok has several poems on the theme, the airplane and its pilot being taken as the instrument of "civilization" in the unsuccessful quest for the freedom which "culture" may be said to promise. A poem begun in 1910 and called "Aviator" was revised in 1912, following the death of a pilot named Smit[h] whom Blok saw killed at an aviation exhibition in May 1911. The poem is weak, but it does contain certain interesting metaphors and awareness of psychic experience. In the first line the plane is called a "rolling stone pushed off into freedom." The stanza in which the poet asks the dead, disfigured pilot what happened, why he went up and came to disaster, takes up precisely that dramatic use of psychic experience which Dostoevsky exploited:

Или восторг самозабвенья
Губительный изведал ты?
Безумно возалкал паденья
И сам остановил винты?

Or did you experience the disastrous
Ecstasy of self-oblivion?
Did you madly crave a fall
And yourself turn off the motor?

The correspondence with Dostoevsky's psychology is striking, especially if one takes a part of the story "Vlas" as given in *The Diary of a Writer* for 1873:

[The hero has] a need to go beyond limits, a need for the sensation of dying, for going up to the very brink, for hanging over the abyss, for looking into its depths and, in certain cases but by no means rare ones, for hurling himself into it like a crazy man, head first.

It is not unlike the experience given in the Chairman's song in Pushkin's *Pir vo vremia chumy* (Feast in the Time of Plague) (1830):

Есть упоение в бою,
И бездны мрачной на краю,
И в разъяренном океане —

. . .

Всё, всё, что гибелью грозит,
Для сердца смертного таит
Неизъяснимы наслажденья —...

There is an ecstasy in battle
And on the edge of a dark abyss,
And in the ocean white with rage—

. . .

Everything that threatens ruin
Conceals inexplicable delights
For the mortal heart—...

Blok is dealing with the moment of escape *from* liberation by technical advances, the escape *into* the absolute freedom of self-consummation. In psychological terms, it is very much analogous to the Christian concept that he who would save his life must lose it. Because there is no heaven for Blok, salvation is not of but in the soul, which remains the lyric point of reference. The understanding is worked out dramatically by correlation of various valueless (because impulsive) psychic moments. The moments are positions in conversation or in the exposition of a semiphilosophical scheme, held together by an understanding which assumes that the apotheosis or self-destruction of the main figure is the central incident, the key to meaning.

Blok's poem "Kometa" (The Comet) (1910), a variation on this theme, presents the comet as the natural agent of this necessary destruction of which "civilization" is unaware:

Ты нам грозишь последним часом,
Из синей вечности звезда!

. . .

Наш мир, раскинув хвост павлиний,
Как ты, исполнен буйством грез:
Через Симплон, моря, пустыни,
Сквозь алый вихрь небесных роз,
Сквозь ночь, сквозь мглу — стремят отныне
Полет — стада стальных стрекоз!

. . .

Но гибель не страшна герою,
Пока безумствует мечта![21]

You threaten us with our final hour,
Star from deep blue eternity!

. . .

Our world has spread its peacock tail,
Like you is filled with roaring dreams:
Across the Simplon Pass, seas and deserts,
Through the scarlet vertigo of heavenly roses,
Through the night, through the haze there rush now
Flocks in flight of steel dragonflies.

. . .

But ruin does not terrify the hero
As long as his dream raves wildly.

This is not to say that Blok was so overcome by the aviation feats and failures that he began to write only morose poetry and only about the end of the world. He had always had a sense of humor and, as was then fashionable, frequently corresponded with friends in light verse. In 1905 he wrote an excellent parody, in Bal'mont's style, of a series of letters Bal'mont published in *The Balance* on his travels in Mexico. The poem begins (and ends):

Я бандит, я бандит!
Поднося мне яду склянку
Говорила Мексиканка:
— У тебя печальный вид.
— Верно ты ходил в Пампасы —
Загрязненные лампасы —
Стыд!
Увлеченный,
Упоенный,
Озираясь,
Упиваясь,
С Мексиканкой обнимаясь,
Я — веселый
Целовал
Мексиканские подолы,
. . .
И во сне меня фламинго
В Сан-Доминго
Пригласил.[22]

I'm a bandit, I'm a bandit!
Bringing me a phial of poison
The Mexican girl said:
"You have a sad look.
You must have been in the Pampas—
Your trouser stripes are muddy—
Shame!"
Distracted,
Ecstatic,
Looking round,
Getting drunk,
Necking with the Mexican,
I was happy,
Kissed
The Mexican skirts,
. . .

And in a dream a flamingo
Invited me
To San Domingo.

In January 1913 Blok wrote two parodies of his own work which he read at a literary gathering one evening. According to Sadovskii, Blok remarked before reading, "This is the way I wrote ten years ago":

Вечность ли вздохнула над березами кудрявыми?
Облака прозрачные на закат сбежали.
Синих елок крестики сделались кровавыми,
Крестики зеленые розовыми стали.

Встал я и задумался над ярким мухомором.
Что ж в груди затеплилось скрытое рыданье?
Мне не стыдно плакать под небесным взором:
В светлом одиночестве сладостно страданье.[23]

Did eternity sigh over the curly birches?
The limpid clouds ran down to set.
The tops of the blue firs became blood-red,
The green tops became rose-colored.

I arose and fell to thinking over a brilliant death-cup.
What of the hidden sobbing that began to gleam in my breast?
I was not ashamed to weep under the gaze of heaven:
In bright loneliness suffering is sweet.

Blok's poetry had changed. The structure of the later poems, Orlov has said, is based "completely on the rules of dramatic composition." It often takes the form of an interior dialogue breaking into actual dialogue focussed on a specific gesture. This is clear in the poem "A Woman," written in August 1914 (included in the section "Various Poems") and dedicated to Strindberg, whose work had much impressed Blok in 1911–12. In the poem, a woman, who functions as narrator, reports that she has thought seriously of suicide and goes to a graveyard where she by chance meets a man. The woman reflects on what it is about her mournfulness that has attracted the man—or is he just lonely, too?—and is ready to defend her loneliness by reproaching him, when he quietly says from over her shoulder that his child lies buried there. She excuses herself. He hands her a bouquet of flowers she has forgotten. She offers them for the child, but he replies that she needs them more. She says:

Да, я винюсь в своей ошибке,
Но... не прощу до смерти (нет!)
Той снисходительной улыбки,
С которой он смотрел мне вслед![24]

Yes, I admit I was wrong,
But... I never, *never* will forgive
That condescending smile
With which he watched me go!

Dramatic movement is also apparent, but not so clear because of the complicated shifts of viewpoint, in the poem "The Snowy Petersburg Twilight," written in March 1914 and printed in the section "Harps and Violins." In this poem there is no sentimental psychologizing: the tensions are real, not melodramatic, and the poem is characterized by a certain beauty and suppleness:

Петербу́ргские су́мерки сне́жные.
Взгля́д на у́лице, ро́зы в дому́...
Мы́сли — то́чно у де́вушки не́жные,
А о чём, — и сама́ не пойму́...

Всё гляжу́сь в мое зе́ркало со́нное...
(Он, должно́ быть, гляди́тся в окно́...)
Вон лицо́ моё — зло́е, влюблённое!
А́х, как мне надое́ло оно́!...

Запева́ния ни́зкого го́лоса,
Снежно-бе́лые ру́ки мои́.
Мои то́нкие ры́жие во́лосы, —
Как давно́ они ста́ли ничьи́!

Му́ж ушёл. Све́т тако́й безобра́зный...
Всё же кро́вь розове́ет на све́т...
Посмотрю́-ка, он та́м или не́т?
Так и е́сть... ах, како́й неотвя́зный!

The snowy Petersburg twilight.
Somebody's glance in the street; in the house, roses...
Thoughts—tender as a girl's,
But of what, I myself don't understand...

I keep looking in my dreamy mirror...
(He, I suppose, looks in the window...)
There it is, my face—evil, enamored!
Ah, how it bores me!

Tunes carried by a low voice,
My snow-white hands,
My fine red hair—
How long they have been nobody's!

My husband left. The world is so hideous...
But blood still shines pink in the light...
I'll see if he's there or not?
So he is... ah, how importunate!

This poem is difficult because it presses into very little a whole intricate series of desires and frustrations. A lapse into sentimental cliché—"my snow-white hands"—is rescued by the striking "my fine red hair." The poem is in anapestic trimeter with alternating dactyllic (two hypercatalectic syllables) and masculine rhymes, except for the last stanza which is a b b a feminine (one hypercatalectic syllable) and masculine. The stress pattern varies only in that quite a few of the first syllables receive a half-stress and one expected first stress is omitted (in the eighth line). No line is run-on; the thirteenth line is two sentences. The poem has a ballad-like quality and a Nekrasov-like pathos. The meter and the alternating rhyme pattern create a "moving" rhythm. The dramatic tension is between the motion of the poem and the prosaically ironic bitterness of its content. Taking the poem as a piece, the last line, for example, gives a fresh and dreadful interpretation to the usual symbols of affection. Love is turned on itself. The dialogue of the lady with herself is paralleled by the movement of her emotion and is played off against it.

Ophelia and Hamlet are used as animated figures in a series of Blok's early poems on love. The Beautiful Lady is from the start carried far from the *amour courtois* tradition where she began.[25] Harlequin, Pierrot, and Columbine are given roles quite different from those in old comedy: the buffoonery and absurdity are used to point up an ironic pathos, a senseless and hopeless loss. The so-called "gypsy" motifs, taken chiefly from Grigor'ev's poetry, and the Carmen story are invested with a greater reality, a liberation in song. Solveig is made to stand for more than Ibsen made her. On an intimate level, Nastasia Filipovna of Dostoevsky's *The Idiot* is used in Blok's poetry—in the cycle "Faina" and in the play *Pesnia sud'by* (The Song of Fate)—as an image of overwhelming attraction.

In the "Carmen" cycle, the seventh section of the third book, the idea of love is altered into a concept of personal satisfaction beyond the limits of ordinary life but within the framework of ordinary life: that is, it is celebrated as belonging to that *other* world where such gratification is plausible. Consequently, it is associated with images of escape and travel—the road or the journey—and images of peace and ease—of whiteness, simplicity, and what is "beyond the storm of life":

За бурей жизни, за тревогой,
За грустью всех измен —
Пусть эта мысль предстанет строгой,
Простой и белой, как дорога,
Как дальний путь, Кармен.[26]

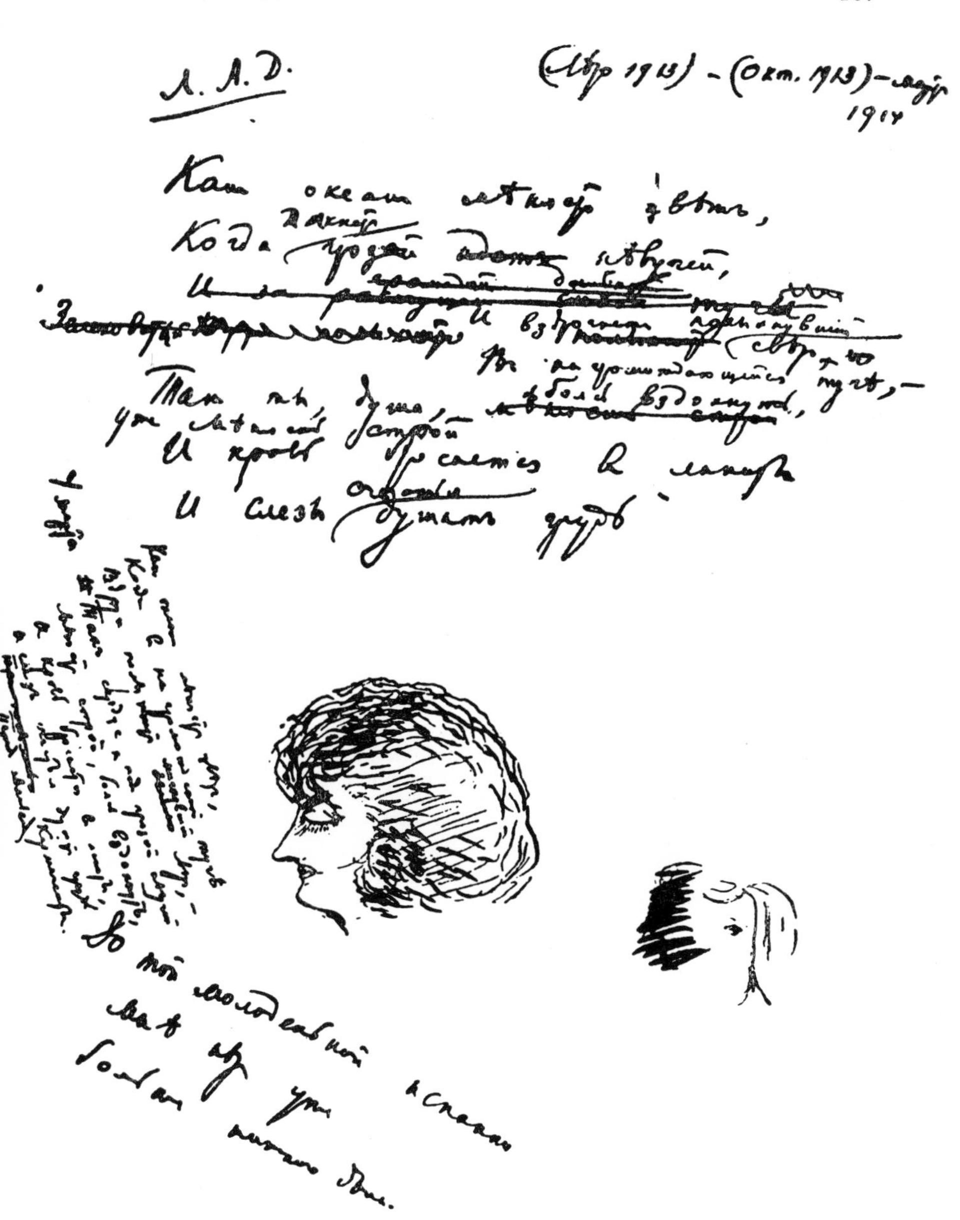

A page of manuscript from the *Carmen* cycle, with the poet's sketch of Liubov' Del'mas.

Beyond the storm of life, beyond anxiety,
  Beyond the sadness of all infidelities—
Let this thought appear severe,
  Plain and white, like a highway,
  Like a distant journey, Carmen.

The poems in the cycle were all written in March 1914 for Liubov' Del'mas, with whom Blok had an affair in the winter 1913–14. The poems, like the affair itself, represent an escape for Blok from personal failures and the return of the possibility that that personal freedom which he had mocked himself for having indulged in, as illusion, was after all real. In the final poem of the cycle, "No, You Never Were Mine and Will Never Be Anyone's," he says that the possibility of the lady's impossibility was what lured him to her and—that it was why he was her "admirer and a poet." He understands the sensual delights with the lady as one side of the coin, and the fusion, in surrender, of independent, transcendental worlds, as the other. The heavens repeat his and his lady's love:

Здесь — страшная печать отверженности женской
За прелесть дивную — постичь ее нет сил.
Там — дикий сплав миров, где часть души вселенской
Рыдает, исходя гармонией светил.

. . .

И этот мир тебе — лишь красный облак дыма,
Где что-то жжет, поет, тревожит и горит!

И в зареве его — твоя безумна младость...
Всё — музыка и свет: нет счастья, нет измен...
Мелодией одной звучат печаль и радость...
Но я люблю тебя: я сам такой, Кармен.[27]

Here—the terrible imprint of feminine rejection
For marvelous charm—one lacks the power to understand it.
There—a wild fusion of worlds in which a part of the universal soul
Sobs, melting into the harmony of the luminous stars.

. . .

This world to you is only a red cloud of smoke
Where something scorches, sings, disturbs, and is aflame!

And in its glow there is your mad youthfulness...
Everything is music and light: there is no happiness, no infidelity...
Sorrow and joy are one melody...
But I love you: I am myself like that, *Carmen.*

The poem is a celebration of the lady's freedom—she is a law unto herself, the poet says, flying past him to other constellations—to which the poet says he is adequate analogy, presumably because the music of his poetry, like the music of the opera, is not subject to the moral standards to which the stories of *Carmen* and of the poet and the singer are subject. Both the poet and the lady have other rôles through which to overcome the limitations people ordinarily impose on themselves. The life of the world is preserved by the music both of the opera and of the poem.

Poetry is equally an effort to preserve freedom from being lost or confounded in the failures and imperfections of the actual world. "The Nightingale Garden," finished in 1915, was originally planned as a short lyric but developed into a quasi-narrative poem as Blok worked on it in 1914–15. The garden is the condition of freedom, harmony, and beauty, untouched by the world, which the poet rides by on his donkey and subsequently enters—or is it only a dream? It is a place of unreal peace which, after having returned to the real world, the poet cannot say he has actually experienced, especially when he sees, going over the path he went, a workman with a pick "driving another donkey." It was the poet's own donkey's cry that in the morning from outside the garden ended his "enchanted dream," his night in the garden. The difficulty about the garden is not that one cannot stay there—cannot endure the peace and is called back to the things of this world—but that one can never know if one has really been there, because there is nothing in this world by which to measure it, it being precisely the opposite of what this world is.

Russia, of course, is part of this world, and in the cycle "My Native Land" Blok definitely identifies himself with Russia and his time with all preceding periods of Russian culture and civilization. In his article "Bezvremen'e" (Hard Times) (1906), he takes up the theme of the individual's responsibility for demoniacally cutting through the spider web of stagnation that has wrapped itself around Russia. The earlier, 1905 poem "Osenniaia volia" (Autumn Freedom), from Blok's second book, with its opening line and meter very similar to Lermontov's "Vykhozhu odin ia na dorogu" (Alone I Set Out on the Road) (1841), introduces the theme of the beautiful Russian countryside confounded with the "voice of drunken Rus'" to both of which the poet is committed:

Запою ли про свою удачу,
Как я молодость сгубил в хмелю...
Над печалью нив твоих заплачу,
Твой простор навеки полюблю...

Shall I begin to sing of my own good luck,
How I wasted my youth in intoxication...
I shall weep over the sorrow of your cornfields,
I shall forever love your vastness...

The cycle "My Native Land" is the development of the theme of the fate of Russia. It stands outside Blok's other poems and sections by its "patriotic" content, much in the tradition of Tiutchev, Solov'ëv and Khomiakov, and by the kind of dramatic personification of the country and the countryside. Russia is called a bride, a wife, containing potential natural resources out of which its own triumph shall come (this is specifically allegoric use of the mother—child theme). Russia is the child of Gogol and "beckons to us from the future," for Gogol, Blok says, was first to see the beauty and the music as an harmonic principle behind the triviality and the perversions of life. Real Russia lies still ahead, beyond the stagnation and staleness, somewhere, somehow, at the end of the road, that yellow, wild, steppe, night, long road, which runs like a musical theme through the cycle on Russia, leading those "who have no real life" to reality itself.

The fate of Russia is involved, on the one hand, with the symbol of Christ (the poem "Zadebrennye lesom kruchi"):

И капли ржавые, лесные,
Родясь в глуши и темноте,
Несут испуганной России
Весть о сжигающем Христе.

And the rusty, forest drops,
Born in a deep, dark thicket,
Carry to frightened Russia
The news of Christ the consuming fire.

and, on the other hand, with the natural world and Russian history (the poem "Reka raskinulas'..."):

Река раскинулась. Течет, грустит лениво
И моет берега.
Над скудной глиной желтого обрыва
В степи грустяат стога.

О, Русь моя! Жена моя! До боли
Нам ясен долгий путь!
Наш путь — стрелой татарской древней воли
Пронзил нам грудь.

. . .

Покой нам только снится
Сквозь кровь и пыль...
Летит, летит степная кобылица
И мнет ковыль...

И нет конца! Мелькают версты, кручи...
  Останови!
Идут, идут испуганные тучи,
  Закат в крови!

Закат в крови! Из сердца кровь струится!
  Плачь, сердце, плачь...
Покоя нет! Степная кобылица
  Несется вскачь!

The river spread out. It flows along, lazily sad,
  And washes the shores.
Above the bare clay of the yellow precipice
  The haycocks are melancholy on the steppe.

O, my Russia! my wife! The long road
  Ahead is so clear it is painful!
Our road has pierced our heart
  Like an arrow of ancient Tartar freedom.

. . .

We only dream of peace
  Through blood and dust...
The steppe mare flies on and on
  And tramples the feathergrass...

There is no end! Versts, ravines fly by...
  Rein in!
The frightened clouds go on and on,
  The sunset in blood!

The sunset in blood! Blood streams from the heart!
  Weep, heart, weep...
There is no peace! The steppe mare
  Gallops on!

This poem is the first of a series of four written in June and July, 1908, and called "On the Battlefield of Kulikovo," the 1380 defeat of the Tartars by a confederacy of Moscow princes under Dmitri Donskoi, marking the end of Tartar hegemony and the beginning of the rise of the Muscovite principality. The first stanza of the poem, with its image of yellow clay, recurrent in Blok's poems, and the second, with its thematic use of the letters R, U, and S of the word for Old Russia (*Rus'*), with its alternating long and short feminine- and masculine-rhymed lines, establish a tone from which the poem moves to a crescendo, conveying by its rhythms and repetitions a feeling of anxiety.

The historic past cannot be forgotten, Blok repeats in a poem to Zinaida Gippius, especially by "us, the children of Russia's terrible years." Although the crow may caw over the deathbed of those who are now living, the hope remains real that those to come will be able to accomplish the perfection so long unfulfilled yet still possible:

Те, кто достойней, боже, боже,
Да узрят царствие твое![28]

Lord, Lord, may those who are more worthy
Perceive your heavenly kingdom!

In a very moving, short poem, "Korshun" (The Kite) (1916), the last two lines of which are obviously imitative of the style and tone of folk poetry, Blok suggests that there is, unfortunately, no guarantee of anything. Between the failure of the past and the hope for the future there is only this present anxiety:

Идут века, шумит война,
Встает мятеж, горят деревни,
А ты всё та ж, моя страна,
В красе заплаканной и древней. —
Доколе матери тужить?
Доколе коршуну кружить?

Ages pass, war roars on,
Rebellion rises, villages burn,
And you are still the same, my land,
In a tear-stained, ancient beauty.
How long shall the mother grieve?
How long shall the black kite gyre?

What can a man believe? And how shall it be said? In the poem "Bylo to v tëmnykh Karpatakh" (It Happened in the Dark Carpathians) (1913) in the final section, "What the Wind Sings About," Blok suggests that the faith is in the power of the fiction itself. The beauty of the fantasy, like the strength and grace of the wind, is the unique and private guarantee of whatever there is to come. Nobody can say that something *will* come; nobody can say that it will not. It is a question of conviction: whether or not other people admit the plausibility of your faith or are willing to accept your story of it, its conformity with reality—with what the wind sings—is vindication beforehand. The poem begins, in the manner of folk recitative, with an eight-line introduction "locating" the "events" and telling how the author heard about them. The verse is dactyllic trimeter. The body of the poem (twenty-six lines) then follows. There are no "events"; it is an intensely lyric poem, in the form of "advice" to a friend and an assertion of faith. The middle part of the poem is in iambic verse of differing length—some lines have one stress, some have five. The last five lines, again varying in length but leading up to a final one-stress line, are anapestic. The three meters together and the movement from one to another, culminating in the final section, give the effect of the music of the wind.

Верь, друг мой, сказкам: я привык
  Вникать
В чудесный их язык
  И постигать
В обрывках слов
  Туманный ход
  Иных миров,

. . .

Жди, старый друг, терпи, терпи,
Терпеть недолго, крепче спи,
  Всё равно, всё пройдет,
Всё равно ведь никто не поймет,
Ни тебя не поймет, ни меня,
  Ни что ветер поет
    Нам, звеня...

Believe fairy-tales, my friend: I am accustomed
  To penetrate
Into their marvellous language
  And to comprehend
In scraps of words
  The foggy march
  Of other worlds,

. . .

Wait, old friend, be patient, patient,
You haven't long to wait; sleep more soundly.
  It doesn't matter, it will all pass,
It doesn't matter that no one understands,
Doesn't understand you or me,
  Or what the wind sings
    To us as it rings...

As measured by the specifics of versification, Blok's poetry, from book to book—that is, as time went on—moves toward drama. In the first book, for example, as Nikitina and Shuvalov have computed, there is approximately one epithet every two lines; in the second, one every two-and-one-half lines; in the third, one every three-and-one-half lines. The verbs take over from the adjectives. But, from the point of view of faith—from the dichotomy between the "ideal" and the "real"—what the poetry "does" is more important. Although the "new man"—the aviator or the artist, each an aspect of the other—cannot absolve himself of the sins of his fathers and must also be burdened with his own inventions, as Baudelaire was burdened, still art has before it the task of moral purgation and philosophic revivification, that is, of creating and demonstrating a beautiful world.

I am chary of any sort of "art for art's sake," because such a tendency contradicts the very essence of art and because, if we pursue it, we ultimately lose all art. Art arises from the eternal interaction of two musics—the music of the creative personality and the music which resounds in the depths of the popular psyche, the soul of the *masses.* Great art arises only from the union of these two electric currents.

By 1919, however, when Blok jotted down this thought in his diary, all his poetry, except for a few little pieces and some unsuccessful extensions of *Retribution,* was behind him.

VII

Retribution

A NARRATIVE

My story will be sad.—A. Pushkin

Serious innovations in art proceed from necessity—from the incapacity of older forms adequately to communicate a new sensibility and from the artist's compulsion to communicate his vision of reality. The form and the content of the vision are significantly indistinguishable.[1] Of all Blok's work the long poem *Retribution* most clearly binds the two. Its mystery is that of a poem adequately adjusted to the several modes of action it mimes.

According to early plans, the poem was to have been in four chapters with a prologue and an epilogue. The first chapter was to deal with the "father"; the second, with the "son's" childhood and youth; the third, with the "father's" death; and the fourth, with the Russo-Japanese War and the 1905 Revolution, in which the "son" was to die. Each chapter was to deal with the family "clan" and, as Blok writes in the introduction, was to be framed by "description of events of world-wide significance."[2] As one of his memoirists said, Blok "wanted to see in *Retribution* the return to Russian poetry of the poem with a plot and real life."[3]

The final plan given in the introduction includes some modifications. The first chapter is a study of an educated, liberal Russian family during the period of the Russo-Turkish War of 1877–78 and the People's Freedom movement, and of the appearance of a "demon," the first harbinger of "individualism, a man like Byron, with unearthly impulses and desires, dulled however by the time's disease, the incipient *fin de siècle*." The second chapter, dealing with the turn of the century and unfinished except for an introduction, was to have dealt with the demon's son, another member of the long family tree, who also vanished, leaving a daughter behind. The third chapter is a study of the father's death—the center of the poem. The scene shifts to Warsaw, to the end of the first decade of the twentieth century, to the motifs of repression and resurrection in both a political and a metaphysical sense. "Here, by the father's fresh grave, the son's development and life-path end." The son yields to *his* son, who was supposed to have been the subject of the epilogue and to have prepared to sacrifice himself for freedom. But, like the second chapter, or like the fourth chapter proposed earlier, the epilogue was never written. It was to be a poem about the provenience, understanding, position, and legacy of a sensitive man of Blok's time. The epilogue about the hero's son was not possible, because one can allegorize but not dramatize the future.[4]

We know that the poem was never completed in two senses: Blok did not stop trying to add to it, and he was dissatisfied with large sections of it. An addition to the 1921 revised draft of the second chapter was found on his desk the day he died. The poem, however, is not unfinished. Blok could not extend it or radically change it because the generative concept in the poem had been, like an electric circuit, closed, as the terminal lines from *Brand*, apposite to the epigraph, indicate. Blok kept coming back, as he put it, to his hatred for the idea of progress and his bewilderment at how to replace the broken shibboleth, convinced that some such central idea must exist. The poem is epic and lyric at once. It is description of a society's manners. It is the story of the failures of love between a series of two men, between fathers and sons, and between these men and their society. It is a psychological self-study of a liberal opposed to the history of his time. It is an effort to realize a man's consciousness in a self-generating—a "musical"—form. Morally, it is an analysis of the war that is revenge.

The idea of the poem was suggested to Blok by his father's death, and he began a poem about that called "December 1, 1909" the day his father died. He soon changed the title to "Father." The poem he was working on is what we would call early drafts of the present third chapter, or focus, of *Retribution.* He even called the hero Dmitrii, as he called his wife's little boy and, he said, "as they once wanted to call me." In the several years that followed, he revised certain sections and printed some as separate lyric poems, for example, "When We Two Met" included in the cycle "Iambs." He was continually cutting down his "real" poem to its dramatic themes.

In its final, definitive form, *Retribution* is 1573 lines long; the first chapter is about two-thirds of the poem. The prologue specifies certain problems of art: first, the relation of the poet to his poetry and of both to society; second, the cognitive function of art—that its definitions and dramatizations of life, such as the first line ("Life is without beginning or end" [Zhizn'—bez nachala i kontsa]), or the Notung symbol, or the Salome story, express meaning adequately; and, third, the determination of the discrepancies between what is and what ought to be, a determination, in the name of ultimate freedom, which it is the unique function of artistic images to carry:

> Пусть жила жизни глубока:
> Алмаз горит издалека —
> Дроби, мой гневный ямб, каменья!
>
> Let the vein of life be deep:
> The diamond brightly burns afar—
> My angry iamb, smash the stones!

The first chapter is an historical survey of the 1870s and 1880s from the viewpoint of a Russian family. It begins with a catalogue of what Blok considers the characteristics of that time distinguishing it from the early years of the twentieth century—congresses, strikes, money-making, parlor conversation, bourgeois manners and morals, and the "humanistic haze" contrasted to machines, airplanes, speed and confusion, and the alienation of men from society and from themselves. The poem then describes the enthusiastic return of Russian troops to Moscow from the Russo-Turkish War of 1877–78, summarizing what the war and the return from the war have meant both to the soldiers who went and to their families who stayed behind. The reader is taken into the drawing room of a family of fashionable society, where guests are arriving for the evening. Someone lights a cigarette; a lady sits patiently. All are waiting for someone. The bell rings. The expected guest arrives:

> В своих движениях уверен
> И статен; мужественный вид;
> Одет совсем, как иностранец,
> Изысканно...
>
> Confident in every gesture
> And stately; a masculine appearance;
> Dressed completely like a foreigner,
> With refinement...

The party continues, fading into the night, into the poet's own sense of responsibility for "fixing" the meaning of manners, the modes of social communication, in a generalization of social behavior.

"That's what my family was like" (Tak bylo i s moei sem'ëi), the poet says, introducing a long "stanza" of autobiography, which is followed by a thumbnail sketch of the head of the family, a sketch delimited by the opening line: "The life of the old is going down" (Zhizn' starshikh blizitsia k zakatu). The man had three daughters, one of whom marries and lives at first with her husband in her family home. The husband slowly shifts from concern over "the cursed questions" to "doing his duty" as an honest official. The society they move in is the society in which Blok's maternal grandfather Beketov, the rector of the university, moves, a society in which Dostoevsky is looking for material for his *Diary* and Polonskii reads his poems. In this society suddenly appears "a demon," a "new Byron," "so interesting and so intelligent," a mixture of "Constant and Pushkin, Stein and Flaubert" (Blok's father), who is invited to the Beketovs and courts the youngest daughter. A rather epigrammatic description of him follows:

Свобода, право, идеал —
Всё было для него не шуткой,
Ему лишь было втайне жутко:
Он, утверждая, отрицал
И утверждал он, отрицая.

Freedom, justice, ideals—
These all were real for him,
Only he was secretly frightened:
Asserting something, he denied it,
And he asserted by denial.

Suddenly, words fail the hero—and Blok the poet digresses, as he does frequently throughout the poem, on problems of language and composition that confront him:

(О, пыль словесная! Что нужды
В тебе? — Утешишь ты едва ль,
Едва ли разрешишь ты муки!) —

O, verbal dust! What purpose can you
Serve? You do not really comfort,
You do not really ease our pains!

The hero and the daughter marry: he spoils her life, tyrannizing over her—and Blok suggests that this is the emotional catastrophe typical of the times. "My Byron" finishes a "brilliant dissertation" and takes his young bride with him to his professorial home in Warsaw. Relations between them break, and the daughter returns to her father's house in Russia, carrying a child in her arms.

The introduction to the second chapter—108 lines in four sections, and all there is of the second chapter—deals with the end of the 1880s, the 1890s, and the beginning of the twentieth century. The introduction does not advance the poem's "plot." Rather, it is an effort to catch up the spirit and psychology of an age in transition, of a time of change in which people sense that things must be different but cannot imagine precisely how.

The third chapter, 460 lines, is the center of the poem. It begins "in the middle of things": the father lies dying in a Warsaw hospital, the son is hurrying to him. Excellent, lyric description of the dead man (he dies just before the son arrives), of the hospital, of Warsaw and the landscape, of the cold winter and of the funeral and the cemetery alternates with summaries of the relations between the son and dead father, their common history, ideals and efforts, and intellectual intentions and possibilities of life in Russia at that time, just before the First World War. The chapter (also, the poem) ends with a final stanza recapitulating the dominant musical and literary themes of the whole poem, as set out specifically in the prologue.

The poem's epigraph—*iunost'—eto vozmezdie* (Youth—that is retribution)—comes from one of Solness's speeches in the Russian translation of *The Master Builder.* "The younger generation—it means retribution," Solness says to Hilda in the first act and keeps repeating throughout the play.[5] "I'm afraid of retribution, Hilda," he says to her in the last act just before he climbs the tower and falls. Ibsen's play is a passionate attempt to penetrate the psychological masks of the obsolete mind of a powerful man, a mind and a man supported by status and profession but challenged by the impulsive, intuitive brilliance of actuality.

The penultimate line of *Retribution*—"Than the *quantum satis* of Brand's will"—refers to what Ibsen intended as a great poem.[6] Ibsen's is a poem of ethics and passion, an innovation to which Blok considered his poem more than adequate successor. Ibsen's is a national poem, the epitome of a society, of an era, and of a consciousness, which Blok, fifty years later, thought he readvanced (that is, refined, redefined, and reanimated). The antibureaucratic protest Ibsen makes in *Brand* Blok makes more pervasively —bureaucracy being by then more pervasive—in *Retribution.* Ibsen said, as Jaeger quotes him: "The State crushes Individuality; away with the State.... Undermine the notion of the State, let free will and spiritual affinity be the only recognized basis of union, and you will have a liberty worthy of the name." This represents Blok's politics not only in *Retribution* but also in other poems and, we know historically, in his own social activity. The name Brand is an obvious identification of the rebel, the new prophet of "being oneself," as given in *Peer Gynt* also. Ibsen said, "I have studied men and human fate and drawn the philosophy out of them for myself." Blok argued that, by the objectivity of his poem's masks, he had made the same understanding of experience.

The irony in Blok's poem is reinforcement of the perceptions of that consciousness which requires faith but finds none available. An example of it is Blok's use of Brand's tag "quantum satis," which Blok ties in with the will of God and the over-all plan of the world. It is a dramatic tag; it functions as the priestly or professional label; it identifies that bourgeois satiety which Blok, like Ibsen, hates; it marks the child of sin and, therefore, a child lost or at least a victim, a sacrifice; it equally suggests the effort to penetrate frustration in the name of self-validation. The complexity of life requires more real responses than the assertion of ego or merely political protest. The meaning, unlike the perceptible beauty, is a remote artifact, the object of this poem.

In Blok's notebook drafts there is a page on which he drew a caricature of his father leaning on a balustrade and entitled "The Prisoner at the Bar." In the final poem, both the actual figure and image (that is, "symbol") of the father establish a convenient psychological focus through which to reconstitute history and to organize the poem's emotional content. It is Blok's most successful dramatic expostulation of a personal or lyric ambivalence. The poet seems to be in continual conversation or communication with another personality. In the third chapter he is clearly in conflict with it. In so far as the relationship is a device it is not new, of course. It is a device which Blok used with increasing control and precision in elucidating impulses and motives. In this poem, of which he himself is the invisible hero and which begins with his addressing himself—the man in him talking to the poet in him—his biological, historical, emotional, and intellectual commitment to his father (expressed as the "realness" of his father to him) establishes tension, gives the poem both intimacy and scope, reinforces by its immediacy that struggle for power and liberation of which Blok feels obliged to determine the meaning.

Blok formally identifies the genesis of his poem with 1910, the year, he says, of the deaths of Kommissarzhevskaia, Vrubel, and Tolstoy, and of the death—the "crisis"—of Symbolism. Specifically, he associates the year with the development of *literary* movements hostile to Symbolism and to each other. He refers to the following years as further examples of in-

Бывало, всехъ по вечерамъ
Онъ очаровывалъ беседой

Онъ утверждалъ, отрицалъ,
[illegible]

Однажды Достоевский встретилъ
Его на вечере

А дамы [illegible] [illegible]
[illegible]
Не лорда Байрона похожъ

Но не несла ни бурь, ни счастья
Ему судьба. Быть может, онъ
Лишь тайной и преступной страстью
Былъ съ лордомъ Байрономъ сравненъ

Подсудимый

A page of the manuscript of *Retribution*, with Blok's sketch of his father entitled "The Prisoner at the Bar."

creasing intellectual skepticism and of a kind of emasculation of the personal and technical power of the poet. He seems to have assumed division of history into two parts and then lived to experience the continuation of the fact of division. Political events are natural: "That year [1911] the summer was exceptionally hot, so that the grass burned, [and] in London there were the glorious railway workers' strikes." Artistic and physical phenomena are equally aesthetic: "I'll never forget the struggle of the hideous Russian heavyweight wrestler with the Dutchman whose muscle-system was the most perfect musical instrument of rare beauty." The work of his poem was to locate these diverse and seemingly incoherent facts or appearances in a single, real system,[7] to include also the newly heard, strident voice of Strindberg, the danger of war and the dilemmas of disarmament, the murders of Andrei Iushchinskii and Stolypin in Kiev, the introduction of aviation and its spectacular, horrible failures. All of these facts or appearances, he said, "create a single musical impetus... [of which] the essential rhythmic expression... is the *iamb.*"[8] The poem's meter is the instrument which presses the disparate events together, the string on which the beads are hung. The separate events are made meaningful by the measure and the method of the verse. The poem is, like Pushkin's *Evgenii Onegin*, a portrait of a society and its most representative individualities bound and exposed, like the poem itself, in terms of all their qualifying properties and modified by the possibilities presented by narration as a literary form and by the lyric expression following as necessity from the poet's alienation. The poem is a study of the meaning of a society as revealed in its essential manners. The poem's success continues to be the similarity between it and its referents.[9]

Blok's statement in the introduction to *Retribution* that "...its plan appeared to me as a series of concentric circles becoming tighter and tighter, the smallest of which... began again to live its own independent life... and to affect the periphery,"[10] suggests an idea of a system like the one expounded in his "General Plan of the *Historical Scenes.*" He did not distinguish ultimately between perception and meaning, between history and his poem: "Such was the life of the rough sketch which drew itself in my mind—only now do I try to translate it into consciousness and into language." In the introduction to *Retribution* he refers to a "musical and muscular consciousness" in which the plan of his poem had existed prior to rational effort of expression: "At that time all the poem's movement and development were for me closely connected with the development of a muscular system." The poem's development is analogous, as he puts it, to the development of the biceps from "systematic manual labor" and gradually of the "finer network" of chest and back muscles: "Such a rhythmic and gradual development of the muscles had to be the rhythm of the entire poem. The poem's basis, idea, and theme are tied to this." Translated, Blok's muscle system is a coordinated body of experiences invoked and of responses provoked by the intellectual progress of the poem. It remains, however, chiefly independent of the final poem, an instrument of construction, something other than a key to meaning. As he wrote his mother in February 1911:

> Wrestling and strengthening of muscles strongly attract me...; rather unusual for me... this is connected with artistic creativity. I'm capable of reading with pleasure articles on the peasant problem and the worst novels of Breshko-Breshkovskii, who's closer to Dante than Valerii Briusov is.... As explanation, I can say that my *Europeanism* lies in this. Europe must give form and flesh to that deep and elusive content which every Russian soul is filled with. Hence the continual need for form, my need in particular. Form is the flesh of an idea; not the last place in the world orchestra of the arts is occupied by the art of "light athletics" and by that very "French wrestling" which is the exact duplicate of ancient wrestling in Greece and Rome....
>
> I've seen only one artist of real genius, the Hollander Van Ril. He inspires me in working on the poem much more than Viacheslav Ivanov. Besides, real art in our time (and probably in any) can come about only when (1) you have an immediate (not a literary) relation with the world, and (2) your own art is akin to that of others (for me personally—to music, painting, architecture and gymnastics).

Blok's rhythmic inventiveness, on the other hand, taking the mazurka as symbolic of the essential gestures of individual responsiveness, imagination, and communication, does lead to a "system" which is partially the poem and partially our experiences of it. It is an attempt at guaranteeing the vitality of as many extensions of our modern selves as possible during a series of specific historical or political manoeuvers.

The entire poem is animated by the "...leit-motif of retribution; this leit-motif is the *mazurka*, a dance which carried along Marina,[11] dreaming of the Russian throne, ...and carried along Mickiewicz at Russian and Parisian balls." The mazurka moves like a motion-picture camera:

> In the first chapter this dance is heard lightly, coming through the windows of a Petersburg apartment in the remote 1870s; in the second chapter, the dance thunders at the ball, mingling with the tinkling of officers' spurs, an analogy to the bubbles of the *fin de siècle* champagne, the celebrated *veuve Cliquot*: still more

obscure are the gypsy, Apukhtin years; and finally in the third chapter the mazurka breaks loose: ...the voice of Retribution is clearly heard.

In the plan of *Retribution* that Blok wrote out February 21, 1913, the mazurkas are divided into three sections. The first is in the second chapter about Petersburg in the 1890s; the second, in the third chapter about the father's death and "Her" appearance; the third, in the epilogue about the events that were to follow the son's death. "There are two leit-motifs: one—that life goes on, like infantry, hopelessly; the other—the mazurka." Music for Blok is the basic principle in the organization of emotion in meaning and beauty.[12]

Retribution is shaped by the rhythmic recurrence of themes and variations. Lexical repetitions, repeated images and metaphors (especially of light, color, size, shape, and time) as in all Blok's poems, help establish the pattern. Unlike his other poems, however, this poem is built on the combination of variations of iambic meter and the idea of the mazurka rhythm, which Blok described in preparing the poem[13] as a series of three triplets and a final two-beat burden: tsýntsyrny—tsýntsyrny—tsýntsyrny—tsytsy. Each chapter is, or was to be (the second chapter was never written) a three-movement tone poem in which the first movement presents the dominant theme and the burden is interposed as either a lyric or rhetorical contrast to the syncopated development of the dramatic and narrative themes. In narrative or descriptive passages, the iambic meter approaches conversational rhythms. The syntax is colloquial, and the verse, which throughout the poem is not organized in formal stanzas, tends to form paragraphs, as in the description in the first chapter of the guests assemblying and the arrival of the special guest:

Смеркается. Спустились шторы.
Набита комната людьми.
И за прикрытыми дверьми
Идут глухие разговоры,
И эта сдержанная речь
Полна заботы и печали.

. . .

Кого-то ждут... Гремит звонок.
Неспешно отворяя двери,
Гость новый входит на порог:
В своих движениях уверен
И статен; мужественный вид;...

It grows dark. The blinds are drawn.
The room is full of people.

Behind the closed doors
There are barely audible conversations,
And this reserved speech
Is full of care and sorrow.

. . .

They wait for someone... The bell resounds.
Unhurriedly opening the door,
The new guest steps across the threshold:
In his movements confident
And noble; a masculine appearance;...

The standard iambic tetrameter is, of course, eight (or nine, with feminine ending) alternately unstressed and stressed syllables. The omission of stress on the sixth syllable is the most typical general modification, and it forms what might be called the "typical" line of this poem. However, absence or presence of "standard" stresses does not itself indicate the difference between the descriptive and the dramatic passages. Rather, the difference is one of rhythmic movement through the syntax of several lines and the pattern of the rhyme. The usual rhyme pattern is a b b a or a b a b, but the "paragraph" in the first chapter in which Dostoevsky in Anna Vrevskaia's salon notices the "Byronic demon,"[14] Blok's father, is introduced by two couplets, deliberately evocative of *Evgenii Onegin:*

Средь пожилых людей и чинных,
Среди зеленых и невинных —
В салоне Вревской был, как свой,
Один ученый молодой.

Among the elder and sedate,
Among the green and innocent,
At home in Vrevskaia's salon,
There was one scholarly young man.

In one part of the long description of the demon, the evocation of *Evgenii Onegin* is even more carefully stipulated. A tone of sarcastic lightness is affirmed by the rhyming of a foreign word—here, a proper name—with a normal Russian word:

Хоть он юристом был,
Но поэтическим примером
Не брезговал: Констан дружил
В нем с Пушкиным, и Штейн — с Флобером.[15]

Although he was a lawyer,
He did not disdain to turn
To poetry: in him Constant joined
Pushkin; and Stein, Flaubert.

The lyric, emotional, or formal "digressions" from the narrative plot are characterized by a tightening of the rhythmic movement: sometimes the verse becomes "regular," as in the following:

> В ком смутно брезжит память эта,
> Тот странен и с людьми несхож:
> Всю жизнь его — уже поэта
> Священная объемлет дрожь,...
>
> He in whom this memory vaguely dawns
> Is strange and different from other people:
> His whole life—but already
> A sacred trembling surrounds the poet,...

More usually, the metric structure itself does not significantly change (it is predominantly a three-stress iambic tetrameter line), but the lines move at a different pace, and the intensity is grasped by a strong spondee that ends the section:

> Ответит телеграфный провод,
> Иль вздернет Пан взбешенный повод,
> И четко повторит чугун
> Удары мерзлого копыта
> По опустелой мостовой...
> И вновь, поникнув головой,
> Безмолвен Пан, тоской убитый...
> И, странствуя на злом коне,
> Бряцает шпорою кровавой...
> Месть! Месть! — Так эхо над Варшавой
> Звенит в холодном чугуне!
>
> The telegraph wire answers,
> Or the infuriated Pan puts up the reins,
> And the cast iron clearly repeats
> The blows of the frozen hoof
> On the empty pavement...
> Once again, hanging his head,
> The Pan is silent, defeated by languor...
> And traveling on an evil horse,
> He clanks his bloody spurs...
> Revenge! Revenge!—That's how the echo over Warsaw
> Rattles in the cold cast iron!

The last two lines are only a very slight alteration of the thirteenth and fourteenth lines of this same, third chapter. They may be said to frame the idea of the rhythmic unity or intensity which, Blok said, is best represented by the mazurka. Although metric analysis of the verse sheds no light on such rhythmic movement—which Blok said was to be found in the voice of retribution breaking loose in this chapter—a dramatic reading of the lines, that is, a reading of the passage just quoted according to its actual accents, run-on lines and pauses, suggests something of the mazurka—here, its final, hard energy.

The mazurka is not only a mobile and infectious dance music but also has an immediate association with Poland, where Blok's father—and the father in the poem—worked and died. It has beauty, opulence, speed, elegance, and ebullient passion. It bears specific relation to the analogous moment of the dancing in *Evgenii Onegin:*

> The mazurka resounded. It used to be that
> When the mazurka's thunder rolled
> Everything in the great hall trembled...;
> Not so now:... (ch. V, stanza XLII)

In Pushkin's poem, the iambic meter is classically organized to describe and to comment. In Blok's poem, the classical tetrameter, very much the same sort of verse as in *Evgenii Onegin*, or, more specifically, "Mednyi vsadnik" (The Bronze Horseman), and not organized into formal stanzas, expands and contracts readily in reproduction both of the social mazurka and the gestures behind it. The mazurka is still, as for Pushkin, a symbol of grace and vitality, but the time of the mazurka is not part of present conventions. The movement of the mazurka is an analogy to the movement of history, a developing spiral of moments always moving toward the present in which choice and judgment are real: "The life of the old is going down."

The introduction to *Retribution* is a warning on how to read the poem: namely, one should read it, as if experiencing music, as a response, alien to its provocation, which assumes in its emotional order reality of events and the moral efficacy of a nonlogical form. In other words, we are warned against a nondramatic reading of a formally lyric poem. In this sense, the poem, like any moral narrative, is an extended effort to define the assumptions epitomized arbitrarily by the title. Locating the title in its context takes us to drama.

The poem was never satisfactorily expanded, as one may deduce from reading the "Prologue," because of the absense of a system in terms of which adequately to locate and to correlate the several personae and sequence of historical moments. The scope of the poem is only as wide as Blok's dramatic experiences:

И в алом от зари притворе
Свою обедню отслужу.

And behind the parvis, vermillion from the sunrise
I will say my morning mass.

The "musical" organization of events establishes satisfactory aesthetic correspondences but not necessarily ethical or philosophic. The musical organization is incapable of organizing such an expanse of thoughts and things. Also, the fact that the author is the protagonist, in some places technically and in others emotionally, limits the poem to lyric experience. That is, the poem's dramatic material does not contain self-sustaining images that infallibly transmit the equivalent of the required emotion. There are symbols in the poem, but, like the figure of the father or the semivisualized concept of retaliation, they are bundles of meaning or perceptions or interpreted emotion. The chief limitation of the poem is the limitation of the lyric attitude of a half-illusioned idealist who, because there is no community of values on which he can rely and because he is not in a position to invent a system, cannot extend the essential drama of experience beyond the modes which he discovers in himself. Although he presents them objectively in his poem, as if eliminating his personality through his art, the delimited frame of reference continually forces him back on himself. What may on the surface seem to be self-celebration is actually only a use of self as agent in an aesthetic attempt to expunge the self in definition of a real, transcendent, meaningful scheme.

The first line of *Retribution,* a kind of epigram, moves us to dramatic experience itself—

Life is without beginning or end.

—provided we follow it, as Blok does, as closely as possible into an experience of life. Unlike us, the artist is required, the poem says, to believe in beginnings and ends and to describe the indifferent environmental forces that, if unopposed or uncontrolled ("chance," line two, versus "hell and heaven," line seven), prevent meaning. The poet is judge, and his art is conscious standard. Intuition is irrelevant after the fact, which is the poem or any part, regardless of its involvement beforehand. By making beginnings and ends the poet creates something which cannot be wholly explained by anything prior to the poem itself. In the lines referring to the poet's responsibility—

Тебе дано бесстрастной мерой
Измерить всё, что видишь ты.

You are endowed with a dispassionate standard
For measuring everything you see.

Blok makes his attitude toward the poet's function and the function of poetry as concrete and as general as possible. Poetry is its own efficient form and content. Because a poem is the focus of all relevant experiences and the only center of meaning, the poem, like a fact, is what holds good for all observers.

It is historically interesting that Blok suggested this and that he suggested it in the beginning of this poem. This attitude helps explain his continual dissatisfaction with *Retribution*. He was afraid that there was still too much left outside which might be brought against the poem to prove its limitations as a standard. Lines ten through sixteen of the "Prologue" are a definition of scope:

Твой взгляд — да будет тверд и ясен.
Сотри случайные черты —
И ты увидишь: мир прекрасен.
Познай, где свет, — поймешь, где тьма.
Пускай же всё пройдет неспешно,
Что в мире свято, что в нем грешно,
Сквозь жар души, сквозь хлад ума.

Let your look be firm and clear.
Erase the accidental features
And you will see: the world is beautiful.
Know where there is light—you will understand where there is darkness.
Let everything go by unhurriedly,
The sacred and profane things in the world,
Through the fire of the soul, through the cold of reason.

Behind both the definition and the dramatization of it is the fear of failure, of exclusiveness, of insensitivity, of ignorance.

The idea like a motif runs in images through the poem. At the beginning of the introduction to the second chapter, for example, it is given as an image of an institutional or social idea:

В те годы дальние, глухие,
В сердцах царили сон и мгла:
Победоносцев ная Россией
Простер совиные крыла,
И не было ни дня, ни ночи,
А только — тень огромных крыл;...

In those distant, muted years
Dream and darkness reigned in hearts:

Over Russia, Pobedonostsev
Stretched out his owl-like wings,
And there was neither day nor night
But only the shadow of the enormous wings;...

The metaphoric use of the owl is clearly conscious. The idea of inadequacy occurs also at the end of the poem where the notion of measure is put against the rational concept of satisfaction and order given as an aspect of will, because from Blok's point of view all relations are essentially aesthetic. The line: "And the world is beautiful as always" (A mir—prekrasen, kak vsegda), does not mean that the world is merely beautiful or even precisely beautiful. The world the poem has created, unlike the world it is about, is beautiful because of the precision which it is the office of the poem to create. The limitation and the failure of the poem—in so far as it may be said to fail—follow from the difficulty of delimiting that circle within which, as James said, relations shall appear to end.

The poem uses relatively few outside references in view of its effort at inclusiveness. Wagner's *Ring*, the Salomé story, Lucifer's fall and the legendary fathering of Cain, the *Song of Roland*, Griboedov's *Woe from Wit*, Harpagon in *The Miser*, a novel by Flaubert, an article by Dobroliubov, Dostoevsky and his *Diary of a Writer*, Saltykov-Shchedrin, Constant, Byron—these are nearly all of the direct "literary" references. Other references are to relatives, kings, streets, restaurants, army battles, political events and uprisings—what might be called "real-life" materials. None of the references is recondite, and all either are taken as being in themselves dramatic or are dramatized in Blok's poem. The Siegfried-Notung story, for example, is redramatized in a few lines, and images in the synopsis are then further expanded—for example, the sword. The reference to the Lucifer legend must be known: it is against the Cain-Abel story and the Hebraic legend that Cain was the son of Lucifer and Eve that Blok plays the line "Sons are reflected in their fathers" (Syny otrazheny v otsakh), the reversal or irony he needs in order to establish his position and the validity of his poetic attitude.[16] The horn of Roland shows use of another, specifically literary but also real moment to extend the scope of this poem and to emphasize by apposition to the old poem the dilemma of the "last" individual of a declining society and the poet's job, which Gol'tsev said Blok considered "...the explication of those laws and conformity to law which influence human development." It is what Blok indicated had been his interest and attitude when, speaking about a performance of Schiller's

Don Carlos, he said that "what about men especially interests great writers is man himself." And the connection between *Retribution* and Pushkin's "The Bronze Horseman" is made particularly clear not only by Blok's references to Peter the Great in the introduction to the second chapter but also by the way the statue of Copernicus in Warsaw takes on a kind of Animation—is treated at times as if it were alive—as Peter's monument comes to life in Pushkin's poem.[17]

Blok intended *Retribution* to be a great poem: "The poem signifies the transition from the personal to the general. That is its main idea. The formula gives me much leeway; at first glance it is loose, unclear, involving many meanings. But this, I hope, is only at first glance."[18] The poem was to be an analysis of the habits and values of a nation at a turning-point in world history—

Век девятнадцатый, железный,
Воистину жестокий век!

The nineteenth, iron century,
In truth a cruel century.

History is present in contemporary time. By studying a moment, one studies all previous moments also. History is terrible and inexorable. Like an ancient Greek, Blok believes that it is a personal force—he uses the second person singular—hostile or indifferent to individuals and, worst of all, unwinding into irrelevant details, into what seem to be "real" historical moments but are meaningless, harmless accidents:

Век не салонов, а гостиных,
Не Рекамье, — а просто дам.

The era not of salons, but parlors,
Not of Recamier—but simply ladies.

Men and women behave like marionettes. Intellectually, they have run down, and the classical system demonstrating absolute value remains only as a "humanistic haze." Even war has become impersonal and, consequently, absurd:

Там — пушки новые мешают
Сойтись лицом к лицу с врагом.

There the new cannons interfere
With meeting the enemy face to face.

The image of Roland and his horn symbolizes both the fallen hero and the impossibility of heroism after Roland's death.

Despite the restriction on meaningful life and communication, the poet wishes to make his poem large enough to break the restrictions. Roland, for example, is also a romantic figure. The world also is perceived as emotionally animated:

А здесь — по-прежнему в болото
Глядит унылая заря.

But here—the doleful dawn peers
Into the swamp as it has before.

The romanticism is the romanticism of disillusionment, of the impotency of the individual by feeling or by reason to provoke response. One's job is limited to apprehending and properly interpreting the signs:

Кометы грозной и хвостатой
Ужасный призрак в вышине.

The terrible apparition up above
Of a menacing and caudate comet.

Those signs are terrifying which, although ostensibly manufactured to help men, function in such a way that they can have no meaningful interpretation. Unlike the indifferent comets,

Зачем — пропеллер, воя, режет
Туман холодный — и пустой?

Why does the propeller, howling, cut
The cold—and empty—fog?

The image is competent and complete. It is ineffable. The question is unanswerable.

We are encouraged to read the poem as being as "big as life" not only by its literary and political references and by the recurrent motifs from Blok's earlier work which are expanded in it, but also by its specific use of *Evgenii Onegin,* which Blok, by stylization in his own poem, wished to reinvoke for his reader. Some of Blok's early lyrics, such as "The Autumn Day Sinks Slowly Down," as Čiževsky and others have pointed out, are directly imitative of Pushkin's early elegies. While working on *Retribution,* Blok had Pushkin's novel in verse closely in mind. He wrote his mother in June 1916:

Mama, now at last I've finished the "First chapter" of the poem *Retribution.* Including the "Prologue," it makes 1019 lines. If you look at the statistics of poems written in iambic tetrameter, you find that: both parts of Lermontov's *Demon* comprise 1139 lines, and "Boyar Orsha," 1066; Boratynskii's "The Ball" is 658 and "Eda" is 683, and only "Nalozhnitsa" [The Concubine]—in *seven* chapters—is 1208 lines. So if I can still write the second and third chapters and the epilogue, as I plan, the poem could become as big as *Onegin.*

Blok wanted to write for his time the kind of novel in verse that Pushkin had written for his. Descriptions of society, discussions, language, the seasons, places and buildings—all reflect the high esteem in which he held Pushkin's long poem. Lest after having read some one hundred sixty lines of *Retribution*, we still have not perceived the correspondence, Blok reminds us, in imitation of Pushkin in "The Bronze Horseman" and in *Evgenii Onegin:*

Теперь — за мной, читатель мой,
В столицу севера больную,
На отдаленный финский брег!

Now—follow me, my reader,
To the diseased capital of the north,
To the remote Finnish shore!

Even the Church Slavonic form for the word shore, instead of the Russian, is used to emphasize the association. Blok requires the reader to adopt Pushkin's attitude of ironic sympathy. What Pushkin says about his hero Onegin

...but I got used
To his caustic argument,
And to his jokes, half mixed with bile,
And the malice of his grim epigrams.

Blok applies to himself in so far as he is the hero or heroic intrusion in his own poem. Onegin is an unsuccessful aspect of his author animated into art, the self-mockery Pushkin uses to define his own position and talent. Blok's figure of himself as protagonist and as poet is successful exactly in those ways Blok, a man in society, cannot be.

The parallel between *Retribution* and *Evgenii Onegin* is apparent in several general respects: "epic" presentation of an age in terms of generalized characteristics—the study of the meaning of social activity by confrontation of patterns and manners, human involvement in natural events, and the motion of a central individual within a social context; everyday detail and commonplace response to actualize central events of the poem; lyric and moral digressions from the plot; admixture of historical and national material; development of character from the author's viewpoint or as aspects of the author himself; use of the classic, Russian iambic tetrameter (including similar ironic or punning rhymes). At moments, both poets show a common attitude: in many descriptive passages, in which the personae are located by lyric description and moral judgment so that setting, actor, and meaning are perceived as interdependent; in asides; and in instructions to the reader.

Blok's insistence on ultimate justice and merciless irony against himself —that is, self-dramatization and a use of the poem not, as with Pushkin, for disinterested pleasure and understanding, but as an enactment or objectivization of moral law—distinguishes his attitude from Pushkin's. Pushkin's poem, basically classic in form and intent, tends to please; Blok's, basically dramatic and skeptical, tends to teach. Pushkin tells two stories: one about a love quadrangle and one about his own artistic life. *Evgenii Onegin* is Pushkin's effort to guarantee his own social function as a poet and the social function of art. Blok had a moral provocation. He presents his information as a fable or a series of incidents pointed to the justification of his own sensibility and, by analogy, of meaningful life. The poem is Blok's effort to prove the importance of the existence of men. To do it he must go through what is trivial and irrelevant, as similarly Pushkin went through social gestures contradictory to the values of art: superficial conversation, intellectual pretension, self-indulgence, conspicuous consumption, confusion, selfishness, egotism, and merely arbitrary behavior designed to conform to social norms. These unreal gestures become real through the poems. Both poems take on further reality by doubling back on the gestures with formal devices: puns, irony, ambiguity, alteration of context, transfer of response or of emotion, literary reference, and so on.

Essentially it is an issue of form. Blok wrote in his diary toward the end of his life that "Classicism, as distinguished from Romanticism and Naturalism, consists in the fact that the observer is presented a firm carcass. Observers such as myself, who know how to look, fit out this carcass with various kinds of figures." *Evgenii Onegin* has a firm carcass defined by specific metric, stanzaic, and structural organization. *Retribution* is organized on a principle of perception, epitomized by the musical development of themes. It is less formal than *Evgenii Onegin;* the absence of the second chapter draws attention to a structural imbalance and makes the poem appear more lyric than it is. The movement of the music around which the poem is built is partially fractured, weakening the musical scheme as an aesthetic principle and exposing the substance of the poem—the conscience of the individual—to political and psychological distortion.[19]

It is important to note that in *Retribution* the sense of time as plot is given in the chronological development of a family. If given historically, this would be diffusion or multiplication. In this poem, it is continual narrowing or elimination of unnecessary relatives—that is, of unnecessary moments. As supernatural events, particular deaths, or certain facts are taken as symbols of historical reality, so only certain moments in certain lives are meaningful for the present. What from the son's point of view is most important about the father is his death. The third, final chapter—the end of the mazurka that is the poem, and itself a mazurka—begins from exactly this crucial, dramatic moment. The father is dead; the son, moving:

> Отец лежит в «Аллее Роз»,
> Уже с усталостью не споря,
> А сына поезд мчит в мороз
> От берегов родного моря.
>
> The father lies in the "Alley of Roses,"
> No longer contending with fatigue,
> And the train speeds the son into the cold
> From the shores of his native sea.

The "Alley of Roses" is a street in Warsaw. The image of roses is ironic. The use of roses as image in Blok's poetry has changed from conventional red to black, to a street, or title, of the dead. The rose of love has become the funereal rose, the rood of time. It is winter. Winter is the dead season, the season of the dead. Psychologically, the son is moving through a geography analogous to the father's and to the father himself as part of the son's geography. This is confirmed by the word "native" in the next line. In this sense, the "story" that is autobiography is provocation that becomes irrelevant once the event it provoked has taken place. What the images yield is a series of events intelligible and historically meaningful only in terms of the symbols which re-enact them. The poem aims at direct symbolization of feeling, at presentation of "the morphology of feeling," to use Langer's phrase.

This labor is the essential function of form. In *Retribution* the content —what the poem is "about," the autobiography, the geography, and the history—are made to stand for or to inform on a total understanding:

> Здесь всё, что было, всё, что есть,
> Надуто мстительной химерой.
>
> Here [in Warsaw] everything that was, that is,
> Is inflated with a vindictive chimera.[20]

How Blok proceeds from autobiographical description to a generalization in which the autobiographic moment takes on a symbolic function is seen in the following passage about the father's burial in Volia, a suburb of Warsaw, in a large cemetery also called Volia—which means "will" or "freedom":

По незнакомым площадям
Из города в пустое поле
Все шли за гробом по пятам...
Кладбище называлось: «Воля».
Да! Песнь о воле слышим мы,
Когда могильщик бьет лопатой
По глыбам глины желтоватой;
Когда откроют дверь тюрьмы;
Когда мы изменяем женам,
А жены — нам;...

. . .

Когда проценты с капитала
Освободят от идеала;
Когда... — На кладбище был мир...

Through unknown squares
From town to a barren field
All followed close behind the coffin...
The cemetery was called "Volia."
Indeed! We hear a song of freedom
When the grave-digger pounds his spade
On the clods of yellowish clay;
When a prison door is opened;
When we are unfaithful to our wives,
And our wives to us;...

. . .

When income from one's capital
Frees one from ideals;
When...—Peace filled the cemetry...

Blok overcomes the limits of history by using a historical discovery of reality, symbolized by the Copernicus statue in Warsaw, which he takes as analogous to the one he himself is working on:

Коперник сам лелеет месть,
Склоняясь над пустою сферой.

Copernicus himself cherishes revenge,
Bending over the armillary sphere.

Blok was overcome, and wanted his reader to be, by the terrible indifference and power—the terrible void he associates with Copernicus and Copernicus's brilliance—of the world outside the self. To come to reality is to come, like Hamlet, to revenge:

> «Месть! Месть!» — в холодном чугуне
> Звенит, как эхо, над Варшавой.
>
> "Revenge! Revenge!"—in the cold cast iron
> It rattles like an echo over Warsaw.

If to come to reality is to take revenge, then to hope is to have the continual possibility of discovering another provocation and another method of satisfaction. Simplified, the "idea" seems conventionally Romantic—the self-justification of the individual against an indifferent, self-satisfied, and conventional world—and the "images" of Copernicus, the chimera, the frozen cast-iron world of the nineteenth century may be squeezed into representations of a conventional attitude. Left complex, as given in the poem, the images work out among themselves from image to idea the sense of horror that Blok identifies as reality and that we must identify afresh. It is a vision of such intensity and terror that the visionary, like the reader, is pleased to return to another, harmless version of the experience:

> Лишь рельс в Европу в мокрой мгле
> Поблескивает честной сталью.
>
> Only the rails leading to Europe in the wet haze
> Gleam as honest steel gleams.

A series of words associated with Symbolist poetry and easily found in Blok's work occur in the next passage. Certain devices characteristic of Blok's poetry are also in it: the indefinite subject "someone," lexical repetition, the absence of antecedent for an adjective, alliteration and assonance, and inversions of word order. The passage is "typical" Blok, leading into the description of the dead man in his coffin. The father lies "dry and straight," "calm, yellow, and speechless." "He rests fine now," the son thinks and looks calmly at the open door:

> (С ним кто-то неотлучно рядом
> Глядел туда, где пламя свеч,
> Под веяньем неосторожным
> Склоняясь, озарит тревожно
> Лик желтый, туфли, узость плеч, —
> И, выпрямляясь, слабо чертит
> Другие тени на стене...
> А ночь стоит, стоит в окне...)
> И мыслит сын: «Где ж праздник Смерти?»
>
> . . .

Покойник
Сегодня может спать один.
Ушли родные. Только сын
Склонен ная трупом... Как разбойник
Он хочет осторожно снять
Кольцо с руки оцепенелой.

(Someone inseparably beside him
Looks there, where the candles' flame,
Bending over in the imprudent
Draft, uneasily lights up
The yellow face, the slippers, the narrow shoulders,
And, straightening up, faintly outlines
Other shadows on the wall...
And the night stands, stands in the window...)
The son thinks: "Where is Death's holiday?"

. . .

The dead man
Today may sleep alone.
The relatives are gone. Only the son
Is bent over the body... Like a thief,
He wants very carefully to take
The ring off the benumbed hand.

The night, an image of the most ineluctable mystery of all, death, stands in the window as if always there, dreadfully, as the dead man and the shadows seem suddenly to have been forever dead and shadowy.

One turns from horror to activity, even if the activity confirms the horror. What matters is the personal and literary heritage. The "prayer" in the line: "And came out, having said 'God be with you,'" invokes that mysterious tradition which everyone who cites God feels he needs but can never represent to anyone else. The reader circles around and around "the vulgarity of life without end" and "the evil night [that] relieved the evil day."

The son relives his life with (in) his father only by associations that occur to him after the father's death. There are, as examples, the cry of the crows and the sound of the funeral bells connected with the son's memory of his father's cry of fright when, as a child, he stuck a pin in his father's arm and his memory of his own feelings of guilt:

Этот крик
С внезапной яркостью возник
Здесь, над могилою, на «Воле», —
И сын очнулся...

This cry
Rose up with a sudden brightness
Here, over the grave in the "Volia"—
And the son regained consciousness...

One is free only before one acts: ironically one is always about to be free; one never has been. Suffering is not a problem. The lines:

И женщина навзрыд рыдает
Неудержимо и светло...

And a woman is sobbing
Unconstrainedly and brightly...

mean that the reality of the act, as distinguished from the response to it, is its own illumination. No one knows the woman, the poem says, covered in a veil of mourning. Is she a heavenly beauty or an old, unattractive woman whose tears fall "lazily down her faded cheeks?" Wasn't it she who in the hospital guarded the coffin with the son? She leaves, a crowd of other people gather near by, and the poet expresses pity for the father through the reference to his having received the legacy of Flaubert's *Education sentimentale.* The pity expressed by the woman's tears is consubstantial with the father's death; from her point of view, identical. The woman's tears are uselessly, brilliantly equivalent to death, which is taken by Blok as a constant, the end from which life is illuminated.

When threatened with summation, life vanishes, edged out by the mere hunger of the living ("the homeless dog," for Blok a recurrent image of modern man):

Так жил отец: скупцом, забытым
Людьми, и богом, и собой,
Иль псом бездомным и забитым
В жестокой давке городской.
А сам... Он знал иных мгновений
Незабываемую власть!

Thus the father lived: a miser, forgot
By people, and God, and himself
Or like a homeless, beaten dog
In the cruel, city crowd.
He himself... He knew the unforgettable power
Of other moments!

Contradictions in logic are prevented by modifications of the meaning of the words. At the end of the passage there is a restatement of the theme of the chapter, given this time directly, as in sonata-form:

Revenge! Revenge! That's how the echo over Warsaw
Rattles in the cold cast iron!

A coda follows, moving into the coda of the whole poem. In the third chapter, the mazurka is divided into the son's arrival, the funeral, and the recapitulation of the father's life. It moves around death. The coda of the chapter starts from an assumption of life:

Еще светлы кафе и баръы,
Торгует телом «Новый Свет»...

The cafés and bars are still lit up,
The "New World" is selling bodies...[21]

an assumption which the poet cannot definitively locate:

Но в переулках — жизни нет,
Там тьма и вьюги завыванье...

But in the by-streets there is no life,
Only darkness and the snowstorm's howl...

The images are presented as contrasting themes: the endlessness, the brilliance, the melancholy, the oppression, the Warsaw streets, Copernicus bending over the armillary sphere, the consubstantial shadow, the horror and the awe, the snow, the darkness, the stone, the imaginary garden and the real activity. The coda of the poem moves in on the reader himself, in on a world in which

...окинешь взглядом...
И небо — книгу между книг;

...you look around...
And see the sky—a book between books;

a world which is "beautiful, as always." It is this permanent world we have moved to from the endless and beginning-less life perceived in the present at the beginning of the poem. The last word, "always," keeps us in both, as music keeps us, if we can be kept. As Blok said in his notebooks, "Having reached its limits, poetry, undoubtedly, will drown in music. Music comes before everything, calls everything forth."

Because one can never overcome either the indifference of what is outside oneself or one's own agony—because, as Yeats wrote in *Purgatory*, there is no reconciliation:

O God,
Release my mother's soul from its dream!
Mankind can do no more. Appease
The misery of the living and the remorse of the dead.

—one can never finish one's work. As Blok put it in the final lines he wrote for the third chapter of *Retribution* the summer he died:

Мне пусто, мне постыло жить!
Я не свершил того......
Того, что должен был свершить.

I've nothing left, I hate to live!
I didn't finish that...
That which I had to finish.

VIII

The Twelve

THE 'POEM OF THE REVOLUTION'

The apostles are so artfully made that you could take them for living men.
—N. Gogol

One's usual sense of chronology and politics suggests that Russian poetry after 1917 was quite different from Russian poetry before 1917 and quite different from postwar European poetry. Perhaps the historians and politicians have again persuaded us into oversimplification, because Russian poetry did not change *that* way until the institutionalization of repression under industrial expansion in the late 1920s and early 1930s.

That Briusov early became a Communist Party member was politically exciting to his friends, important for the Party, but not artistically significant. Like any "change," it followed not from the character of the new but from the failure of the old, in this instance, from Briusov's creative attrition. Briusov did not so much become a member of the Party as he stopped being a nonmember, much in the sense that he stopped being a Symbolist when the social principles and patterns which tolerated the aesthetic values associated with Symbolism altered and, in alteration, required fresh satisfaction and different values.

What may be considered to have been the two latent and commingled tendencies in Symbolism, particularly in the work of Blok, split openly under the disintegration of those values and that social cohesiveness (that liberalism) peculiar to Russia between 1900 and 1914, which had understood the world, whether well or badly, as a unity. Futurism and Acmeism are both continuations of aspects of Symbolism, necessary consequences of its discipline and practice in a world of fractured values and chaotic performance.

If Romanticism may for a moment be considered the attempt in art to get away from the things of this world, and Realism, the attempt to get to the things of this world, Futurism may, again for a moment and despite the urbanistic current in it, be labeled the continuation of the Romantic aspect of Symbolism, and Acmeism, despite its exotic current, of the Realistic aspect. Each movement celebrated half of what the Symbolists had celebrated, adjusting history and society to a fresh, vigorous, but unendurably partial understanding. Together, both cited those French and other European writers whom the Symbolists had first praised in the name of the same rejuvenation which Symbolism had come in on, namely, a return to the original roots of poetry. The Acmeists emphasized craftsmanship and concreteness; the Futurists, the ebulliently personal, the general, and the transcendental. The Soviet government's approval of Futurism, particularly of the work of Maiakovskii, and its rejection of other literary programs and examples meant that what was personal, general, and intellectually conservative in Futurism was included as part of the understanding the government's program represented. What was transcendental was quickly limited to metaphoric exaggeration, a politically harmless indulgence.

As organizations, the groups of poets organized as Futurists, Acmeists, Imaginists, Cosmists or whatever, operated after the Symbolists had become passé. As poets, however, they were young contemporaries of the Symbolists and frequently promoted by them, as Blok promoted Kliuev or Esenin. Their success or failure depended not so much on political change (outside of political persecution) as on the maturation of their own talents and on public recognition, often tardy, as it was of Pasternak.

More importantly, the work of this period that used political change to promote itself is, regardless of author, without value now that the "change" is history. Neither Briusov's nor Maiakovskii's, neither Belyi's nor Bednyi's political poetry is of more than topical interest. Bednyi's poetry is cliché. Belyi is remembered chiefly for his prose and for his propaedeutic critical writings, preludes to the more competent work of the Formalist critics. Maiakovskii is a monument of a certain kind of wonderful vitality and imaginativeness. Briusov is associated with an aesthetic movement at the end of the nineteenth century. The one frequently cited example of the successful marriage of art and politics is Blok's *The Twelve*. Its political associations are, however, not so much intentional as merely coincidental. Its design is apolitical. It is a poem about revelation.

The Twelve is in twelve sections. Some are short, some long; some divided into measured stanzas, some in a kind of movement that approximates "free" verse but nonetheless with a coordinating scheme of rhyme and rhythm. The poem was written in the three-week interval January 8 to 28, 1918. It was begun a couple of days before Blok finished his article "Intelligentsiia i Revoliutsiia" (The Intelligentsia and the Revolution).[1]

The opening section is a lyric description of atmosphere, an invocation of setting, in which man and nature are presented as inextricably bound together in a given historical moment. The seemingly insignificant details or desires of ordinary people in their ordinary lives are made to take on meaning by being isolated and frozen (very much in the manner of Dostoevsky) as symbols against an emotional intensity carried by a set of natural images, which themselves are symbols or verge on being symbols. The section is a series of sketches of dramatic oppositions and losses between man and nature and among men themselves. The end of the section turns to the rest of the poem as resolution of the conflicts "pictured" in it.

Черный вечер.
Белый снег.
Ветер, ветер!
На ногах не стоит человек.
Бетер, ветер —
На всем божьем свете!

. . .

Ветер хлесткий!
Не отстает и мороз!
И буржуй на перекрестке
В воротник упрятал нос.

А это кто? — Длинные волосы
И говорит вполголоса:
— Предатели!
— Погибла Россия!
Должно быть, писатель —
Вития...

. . .

Хлеба!
Что впереди?
Проходи!

Черное, черное небо.

Злоба, грустная злоба
Кипит в груди...
Черная злоба, святая злоба...

Товарищ! Гляди
В оба!

Black night.
White snow.
Wind, wind!

A man can't stand up.
        Wind, wind—
All over God's world!

. . .

        The wind is cutting!
        And the cold's as bad!
        The bourgeois on the corner
        Has hid his nose in his collar.
But who's this?—Long hair,
And he says in an undertone:
        "Traitors!
        "Russia's lost!"
Must be a writer—
    Some Cicero...

. . .

        Bread!
        What's ahead?
        Go on!
Black, black the sky.
Spite, mournful spite
    Boils in the heart...
Black spite, holy spite...
        Comrade! Look out
        Both eyes!

The second section introduces the twelve Red Guardsmen as if coming out of the violence of nature and of men. Van'ka, a friend of one of the twelve, is "occupied" with a prostitute, Kat'ka, as a few lines of dialogue among the twelve indicate. The third "stanza" of the section, followed like the other two, by the burden "Eh, eh, without a cross!" is again a description of the emotional content of what the twelve men feel and of what we readers are in this moment to perceive of the total process of change.

The third section, consisting of three four-line songs of which the second was a Russian soldiers' song, is a lyric interlude. The fourth section is a description of Van'ka's seduction of Kat'ka from the point of view and tone of one who has been there before. The words move quickly until consummation of the vulgarity itself, given sardonically in the last word of the section:

Ах, ты, Катя, моя Катя,
    Толстоморденькая...

Ah, you, Katia, my Katia,
    You fat little mug...

In the fifth section, the language is again colloquial—it is slang—but it is not dialogue, and the dominant point of view or attitude is that of the outsider, the poet. The section is a resumé of Katia's professional history. Three people seem to be speaking simultaneously: Katia to herself, remembering; someone, presumably among the twelve, who has known her and wants her; and the poet.

In the sixth section, the center and the climax of the poem, the Red Guardsman Petrukha shoots at Van'ka and Kat'ka. Van'ka escapes; Kat'ka is killed. Petrukha curses her, and he turns, as if with the author, to the revolution at hand, as indicated by the two lines that close the section (The same two lines are the middle couplet in the third stanza of the second section, and a variation of them is part of Petrukha's effort at assuaging his conscience in the tenth section.):

> Революцьонный держите шаг!
> Неугомонный не дремлет враг!
>
> Keep in revolutionary step!
> The indefatigable enemy doesn't nap!

As the troop marches on, in the seventh section, Petrukha begins to feel remorse and guilt, remembering the ecstasy he had experienced with the girl and his commitment to her. His comrades tease him for his regret. The group begins looting, in the excitement of which Petrukha's remorse is momentarily lost.

The remainder of the poem is a series of different sorts of lyric digressions or interruptions of Petrukha's dialogue between self and soul. The eighth section contains two folk songs of lamentation, in wording much like part of the third section, and is the beginning of Petrukha's purgation.

The ninth section is a lyric interlude, quickly identifiable as such by the opening lines, which are from a nineteenth-century Russian romance adapted from a poem by F. N. Glinka, as Chukovskii has pointed out:

> Не слышно шуму городского,
> Над невской башней тишина.
>
> The city noise cannot be heard,
> Calm surrounds the Neva tower.

The image of the bourgeois standing on the street-corner, his collar up around his ears, occurs as in the first section. It is this time coupled with the image of the mangy cur, with which the bourgeois is identified.

The tenth section is, after a short transition, a return to the debate in

Petrukha's mind: what he has lost of himself by the violence of murder and openly sexual commitment and what he owes to himself and to others in terms of the new future the revolution promises.

The eleventh section, which ends with the same burden as the tenth (one word short):

Вперед, вперед,
  Рабочий народ!

Forward, forward,
  Working class!

is a kind of photograph of the twelve men's procession through the snowstorm, the red flag high and foremost. If the twelve men are, as the last two lines of the section suggest is possible, to be taken as the revolutionary movement and the people in revolt, they themselves are so oblivious of the essence of their work and their reform, that we readers cannot be expected to apply such an interpretation to the poem as a whole. Although it is true that Blok in his critical articles often referred to a parallel between the period of the rise of Christianity in Rome and the revolutionary period in Russia that he himself was living through, there is nothing in this poem to support the idea that the twelve Red soldiers are parallels to the Apostles. They are the modern missionaries, but they do not understand the content of their faith, and the only sanction they have is what they themselves have asserted. Any consciousness of their mission on their part is sharply limited and ultimately subverted by their own violence and by their passion for self-satisfaction.

The twelfth section repeats the vocabulary and images of the preceding parts of the poem and the three dominant points of view: the guardsmen's attitude to their adventure, Petrukha's "interior monologue," and the poet's observations and finally moral understanding. The marchers, the dog, the snowstorm, the bullet, the blood—all come together at the end with Christ:

...Так идут державным шагом —
  Позади — голодный пес,
Впереди — с кровавым флагом,
  И за вьюгой невиди́м,
  И от пули невредим,
Нежной поступью надвьюжной,
Снежной россыпью жемчужной,
  В белом венчике из роз —
  Впереди — Исус Христос. —

...So they march in solemn step—
Behind—the hungry dog,
Ahead—with the bloody flag,
Unseen behind the snowstorm,
Unhurt by the bullet,
In gentle tread above the storm,
Dusted with the pearly snow,
In a white halo of roses—
Ahead—goes Jesus.

The Twelve contradicts the usual political interpretation of art which asserts the artist's satisfaction with his elaboration of a political theme. *The Twelve* has no political theme. One may give the poem a political reading, of course, but such a reading shows that the poem is neither for nor against the revolution that most people assert it apotheosizes and is against revolution in general, passsively admitting the fact of violence and physical change.

The existence of a political theme would necessarily form the axis of the poem, as it does in Blok's short political lyrics or in "Skify" (The Scythians). There is no political axis in *The Twelve.* On the contrary, the structure of the poem confirms that, whatever it may yield to even contradictory political readings, it is apolitical, using the violence of a political change for its own nonpolitical and nonviolent ends. P. Medvedev, who studied the manuscript, has succinctly stated Blok's composition of it:

It seems that the chapters written on white paper, i. e., those written first, include all the chief moments of the dramatic plot of the poem. This includes the appearance, the "first sortie," of the twelve Red Guardsmen and—as exposition of dramatic action—the conversation between Van'ka and Kat'ka (ch. II), Kat'ka's murder—the climax of the poem (ch. VI)—Petrukha's suffering (ch. VII) and the resolution of his anguish—an original social catharsis: *to the grief of all the bourgeois we will fan the world conflagration* (ch. VIII and ch. XII to line 327). It is very significant that all of chapter XII to the lyric ending with Christ is given in the poem as a continuation of Petrukha's monologue begun in chapter VIII and interrupted by the lyric digression of the intervening chapters....

The writing of the poem began with the central dramatic eposode—the love tragedy of Kat'ka-Petrukha-Van'ka, an original modification of the old romantic plot several times before used by Blok—Columbine-Pierrot-Harlequin.

The Twelve is a series of lyric poems around a central dramatic plot. The dramatic plot, or axis, is interrupted by lyric intervals. The poem is a love story. It is a concatenation of scenes and interludes which in the writing were composed into a total drama. Each section was conceived as a separate poem with separate motifs, a different aspect of the central plot, a separate example of Blok's understanding. Medvedev points out that the poem was written in sections which were later reshuffled into their present order, and that the title itself, which many people have considered provocative of the poem or as a provocative theme, first occurs on the eleventh page of the manuscript, indicating that, like most titles, it was come upon during work on the poem it labels and that, like any good title, its function is to shed other light on, to be still another aspect of, the whole poem.

In short, we have no evidence either inside or outside the poem to contradict Blok's own comment in his notes on the poem that

> ...who interprets *The Twelve* as a political poem is either blind to art or else up to his ears in political mud or possessed with great rancor—whether he be friend or enemy to my poem.
>
> At the same time it would be incorrect to deny any connection between *The Twelve* and politics. The truth is that the poem was written in that exceptional, and always brief, period when a cyclone of revoluton causes a storm on all the seas—of nature, life, and art. On the sea of human life there is also a backwater, like the Markizovaia Pond, which is called politics.

As puzzling to commentators as the politics of the poem is the use of the Christ-figure at the end. Gumilëv, in a public lecture in 1919, was one of the first to say that it disturbed him, that it was a superfluity tacked on for "purely literary effect."[2] Blok himself said then, and wrote in his notebooks and diary, that he was not satisfied with the Christ-figure, but could not imagine an alternative. Why he could not is given in an entry in his diary of 1918:

> The Marxists are the most intelligent critics, and the Bolsheviks are correct in being chary of *The Twelve*. But the artist's "tragedy" remains a tragedy. Besides: *if* there existed in Russia a real clergy and not just a class of morally obtuse people called clergy, it would have long ago "mastered" the fact that "Christ is with the Red Guardsmen." It is hardly possible to dispute this truth so simple for those who have read the Gospel and thought about it....
>
> "The Red Guard" is the "water" on the millwheel of the Cristian church... (As rich Jewery was the water on the millwheel of sovereignty, which not one "monarch" figured out in time).
>
> This is the terror (if they could understand this). This is the weakness of the Red Guard also: mere children in an iron age; an orphan, wooden church at a drunken and bawdy fair.
>
> Did I really "eulogize" [Christ]? (as Kamenev said). I only verified a fact: if you look into the eye of the snow-storm *on this road* you will see "Jesus Christ." But sometimes I myself deeply hate this feminine specter.

Two years later he still supported his poem; in fact, he called it "...whatever it may be, the best I have written. Because then I lived contemporaneously."

It is not adequate to say that the theme of the poem and the poem itself follow from Blok's work on his article "The Intelligentsia and the Revolution" or are verified by the article on Catiline, not merely because the political attitude in the articles is transformed in the poem, but because the political animus of the articles is only facultative in the poem. The fact that the poem is basically a love story not only coordinates it thematically with Blok's other work but also requires us to look more deeply into the poem for its sources and meaning.

The poem's immediate and unusual success depends on its dramatic organization of powerful symbols. Whatever may be the poem's failures in terms of its possibilities, its impact is that of a violent confrontation among essential but disparate symbols that directly apply to actual life.

Psychologically speaking, a symbol is an archaic concept which is a direct consequence of human opposition to change and which is an attempt to restore, at least partially, what has been changed.[3] The aim of the symbol is to repress the painful circumstances of change—that is, of the conditions which gave rise to the symbol—or, at least, to prevent their return. In these terms, all symbols have a historical content and an emotional significance. Although values, as predictions of probabilities of satisfaction, may shift from symbol to symbol, a symbol remains, Margolin says, "...a condensation of the genetic past... and of the future, ...[of a] wish to experience a gratification which was denied in the setting that gave rise to the symbol." Symbols have kernels of grief, of forgotten sadness or loss. They communicate change by naming it as a historical event; they express the anxiety of the disrupted equilibrium concomitant on change and the anxiety that follows awareness of the new experience.

In short, what is considered the psychological function of symbols is, in terms of the content taken up by this poem, very much the same as the ultimate aesthetic function: the organization of the determinate negation of established reality—ultimate freedom—and its actualization. The symbols of the mind in its historic play and the images of art in their systematic elaboration here correspond. This is exactly what we find in the poem.

The symbol of the Christ-figure is excellent illustration both of the success of the correspondence and of the imperfection or inadequacy of the representation and its elaboration. Blok himself suggests this in his diary:

> Religion is junk (priests and so on). The terrible thought nowadays: not that the Red Guardsmen are "unworthy" of Christ, who now goes with them, but that it is precisely He who goes with them, when it ought to be Someone Else.
>
> Romanticism is junk. Everything that's *settled* into dogma, delicate dust, *fantasticality* has become junk. Only *élan* is left.

He says the same thing in his notebook. He says the same thing, sharply, in his letter to Maiakovskii in December, 1918: "Your cry is still only a cry of pain and not of joy (Wagner). In destroying we are still the same slaves of the old world; destruction of tradition is the same tradition." He says it tactfully in his letter in August to Annenkov, who illustrated an edition of *The Twelve:*

> About Christ: He's not at all like that: little, hunched over like a dog from behind, carries the flag precisely and *goes away.* "Christ with the flag"—it's—"like that and not like that." Do you know (I do, by all my life) that when a flag flies in the wind (when it rains or snows or *especially* in the dark of night) then *it* makes you think of some enormous person somehow related to it (he doesn't hold it, carry it, but somehow—I don't know how to put it)...
>
> Or again:... I again looked at the whole picture, looked, and suddenly remembered: Christ... by Dürer! [a self-portrait] (i.e., something completely different from this, an *extraneous* remembrance).[4]

According to Medvedev, the manuscripts confirm the guess that the Christ-figure is a culminating figure, that it runs through all the variants and early versions of the poem and that it is not a sudden invention or addition but an intended functional persona.

In tone the poem is oddly, in moments heretically, religious: the eighth section is composed of two stanzas from an old Russian peasant song (the first stanza and three-fourths of the seventh stanza), four distichs based on imitation of a habitual concept of folk poetry but savagely, ironically directed against bourgeois standards and mores, a line from the Church Slavonic burial service asking mercy, and a last line—"It's boring!" The poem is dramatic, attacking the indifferent, forward movement of an insensate society through the vitality of its lowest and its highest common denominators.

The figure of Christ is both low and high, both immediate, in the sense of suffering, and eschatological, in terms of divinity. Furthermore, the corruption which Blok is moving against has been, as he sees it, largely impelled by a stupid and perverse imitation of Christ, that is, by the inanities and barbarities of standardized religious and intellectual practice and behavior at the expense of what we might call the essential in man and what Blok chooses to organize under the spirit of music.

The difficulty with the Christ-figure is its historical and, therefore, poetic limitation: it is really only half a symbol. It is adequate to the content of the poem but not to the poem's meaning. It carries everything except the notion of ultimate freedom. This is the basic failure of the poem and the cause of our dissatisfaction with it: that it sets out to delimit just such a notion, but, at the end, seems to subvert its own system. The actual Christ-figure is a sensational analogy to an aspect of the freedom the poem is about. Christ *is* the redeemer of both the living and the dead. In terms of meaning, however, neither Christian theory nor Christian practice is adequate to the dilemma dramatized by this poem. The Christ-figure is dramatization of the contrast between the failures of men and the limitations imposed on them by their history of failures.

If one interprets the Christ-figure as a symbol of some principle of liberation or as the herald of a new world, or as manifestation of the concept of redemption through suffering, one restricts the poem to a political signification. The Christ-figure may indeed be taken as a messenger, but rather like the messenger in a Greek tragedy who announces both the pathos and the epiphany, apotheosis *in* suffering, not through it. This is the notion, carried as an image, of real freedom in actual restraint, as distinguished from the idea of liberation. Historical tradition and the processes of religious thought weight interpretation of the Christ-figure on the side of redemption, as opposed to the side of essential freedom. Although Blok uses the figure in this second, and what he would call musical, sense, he was aware that intellectual history imposed the first, and for his purposes unsuccessful, understanding. If we can see the Christ-figure not in terms of a church or a religious doctrine or even as historical agent, but as incarnation of the experience of ignorance and loss and of the concept of ultimate, free reality, it does not present any difficulties to us. The trouble is that because the figure in the poem is not carefully defined —however mysterious it be—and because the figure in our culture comes cluttered with other uses, it is not easy to see it this way.

Necessarily Blok himself, although holding to this notion of passive and essential freedom, described what he had in mind in terms of cycles of retribution and resurrection. Since the revenge–redemption cycle of the 1917 Revolution seemed actualization of his belief, he frequently described it in terms of that belief, thinking it apt description: "A completely new world is upon us, a completely new life is coming." Such description should not be taken literally, although it is a prophetic assertion, any more than that line in the first stanza of *The Twelve* which reads literally, but asserts nothing—

Ветер, ветер
На всем божьем свете!

Wind, wind
All over God's world!

should be construed as involving divinity. The Russian phrase is, rather, equivalent to something like "all over the lot." The word "God's" is used completely colloquially suggesting a particular kind of universality which is not involved in a religious context.

Blok uses Christian symbols in a non-Christian or even antidoctrinaire understanding. In part, they elaborate tersely his notion, fully presented in "Catiline," of the essential analogy between the historical moments of 1917 Russia and Rome after Christ's birth. Chiefly, however, they involve that metaphysic of absolute freedom toward which, he believes, meaningful life must move. In the first section, Blok ridicules the doctrine and the performance of institutionalized religion. Addressing "Comrade Priest," he asks:

Помнишь, как бывало
Брюхом шел вперед,
И крестом сияло
Брюхо на народ?

Remember how you used to go
Belly foremost,
And the belly with its cross
Shone on the people?

In the second section, following introduction of the twelve soldiers, Blok picks up the cross again but in a sharply different sense:

Свобода, свобода,
Эх, эх, без креста!

Freedom, freedom,
Oh, oh, without a cross!

He means without the priest's badge of office, and he means that without the idea of purification and redemption the passion of protest becomes only self-indulgence and self-consummation (Kat'ka and Van'ka). He also means that the idea of freedom of which the cross may be taken as symbol and Christ as agent is really independent of either. Blok understands a dilemma which he cannot resolve and of which this poem is the expression.[5]

The love story of Kat'ka-Petrukha-Van'ka merges into the love story in which Christ is the central figure:

Эх, ех, согреши!
Будет легче для души!

Oh, oh, go ahead and sin!
It'll be easier for your soul!

This is the movement toward freedom, which can be understood only as a contradiction and never actualized. In so far as the poem seeks to preserve the integrity of this paradox—that the necessary quest for freedom destroys the capacity to be free—it is an antirevolutionary poem. The hope for freedom is countered but not controverted by the experience of failure.

Our response to the poem is complicated by the literary and colloquial elements woven into it. Some seem dramatically tied to the poem's movement; others seem affixed, the way children pin the tail on the donkey. D. Strémooukhoff suggested that the method was taken over from Richepin's *Chansons des Gueux*. That is to say that its provenience was literary and French. Blok certainly knew Richepin's work, but, except for a similarity in the use of certain colloquial elements in this poem, and in Richepin's songs, there is nothing to suggest any closer connection. The structure of Blok's poem is very different. Zhirmunskii refers to the correspondence between Vlas's vision in Dostoevsky's story "Vlas" and the appearance of the Christ-figure at the end of Blok's poem. Something of the theme and method of *The Twelve* is evident also in Blok's early work—for example, in the 1904 poem "Fraud"—and in his later work as well—for example, the 1918 project for a play about Christ. It is also probable that Blok's affection for Grigor'ev's work and the gypsy romance had made available to his consciousness certain motifs and types of lyric used in *The Twelve*. Above all, however, the material seems to come from Blok's own sense of the character and vitality of the times: this, he suggests, is what people were occupied with; this is the way they talked; this is the expense.

The second stanza in the third section was, Chukovskii has pointed out, a Russian soldier's *chastushka* or epigrammatic lyric:

Эх, ты, горе -горькое,
Сладкое житье!

Рваное пальтишко,
Австрийское ружье!

Ah, you, bitter-misery,
Sweet life!
A torn greatcoat,
An Austrian gun!

In the eighth section, the first three lines, which are variants of the lines just quoted, and lines thirteen through fifteen, addressed by Petrukha to a real or imagined bourgeois, are from an old Russian folk-song:

Ох, ты, горе-горькое!
Скука скучная,
Смертная!
. . .
Выпью кровушку
За зазнобушку,
Чернобровушку...

Oh, you, bitter-misery!
Boring boredom,
Deadly!
. . .
I'll drink your blood
For my lady-love,
My dark eyes...

Orlov among others has pointed out that the lines in the tenth and eleventh sections—

Forward, forward, forward
Working class!

are a variant of two lines from the revolutionary song "Varshavianka," which had been very popular at the turn of the century.

The poem builds up its impact, in part, by use of then contemporary political slogans, fragments of street conversations, signs on political banners, dialectical expressions and word forms, slang phrases, revolutionary jargon, vulgarisms and obscenities. The language has an immediacy and force about it—much of it is presented as dialogue—that makes it resemble the language of the stage. Its closeness to the reader is further emphasized by the contrasting use of phrases from the liturgy and imitations of the grand style, as in the almost "montage" technique of the last section, for example.

The love story is tied to its time by what the lovers say, by the phrases of straight description of them, and, chiefly, by Blok's comments on it and by the series of parallels he sets up: for example, the twelve soldiers are walking, the lovers are walking, Kat'ka walks the streets for a living, the poor walk begging, and the dog-bourgeois walks behind them all. This sense of motion, this image of walking in all its ramifications, is a symbol combining by a principle of dramatic apposition a series of highly charged, essentially lyric perceptions. Structurally the poem is a concatenation of alternating scenes of exposition and action narrated as if by a chorus, an omniscient but present intermediary. In moments of lyric digression, the judgment of the author is obvious. In moments of dramatic narrative, phrases of the actors stand apart. A number of figures fitted to the play and independent of the author's biases are the objective equivalents of emotional responses, the impersonal symbols which, rubbed against each other by coincidence and violence, generate and carry the poem's meaning. The poem is intensely abstract and directly passionate at the same time. Each aspect is both complementary and disturbing to the other. This is another way of saying that the Christ-figure is a necessary and unsatisfactory symbol of apotheosis: necessary, in that the emotional intensity leads to a culminating definition; unsatisfactory, in that apotheosis is a removal of, and from, actual passion.

From this point of view, *The Twelve* is an example of Blok's life-long fascination with the theater and the possibilities of drama. He knew that the real suffering of real people was essential to tragedy, that the author must do more than extend his consciousness—he must re-enact it totally. He was certain that public desire for mere entertainment would pass and, with it, an author's indifference to theatrical reality and his consequent reliance on a director. He envisioned a return to the immediacy of the Greek theater, characterized, as he put it, by the involvement of an educated and responsive audience and the anamnestic myth, analogous to Plato's, informing the life of the community.

Despite his theory, all his plays are clearly adaptations of the efforts of the late medieval actors' theater—the Harlequin-Pierrot-Columbine triangle and the improvisational, sad buffoonery of the commedia dell'arte tradition—to the essential effort at revelation of the medieval mystery or passion plays. Blok's "biggest" play, *The Rose and the Cross*, rehearsed but not performed by the Moscow Art Theater, is a good illustration, not only because of its development in stages from original idea as a ballet with the lady Châtelaine, a Troubadour, and a "Devil's Emissary" to an opera and finally, after a period in which Blok read extensively in medieval French, Latin, and Italian literature, to a play, but also because of the setting (Languedoc and Brittany in the early twelfth century) and the use of castles and knights (Bertran is called the Knight of Woe) and the series of dove-tailed triangles of relationships. Each triangle, like each person, is emotionally or morally imperfect or corrupt. Out of this imperfection or corruption, the person moves in such a way as to violate another relationship and establish an imperfect triangle analogous to the one left behind, until, at the end, everyone is cut off from the central object of desire, the lady Izora, by death or by having gone away or by failing to understand where one is at all. The play is very much a lesson. In his instructions to the actors of the Moscow Art Theater, Blok set out directly to contradict the obvious: his play is not a historical drama, specifically because upper-class life and morality "of whatever period or whatever nation never differ." History, he says, was merely a convenience he used to represent his plan. The words of the songs are, he says, irrelevant, but the rhythm of them, once met, will remain and will evoke further modulations. The images of sea and of snow, of motion and of dream, of joy and of suffering run throughout the play as throughout a poem. The allegorical figure Joy-Suffering, taken, Blok says, from an old Cornwall dialect song in a collection of Breton folk-songs, is a "poetic" symbol, not a dramatic symbol, an illustration of a point of moral view.

The play is about Bertran, who, Blok says, is "not the hero but the head and the heart of the play." From another point of view, however, it is not about *him* or about an aspect of Christianity at all. It is equally about mystery, about the character Gaetan, whom Blok calls ξένος, the stranger, the man who is here but does not belong. "This is the artist," and he is the real subject. Generalized, of course, he is Everyman alienated in the twentieth century. In a world in which the only significant communication can be, as Blok himself argued, communication by gesture, the hero as symbol has no real role. Really history does not repeat itself, as Blok says in the "General Plan of the *Historical Scenes*," and this play, like *The Twelve*, is an intense, brilliant, but not finally successful effort to cross from myth to theater, to animate myth into theater, to transform allegory into the substance of life and make both sing.

The movement of *The Twelve* is very much like that of the tragic rhythm of drama: a statement of a dilemma or impasse in terms of contrasting or opposing sides or principles; consequent suffering or intensely emotional activity that destroys simultaneously the integrity of both conflicting principles; apotheosis or epiphany in which the sense of loss is sublimated and the change defined by an understanding. It is the movement of that essential music which Blok considered the moving principle of life and which Gogol had identified with God. Blok asked in his diary: "What is a poet? A man who writes in verse? No, of course not. A poet is a carrier of rhythm."

The Twelve is further delimited in scope, however, by the absence of character development and by its predominant lyric tone. Although its success may follow directly from its lack of grandeur, the absence of a sense of greatness (which is not absent in *Retribution*) or merely of size contradicts the dramatic movement. The poem seems too small for what it says it is about. Its symbols, like the Christ-figure, seem to have escaped it.

It is Blok's most popular poem. It is his last important one. It is the final example of those principles of versification and aesthetic understanding which he had long maintained and periodically refined. It is his central example of the interplay between pictures and meaning in poetry, of the fusion of image and idea through the office of symbols. It is a rather successful attempt to bind politics (in the broadest sense) and art, to make each inform on the other, to present poetry as a significant description of what is going on.

In our Western tradition—and this includes Blok's Russia—the image of Christ is that of a hero, a god, and an idea, and at the same time—as Blok would have liked to have used it—of a real value which has never been, and never can be, actualized.

IX

An Era Gone

Blok awaited the thunder-and-lightning.
Like dread or like terrible thirst
For the outcome, its fingers on fire
Lay over his life and verse.
—B. Pasternak

The period from the turn of the century to the World War was one of extreme nonconformism, experimentation, and vitality in the fields of literature, the theater, politics, journalism—in all fields of activity. There was considerable economic expansion and development. There were political reforms and counterreforms, and there was the growth of strong and opposing political parties. There was a proliferation of all sorts of periodicals. Perhaps the period may best be characterized as one of diversity, ferment, and accomplishment. The liberal movement began to bog down in the years after the 1905 Revolution, but those educated Russians, best described as "liberals," who had made extraordinary contributions in all fields of political and cultural activity and who disappeared from politics after the 1917 Revolution did not disappear from prominent positions until the late 1920s—until the institutionalization of a very narrow political "either–or" in the place of that intellectual sophistication which had pervaded society up to the World War, and, in many ways, even after it.

In literature, the period may be said to mark a brilliant and variegated transition from the nineteenth-century tradition to the modernist work of the 1920s. Tolstoy died in 1910, the last of the "giants." The Symbolist movement that had begun in Moscow in the 1890s as a kind of avant-garde coterie whose members were held together, if by nothing else, by a sense of Philistine opposition, became supported financially by the Philistines themselves. The economic expansion had produced a merchant group rich enough to afford the luxury of literature and, given the general atmosphere, desirous of supporting such a sophisticated magazine as *The Balance* or such an arty magazine as *The Golden Fleece*. The poets who had met together with a common enthusiasm for rebellion now met in salons. The single Symbolist movement that had ushered in the literary change gave way to literary factions, cliques, and new figures. Some writers merely repeated the discoveries of the 1890s and the early 1900s; others, like Akhmatova, Pasternak, Gumilëv, who first published before the War, did not become influential until after it. The worsening of conditions during the War not only accentuated the political restiveness and made protest general—and meaningful—but also undercut life with terrible fear. People not only began genuinely to hope for improvement but also began even more deeply to dread disaster. The necessity of political choice dictated by the fact of the 1917 Revolution ended the possibilities for freedom which, as assumption or even as creed, had lain behind the variety and vitality of intellectual activity in the period before the War.

In the magazine *Apollo* in 1913 there appeared a number of articles by Sergei Gorodetskii and Nikolai Gumilëv saying that Symbolism had died and had been replaced by a new movement. Gorodetskii strongly felt that the Acmeists and the new poets who came after the Symbolists had revitalized poetry: "A rose for the Acmeists has again become good in itself, in terms of its own petals, odor, and color, and not by virtue of its conceivable resemblances to mystic love or something else still." In response Blok, admitting that the Symbolist movement had begun to split into factions, said that the basic ideas of Acmeism had come from Symbolism, that Gumilëv and Gorodetskii had taken them over from his and Viacheslav Ivanov's articles in *Apollo*. He felt, he noted in his diary, that both the Acmeists and the Futurists (whom he preferred to the Acmeists) offered a poetry that was technically interesting but not *significantly* descriptive:

> These days we have the disputes of the Futurists with their violent arguments.... The followers of Burliuk, whom I haven't yet seen, frighten me off. I'm afraid that there's more indecency here than anything else (in D. Burliuk).
>
> The Futurists as a whole, most likely, are a more significant phenomenon than the Acmeists. The latter are puny, Gumilëv is weighed down with "taste," his baggage is heavy (from Shakespeare to... Théophile Gautier), and they follow Gorodetskii like a famous pioneer. I think that Gumilëv is frequently baffled and shocked by him.

The sense of ethical unity of purpose, of opposition to reactionary politics and to perversely traditional art, that had held the Symbolists together despite their wide differences of aesthetic theory and practice had been lost once there had come about political liberalization and general acceptance of the principles which the Symbolists had reintroduced to literature and which, in the period 1895–1905, had seemed extremely avant-garde. The sense of mystery, the wonderful influence of music—especially of Wagner's —and the discoveries of the past, of the real tradition in the name of which the Symbolist revolt had occurred—all this was gone. The common agreement among the Symbolists to reject the appeal to a majority was subverted by majority acceptance of their principles.

In part, Symbolism died out from its own virtues: the accomplishment of the poetic reform which had been its main program invisibly subrogated continued effort at reform. The ascetic ideal, an aspect of the mystic or quasi-mystical attitude that accompanied the religious notion of the essential nature of the poetic emotion and that reflected the Symbolists' desire to eschew "a choice between two evils" if both were political, was replaced by different standards of taste and, a bit later, by serious isolation of the artist. The development of the divers Symbolists' talents led them away from each other naturally by conditions of life and the increased desire for satisfaction and the security of fame or reputability. Above all, the emergence of a new group of writers before and during the World War determined the dissolution of the movement. The younger people had grown up, artistically speaking, under Symbolism. The reform had been successful. The young wished to extend, necessarily in a new sense, what the Symbolists had discovered. What the Symbolists had worked so hard to establish as a technical principle—the freedom of creative activity—had become an assumption. The effort of the Symbolists to establish works which create their own public had resulted in a public, limited to be sure, but prepared to accept independent artistic activity and values.

Subsequent political oppression of intellectual activity submerged, without altering, the principles and vitality of the Symbolist movement and the various extensions of it through the 1920s. As Valéry said in the middle of the thirties, apropos of French Symbolism but equally relevant to Russian:

> Everything I have seen produced in literature since that tormented era, in the way of audacities, ventures into an uncertain future, or brusque returns to the past, was indicated, or already attained, or prefigured, or rendered possible, if not probable, by the intense and disorganized efforts carried on at the time.

The introduction of political control into more and more social activities and the extraordinary growth of industrialization and the accompanying bureaucratization, outside Russia as well as in, deprived the serious artist of an audience, of an easily accessible means of communication of complex sensibilities, and of the probability of adequately developing his talent. Civilization won out over culture. Pseudo-gratification in all phases of social life began to be mass-produced for the masses. The lowest common denominator became the universal—and the individual—standard. Valéry said:

> The conditions for the development of talents in depth, in subtlety, in perfection, in exquisite power, have disappeared. Everything is opposed to the possibility of an independent life of art....
>
> "Symbolism" is henceforth the symbol that names the intellectual qualities and conditions most opposed to those which reign, and even govern, today.

In short, Symbolism became, and remains, the symbol of itself.

Appendix

ДВЕНАДЦАТЬ

1

Черный вечер.
Белый снег.
Ветер, ветер!
На ногах не стоит человек.
Ветер, ветер —
На всем божьем свете!

Завивает ветер
Белый снежок.
Под снежком — ледок.
Скользко, тяжко,
Всякий ходок
Скользит — ах, бедняжка!

От здания к зданию
Протянут канат.
На канате — плакат:
«Вся власть Учредительному Собранию!»
Старушка убивается — плачет,
Никак не поймет, что значит,
На что такой плакат,
Такой огромный лоскут?
Сколько бы вышло портянок для ребят,
А всякий — раздет, разут...

Старушка, как курица,
Кой-как перемотнулась через сугроб.
— Ох, Матушка-Заступница!
— Ох, большевики загонят в гроб!

Ветер хлесткий!
Не отстает и мороз!
И буржуй на перекрестке
В воротник упрятал нос.

А это кто? — Длинные волосы
И говорит вполголоса:
        — Предатели!
        Погибла Россия!
Должно быть, писатель —
            Вития...

А вон и долгополый —
Сторонкой — за сугроьб...
Что нынче невеселый,
        Товарищ поп?

Помнишь, как бывало
Брюхом шел вперед,
И крестом сияло
Брюхо на народ?

Вон барыня в каракуле
К другой подвернулась:
— Ужь мы плакали, плакали...
        Поскользнулась
И — бац — растянулась!

            Ай, ай!
        Тяни, подымай!

        Ветер веселый
        И зол, и рад.
        Кру́тит подолы,
        Прохожих косит,
        Рвет, мнет и носит
        Большой плакат:
«Вся власть Учредительному Собранию»...
        И слова доносит:

...И у наз было собрание...
...Вот в этом здании...
        ...Обсудили —

        Постановили:
На время — десять, на́ ночь — двадцать пять...
...И меньше — ни с кого не брать...
...Пойдем спать...

        Поздний вечер.
        Пустеет улица.
        Один бродяга
        Сутулится,
Да свищет ветер...

        Эй, бедняга!
            Походи —
        Поцелуемся...

Хлеба!
Что впереди?
Проходи!

Черное, черное небо.

Злоба, грустная злоба
Кипит в груди...
Черная злоба, святая злоба...

Товарищ! Гляди
В оба!

2

Гуляет ветер, порхает снег.
Идут двенадцать человек.

Винтовок черные ремни,
Кругом — огни, огни, огни...

В зубах — цыгарка, примят картуз,
На спину б надо бубновый туз!

Свобода, свобода,
Эх, эх, без креста!

Тра-та-та!

Холодно, товарищи, холодно!

— А Ванька с Катькой — в кабаке...
— У ей керенки есть в чулке!

— Ванюшка сам теперь богат...
— Был Ванька наш, а стал солдат!

— Ну, Ванька, сукин сын, буржуй,
Мою, попробуй, поцелуй!

Свобода, свобода,
Эх, эх, без креста!
Катька с Ванькой занята —
Чем, чем занята?...

Тра-та-та!

Кругом — огни, огни, огни...
Оплечь — ружейные ремни...

Революцьонный держите шаг!
Неугомонный не дремлет враг!

Товарищ, винтовку держи, не трусь!
Пальнем-ка пулей в Святую Русь —

В кондовýю,
В избянýю,
В толстозадую!

Эх, эх, без креста!

3

Как пошли наши ребята
В красной гвардии служить —
В красной гвардии служить —
Буйну голову сложить!

Эх ты, горе-горькое,
Сладкое житье!
Рваное пальтишко,
Австрийское ружье!

Мы на горе всем буржуям
Мировой пожар раздуем,
Мировой пожар в крови —
Господи, благослови!

4

Снег крутит, лихач кричит,
Ванька с Катькою летит —
Електрический фонарик
На оглобельках...
Ах, ах, пади!...

Он в шинелишке солдатской
С физиономией дурацкой
Крутит, крутит черный ус,
Да покручивает,
Да пошучивает...

Вот так Ванька — он плечист!
Вот так Ванька — он речист!
Катьку-дуру обнимает,
Заговаривает...

Запрокинулась лицом,
Зубки блешут жемчугом...
Ах, ты, Катя, моя Катя,
Толстоморденькая...

5

У тебя на шее, Катя,
Шрам не зажил от ножа.
У тебя под грудью, Катя,
Та царапина свежа!

Эх, эх, попляши!
Больно ножки хороши!

В кружевном белье ходила —
Походи-ка, походи!
С офицерами блудила —
Поблуди-ка, поблуди!

Эх, эх, поблуди!
Сердце ёкнуло в груди!

Помнишь, Катя, офицера —
Не ушел он от ножа...
Аль не вспомнила, холера?
Али память не свежа?

Эх, эх, освежи,
Спать с собою положи!

Гетры серые носила,
Шоколад Миньон жрала,
С юнкерьем гулять ходила —
С солдатьем теперь пошла?

Эх, эх, согреши!
Будет легче для души!

6

...Опять навстречу несется вскачь,
Летит, вопит, орет лихач...

Стой, стой! Андрюха, помогай!
Петруха, сзаду забегай!...

Трах-тарарах-тах-тах-тах-тах!
Вскрутился к небу снежный прах!...

Лихач — и с Ванькой — наутек...
Еще разок! Взводи курок!...

Трах-тарарах! Ты будешь знать,
. . . .
Как с девочкой чужой гулять!...

Утек, подлец! Ужо, постой,
Расправлюсь завтра я с тобой!

А Катька где? — Мертва, мертва!
Простреленная голова!

Что, Катька, рада? — Ни гу-гу...
Лежи ты, падаль, на снегу!...

Революцьонный держите шаг!
Неугомонный не дремлет враг!

7

И опять идут двенадцать,
За плечами — ружьеца.
Лишь у бедного убийцы
Не видать совсем лица...

Всё быстрее и быстрее
Уторапливает шаг.
Замотал платок на шее —
Не оправиться никак...

— Что, товарищ, ты не весел?
— Что, дружок, оторопел?
— Что, Петруха, нос повесил,
Или Катьку пожалел?

— Ох, товарищи, родные,
Эту девку я любил...
Ночки черные, хмельные
С этой девкой проводил...

— Из-за удали бедовой
В огневых ее очах,
Из-за родинки пунцовой
Возле правого плеча,
Загубил я, бестолковый,
Загубил я сгоряча... ах!

— Ишь, стервец, завел шарманку,
Что ты, Петька, баба что ль?
— Верно, душу наизнанку
Вздумал вывернуть? Изволь!
— Поддержи свою осанку!
— Над собой держи контроль!
— Не такое нынче время,
Чтобы няньчиться с тобой!

Потяжеле будет бремя
Нам, товарищ дорогой!

И Петруха замедляет
Торопливыс шаги...

Он головку вскидава́ет,
Он опять повеселел...

Эх, эх!
Позабавиться не грех!

Запирайте етажи,
Нынче будут грабежи!

Отмыкайте погреба —
Гуляет нынче голытьба!

8

Ох ты, горе-горькое!
Скука скучная,
Смертная!

Ужь я времячко
Проведу, проведу...

Ужь я темячко
Почешу, почешу...

Ужь я семячки
Полущу, полущу...

Ужь я ножичком
Полосну, полосну!...

Ты лети, буржуй, воробышком!
Выпью кровушку
За зазнобушку,
Чернобровушку...

Упокой, господи, душу рабы твоея...

Скучно!

9

Не слышно шуму городского,
Над невской башней тишина,
И больше нет городового —
Гуляй, ребята, без вина!

Стоит буржуй на перекрестке
И в воротник упрятал нос.
А рядом жмется шерстью жесткой
Поджавший хвост паршивый пес.

Стоит буржуй, как пес голодный,
Стоит безмолвный, как вопрос.
И старый мир, как пес безродный,
Стоит за ним, поджавши хвост.

10

Разыгралась чтой-то вьюга,
    Ой, вьюга́, ой, вьюга́!
Не видать совсем друг друга
    За четыре за шага!

Снег воронкой завился,
Снег столбушкой поднялся...

— Ох, пурга какая, спасе!
— Петька! Эй, не завирайся!
От чего тебя упас
Золотой иконостас?
Бессознательный ты, право,
Рассуди, подумай здраво —
Али руки не в крови
Из-за Катькиной любви?
— Шаг держи революцьонный!
Близок враг неугомонный!

    Вперед, вперед, вперед,
        Рабочий народ!

11

...И идут без имени святого
    Все двенадцать — вдаль.
        Ко всему готовы,
        Ничего не жаль...

Их винтовочки стальные
На незримого врага...
В переулочки глухие,
Где одна пылит пурга...
Да в сугробы пуховые —
Не утянешь сапога...

    В очи бьется
    Красный флаг.

Раздается
Мерный шаг.

Вот — проснется
Лютый враг...

И вьюга́ пылит им в очи
Дни и ночи
Напролет...

Вперед, вперед,
Рабочий народ!

12

...Вдаль идут державным шагом...
— Кто еще там? выходи!
Это — ветер с красным флагом
Разыгрался впереди...

Впереди — сугроб холодный,
— Кто в сугробе — выходи!...
Только нищий пес голодный
Ковыляет позади...

— Отвяжись ты, шелудивый,
Я штыком пощекочу!
Старый мир, как пес паршивый,
Провались — поколочу!

...Скалит зубы — волк голодный —
Хвост поджал — не отстает —
Пес холодный — пес безродный...
— Эй, откликнись, кто идет?

— Кто там машет красным флагом?
— Приглядись-ка, эка тьма!
— Кто там ходит беглым шагом,
Хоронясь за все дома?

— Всё равно, тебя добуду,
Лучше сдайся мне живьем!
— Эй, товарищ, будет худо,
Выходи, стрелять начнем!

Трах-тах-тах! — И только эхо
Откликается в домах...
Только вьюга долгим смехом
Заливается в снегах...

Трах-тах-тах!
Трах-тах-тах...

...Так идут державным шагом —
Позади — голодный пес,
Впереди — с кровавым флагом,
И за вьюгой невиди́м,
И от пули невредим,
Нежной поступью надвьюжной,
Снежной россыпью жемчужной,
В белом венчике из роз —
Впереди — Исус Христос.

ABBREVIATIONS IN NOTES

Notes

Pol. sobr. soch.	*Sobranie sochinenii* (Complete Works), 12 vols.
Sobr. stikh.	*Polnoe sobranie stikhotvorenii v dvukh tomakh* (Complete Poems in Two Volumes)
Soch.	*Sochineniia v odnom tome* (Selected Works)

I: AN ARTISTIC METHOD

1. G. Adamovich, "Aleksandr Blok," *Sovremennye zapiski*, XLVII, pp. 288–89. The Russians used the term "decadent" chiefly in four ways: first, like the French, as a label for the "modernist" school; second, pejoratively by those who for one reason or another were hostile to the Symbolist movement; third, by the Symbolists themselves as a label for second-rate "bohemian" imitators; and fourth, by the Symbolists again in an ironic sense as a description of themselves. To take the word as Plekhanov took it or as the conservatives used it is to misinterpret the attitude of the entire movement. "There is only one absolute decadence; it consists in a lowering of vitality.... A phenomenon generally overlooked is the consciousness or sensation that every period has experienced of its own vital level." J. Ortega y Gasset, *The Revolt of the Masses* (New York, 1952), p. 31. See E. Bellot, *Notes sur le symbolisme* (Paris, 1908) and the review of it in *Vesy*, 1909, No. 1; also, S. Solov'ëv, "Simvolizm i dekadentstvo" *Vesy*, 1909, No. 5.

2. For example, consider Mallarmé's

Une dentelle s'abolit
Dans le doute du Jeu suprême
A n'entr'ouvrir comme un blasphème
Qu'absence éternelle de lit.

Valerii Briusov used the first two lines as epigraph to the first volume of his and Miropol'skii's translations of French Symbolist poetry, *Russkie simvolisty.* In the second volume (p. 12), Briusov stated the way the juxtaposition of images was designed to work: "The connections given this way are always more or less accidental, so that one must regard them as markers of an invisible path open to the reader's imagination."

Earlier, of course, Baudelaire had stated, "In the work of the best poets there is not a metaphor, a simile or an epithet which is not a precise mathematical adaptation for the given condition, because these similes, these metaphors, these epithets are drawn from the ineluctable depths of the *universal analogy* and cannot be drawn forth elsewhere." *L'art romantique* (Paris, n.d.), p. 245.

3. A. Belyi, "Chekhov," *Vesy*, 1904, No. 8, p. 6.

4. V. Briusov "K istorii simvolizma," *Literaturnoe nasledstvo*, XXVII/-XXVIII, p. 272; and "O 'rechi rabskoi,' v zashchitu poezii," *Apollon*, 1910 No. 9, p. 33.

5. V. Briusov, "O 'rechi rabskoi,' v zashchitu poezii," *Apollon*, 1910, No. 9, p. 32; and A. Belyi, "Venok ili venets," *Apollon*, 1910, No. 11, pp. 2–3. See S. Mallarmé, quoted in C. M. Bowra, *The Heritage of Symbolism* p. 15: "I think that the world will be saved by a better literature." See also V. Ivanov, *Borozdy i mezhi*, p. 137: "Russian symbolism could not be, and did not want to be merely art"; M. Voloshin, "Skelet zhivopisi," *Vesy*, 1904, No. 1, p. 42: "Artists are the eyes of mankind"; E. Pound, *ABC of Reading* (Norfolk, Conn.. 1946), p. 32: "Artists are the antennae of the race."

II: A BIOGRAPHICAL SKETCH

1. The influence of the French Symbolists on Blok was real but oblique—oblique partly because time had passed and the Symbolists' discoveries were becoming literary standards and partly because Blok, one of the second generation of Russian Symbolists, heard of the French chiefly through the work of such poets as Briusov and Gippius.

Blok was well acquainted with French literature. He translated Flaubert's *St. Julien l'Hospitalier*, and he worked with his mother and aunt on translations of French poetry (letter to his grandmother, April 11, 1898, in *Pis'ma Aleksandra Bloka k rodnym*, I, 38–39). That he knew the work of the French Symbolists well is supported by a comment in a letter to his father: "Besides, I can write an article on the French Symbolists for the newspaper *Slovo*" (letter to his father, March 28, 1905, in *Pis'ma...k rodnym*, I, 133). Blok was influenced by Baudelaire not only in general attitude, as suggested by the epigraph from Baudelaire to Blok's early poem "Odnoi tebe, tebe odnoi," but also in terms of specific constructs. In the following quotations one sees the ever-present danger of rhetoric common to both poets' work: Baudelaire's spectacular dramatization of sensual response and Blok's reliance on an "a priori" concept to vitalize a poem, a reliance which is not successful. This particular Blok poem is possible precisely because of Baudelaire's work; it uses Baudelaire's discoveries about imagery redundantly.

My sister, swimming side by side,
We'll flee without respite or release
Toward the heaven of my dreams.

(C. Baudelaire, "Le vin des amants," in *Les Fleurs du Mal* [Paris: n.d.], p. 130).

Your ardent form, your smoky outline
Swam to me through the dusk of a lie...

. . .

When, telling fortunes, scarcely visible,
There rose before me like thin haze
That phantom, that invisible...

(A. Blok, "Cherez dvenadtsat' let," in A. Blok, *Pol. sobr. soch.*, III, 136).

III: BLOK'S CRITICAL POSITION

CULTURE VS. CIVILIZATION

1. He said that Rimbaud's influence in Russia was most strongly and directly perceptible in the work of Alexander Dobroliubov. Blok in "The Annunciation" ("S plech upali tiazhkikh dve kosy") and Dobroliubov in "The Brave Night Before You" ("upala kosa do kolen") use the same image to convey a girl's, the Fiancée's, consent to and healthy innocence in the sexual act.
2. The transcendental personality is presumably female.
3. A. Blok, "S ploshchadi na 'Lug zelënyi.'" I would draw attention not only to the reference to Poe but also to the identification of actuality with the motif of color and the moral use of color and to the use of words like "vertigo" and "hysteria" in just the sense that Baudelaire and Rimbaud used them.
4. S. K. Makovskii "Aleksandr Blok," p. 7.
5. A. Blok, "Vstuplenie," *Molniia iskusstva* (neokonchennaia kniga "Ital'ianskikh vpechatlenii"). Apropos of a comparison of his trip through dead, modern Italy with its rich past to Dante's trip through Hell, he piercingly comments: "History astounds and oppresses" (Nemye svideteli.).
6. "This... vision was quite unexpected, rather bookish and not particularly necessary: not necessary because at that moment for me it was aesthetic; but aesthetics loses meaning for a person who feels himself on a summit and about to fall." (A. Blok, "Prizrak Rima i Monte Luca"). The next quotation in the text is from this same article.
7. A. Blok, "Otvet na anketu soiuza deiatelei khudozhestvennoi literatury."
8. Blok would say that the essential content of history is involved in this composition of analogies. For example, in "Catiline" Blok flatly denies the validity—the correspondence to reality—of any self-contained, intellectual scheme and insists on the coincidence of the decline of Rome and the rise of Christianity and the decline of Russia and the rise of Socialism-Communism. Knowing this, one is not surprised by the symbol of Christ at the end of *The Twelve;* it is an attempt to revivify an image of actuality through an analogous act of art.
9. H. Marcuse, *Eros and Civilization* (Boston, 1955), p. 58.
10. Blok nowhere suggests even the possibility of certainty, that is, of absolute knowledge. Cognition is only of a moment of reality, both actual and transcendent, which a symbol contains. Consequently, several meanings, even contradictory meanings, may be simultaneously verifiable.
11. A. Blok, "Obshchii plan 'Istoricheskikh kartin,'" *Pol. sobr. soch.*, XII, 169–72.

IV: POEMS

1898–1904

1. The phrase "novel in verse" comes from Pushkin's *Evgenii Onegin*, of which it is the subtitle. It is interesting that this preface is dated January 9, 1911, just a few weeks before Blok wrote the first draft of parts of *Retribution*. See *infra*, ch. 6.

2. As Blok wrote to Makovskii, the editor of *Apollon* (letter to Makovskii in S. K. Makovskii, "Blok", p. 13): "All my grammatical negligence in poetry is not accidental, there lying behind it what I internally cannot sacrifice; in other words, that's the way 'it came to me.'"

3. For an illustration of the exceptions see *Sobr. stikh.*, II, 453, No. 567.

4. On August 15, 1918, the day he wrote this introduction, Blok also noted (*Zapisnye knizhki*, p. 201) that: "I thought, as once Dante did, of filling in the gaps between the lines in *Verses about the Beautiful Lady* with a simple explanation of events. But by nighttime I was tired. Is this effort really too much for my feeble mind?" Later that August he wrote down what he remembered applied to the poems from 1897 to 1901, including a detailed "commentary" on the poems of the first half of 1901 (*Dnevnik Al. Bloka, 1917–1921*, pp. 122 ff.).

5. Blok, letter to father, October 29, 1904; "Dear Papa. Today I finally received [a copy of] my first book, which I send you.... I hoped for a 'noble modesty,' and therefore tried to avoid dedication to 'famous figures,' if you don't include my teacher, Val. Briusov, and my kind and close friend, Andrei Belyi. As for Vl. Solov'ëv, he would be too well located in an epigraph. I feel I'm so much indebted to his poetry that it was better to keep quiet about the 'bright daughter of dark chaos' and not quote him. But the surrounding chaos and 'literary' stupidity require it. I'll sometime meet Vl. Solov'ëv personally, but sooner in the vast and bright window of the sky than in a book-shop window lit up by multi-colored 'gases.'"

6. Blok, "Zametki o Gamlete," *Pol. sobr. soch.*, XII, 255. I think also of Blok's apt comment on *Othello:* "The tragedy would not be a tragedy, but rather a mystery (it has all the elements of a mystery in it) if there were not a third person just as important as the first two—Iago." (*Ibid.*, p. 208).

7. Instanced in K. Mochul'skii, *Aleksandr Blok*, p. 71.

8. A. Blok, letter to Belyi, February 3, 1903, about the mystical significance of the number 4; in V. Orlov (ed.), *Aleksandr Blok, Andrei Belyi: Perepiska.* The four poets whom Blok associated with "She" are those whom he felt or wanted to feel closest to.

9. E. F. Nikitina and S. V. Shuvalov, *Poeticheskoe iskusstvo Bloka*, pp. 77–78.

10. Of all the more difficult forms of verse Blok tried only the sonnet. He also wrote some poems more or less loosely based on formal patterns, such as that of the ode.

11. See Nikitina and Shuvalov, *Poeticheskoe iskusstvo Bloka*, p. 107.

12. *Dnevnik Al. Bloka*, II, 134 (September 11/August 29, 1918 *re* March 1901). On Vasili Island the streets are called "lines."

13. V. Orlov, footnote in A. Blok, *Sobr. stikh.*, II, 545.

14. See footnote, *Sobr. stikh.*, I, 629. Again we find, interestingly enough, a correlation between Blok's prose and poetry. See his article "The Girl of the Pink Gate and the Ant-King," *Pol. sobr. soch.*, IX, 24.

15. V. Briusov, *Sovremennoe stikhovedenie* (Leningrad, 1931), p. 305.

16. V. Piast, "O 'pervom tome' Bloka," *Ob Aleksandre Bloke*, p. 227.

17. Nikitina and Shuvalov, *Poeticheskoe iskusstvo Bloka*, p. 66.

18. "Iunosheskii dnevnik Al. Bloka," *Literaturnoe nasledstvo* XXVII/-XXVIII, p. 308.

19. See V. Orlov, footnote, in Blok, *Sobr. stikh.*, I, 629.

20. V. Zhirmunskii, *Rifma, eë istoriia i teoriia*, p. 273.

21. Compare, for example, the regular meter and rhyme of a slightly earlier poem in much the same "form": "Ia ikh khranil v pridele Ioanna," (1902).

V: POEMS

1904–1908

1. V. Orlov, footnote to *Balaganchik*, in *Soch.*, p. 615. Blok and his wife, Viacheslav Ivanov and Belyi hoped that there would be a *theatre intime*, but Belyi found *The Puppet Show* completely unsuitable for such a theater—or for any. See K. V. Mochul'skii, *Aleksandr Blok*, p. 130, and especially A. Belyi, "Simvolicheskii teatr," *Arabeski*, pp. 300–10.

2. Blok, note in N. Volkov, *A. Blok i teatr*, p. 78. For foreign "influence," see P. Medvedev, *Dramy i poemy Al. Bloka*, p. 18. For Chekhov's influence, especially on Blok's *The Ridiculous Man*, see A. R[oskin], "Aleksandr Blok obrashchaetsia k Chekhovu," *Literaturnyi kritik*, No. 2 (1939), p. 233.

3. N. Volkov, *A. Blok i teatr*, p. 78. Blok's letter to Meierhold of December 22, 1906, helps explain what Blok wanted the play to do and what he thought Meierhold could do with the play: "The general tone [of the rehearsal], as I told you, so pleased me that I even discovered new ways of looking at *The Puppet Show*. It seems to me that it is not merely lyric, but that there is in it the skeleton of a play. I myself try "to hide in my pocket" those dissatisfactions which arise in my *lyric* self, built for song only and, consequently, limited. I kick this dissatisfaction away in the name of another and, for me, more necessary music—the music of this *showbooth*, which blows up and thereby "brings to the people" an old hag knocked together out of dead theater canvas, string, carpenter's curses and self-satisfied repletion.... *Every* piece of buffoonery wants to become a battering ram to smash right through all the dead stuff...; at this point "*the hour of mystery must strike*": the substance has become numb, powerless, and submissive; in this sense I "*accept the world*"—the whole world with its stupidity, obliqueness, dead and dry colors, only in order to fool this old bony witch and make her young again: in the embraces of the fool and the buffoon the old world brightens up, becomes young, and its eyes become translucent, depthless.... Believe me, it's important for me to be around your theater, very important that *The Puppet*

Show be put on in your theater. This is for me a *purgative* moment, a way out of lyric isolation. Moreover, I'm completely at ease about the warp of my lyric self because I know and see how *your* theater keeps such a true sense of balance in terms of what must not be sold to the crowd, that blind and easy-sitting theatrical audience—it will never sell—either Maeterlinck or Przybyszewski. In this I feel something of great significance—the presence of real love which *alone* saves us from perfidy." (Blok archive, TSGALI, Moscow, 998–1–1051)

4. A. Zonov, *Sbornik pamiati Kommissarzhevskoi*, p. 76.

5. K. Chukovskii, "Iz vospominanii ob Aleksandre Bloke," in M. Aliger *et al.* (eds.), *Literaturnaia Moskva*, I, 786.

6. V. Zhirmunskii, *Poeziia Aleksandra Bloka*, pp. 85, 89, and 91.

7. Blok, letter to father January 1900 (*Pis'ma Aleksandra Bloka k rodnym*, p. 50): "Writing poems moves rather slowly because drama is a more real field, especially when you're in a company."

8. *V vine* may also be read as "in sin."

9. Blok, *Zapisnye knizhki*, May 19, 1906, p. 58.

10. V. Zhirmunskii, *Poeziia Aleksandra Bloka*, p. 17. See also his *Nemetskii romantizm i sovremennaia mistika.*

11. See the poem "Syroe leto. Ia lezhu" (June 20, 1907), *Zapisnye knizhki*, pp. 71–72.

12. "Angel-khranitel'," When published in Blok's 1908 book of lyrics *The Earth in Snow* the poem had as epigraph a phrase from Vl. Solov'ëv: "My cruel, my delightful friend."

13. O. Tsekhnovitser, "Simvolizm i tsarskaia tsenzura," *Uchënye zapiski, Leningradskogo gosudarstvennogo universiteta*, No. 76, pp. 293–94; V. Orlov, *Blok*, p. 96; Blok, *Sobr. soch.*, I, p. 636.

14. Blok, letter to N. N. Rusov, July 20, 1907, *Vestnik literatury*, X (1921), p. 16.

15. V. Zhirmunskii. *Poeziia Aleksandra Bloka*, p. 60.

A pod maskami bylo zvezdno.
Ulybalas' ch'ia-to povest'.
Korotalas' tikho noch'.

I zadumchivaia sovest',
Tikho plavaia nad bezdnoi,
Uvodila vremia proch'.

16. "O lirike," *Pol. sobr. soch.*, X, 63 and 65.

17. The poem "On the Dunes," although written at the same time (the early summer of 1907), was first printed in *Zolotoe Runo* and not with the others in *Fakely* and is not strictly part of the sequence.

VI: POEMS

1907–1916

1. *Dnevnik Al. Bloka, 1911–1913*, February 10, 1913, p. 177: "It's time to untie my hands, I'm not a schoolboy any more. No more Symbolism—I'm alone

responsible to myself, *alone*—and I can still be younger than the young 'middle-aged' poets burdened with posterity and Acmeism." See also *ibid.*, p. 30 (November 4, 1911).

2. Blok uses "romantic" in the sense often applied to Shakespeare by nineteenth-century critics. His own poetry had at first strong Romantic elements, but these were replaced by dramatic elements as the poetry became more successfully Symbolist. What Blok here equates—symbolism and romanticism—his own work shows to be contradictions.

3. Leconte de Lisle, *Poèmes antiques* (Paris, 1852), p. xi. The change in Blok's work from the idealistic "pure" poems about the Lady to poems not only on overtly political themes but also on the corruption of civilization and the necessity of its reform, as well as Blok's minor, but interesting political efforts seems a striking parallel to Baudelaire's. Gautier praised Baudelaire for having insisted that the only end of art was itself, was to excite in the reader an absolute sensation of beauty. But during the February 1848 uprising Baudelaire published the revolutionary journal *Le salut public* (February 27 and 28, 1848), and in 1852 in a preface to Pierre Dupont's *Chants et chansons* (reprinted in Baudelaire, *L'art romantique*), he called art for art's sake "puérile," asserting that "l'art est désormais inséparable de la morale et de l'utile."

4. Blok, book review of *Polnoe sobranie sochinenii Edgara Po* (trans. by K. Bal'mont), in *Pol. sobr. soch.*, XI, 300–1. Blok refers to Poe's influence on the work of such poets as Baudelaire, Mallarmé and Rossetti and to the excellence of Poe's aesthetic criticism.

Henry Lanz says in *The Physical Basis of Rime*, p. 240: "Through Poe this method [distichs, hemistichs, assonance] penetrated into Russian poetry and found a wide application and further development in Bal'mont's work.... Cf. Bal'mont's translation of "The Raven." Pushkin applied it in some of his ballads. Lermontov and Fet occasionally experimented with it." Cf. Pushkin's "Tri u Budrysa syna," Briusov's "Detskikh plech tvoikh drozhan'e," Voloshin's "Osen'," and B. O. Unbegaun, *Russian Versification*, pp. 69–71.

5. Blok used the first line of this poem as epigraph to his 1898 poem "Odnoi tebe, tebe odnoi." As Herbert Marcuse has pointed out, "In a repressive order, which enforces the equation between normal, socially useful, and good, the manifestations of pleasure for its own sake must appear as *fleurs du mal.*" (Herbert Marcuse, *Eros and Civilization* [Boston, 1955], p. 50).

6. A. Odoevskii's "The Ball" (1826) is "close to 'Dances of Death' in theme and structural devices... [In it] the Decembrist poet describes the secular society of the capital as a crowd of dancing skeletons" (V. Orlov, *Aleksandr Blok*, p. 181).

There seems to be no further connection, however, between Odoevskii's poem and Blok's, which was subtitled "Totentanz" in manuscript and is clearly based on the medieval legend.

7. The device of repetition of thematic material from poem to poem in Blok's work has been discussed above. Andreev has succinctly pointed out (V. Andreev, "Stat'ia o Mandel'shtame," pp. 82–83) that: "In Blok's work we see, for the first time it would seem, the, as always in such instances, unconscious

use of the device of theme and variations for which poems preceding and following the basic theme exist not as originals but as essential and conscious completions in which, often in the same words and expressions, the basic leit-motif is developed. "The Unknown Lady" is an especially clear example of this.... Several years later Pasternak constructed a whole book of poems on this device, *Themes and Variations.*"

8. Nikitina and Shuvalov, *Poeticheskoe iskusstvo Bloka*, p. 68. In Blok's first book, there are 12 examples of inexact rhyme; in the second, 114; in the third, 53.

9. Georgette Donchin, *The Influence of French symbolism on Russian Poetry*, p. 193: "French influence in this case can hardly be denied if one notes that the German romantics used the form very rarely... In the French poetry of the latter half of the 19th century it is widely resorted to."

One may point out, however, that repetition is a feature of several fixed forms, in particular, of the triolet, examples of which may be found in eighteenth-century Russian poetry. A repeated refrain, or burden, is, of course, a regular device of popular song and of Russian Romantic poetry.

10. "Idut chasy, i dni, i gody" (1910). The poem also contains the "truncated" feminine rhyme *stúzha—úzhas.* Most of Blok's imperfect rhymes are of this type.

11. V. Zhirmunskii *Poeziia Aleksandra Bloka*, p. 11. Pasternak's last poetry, like Zabolotskii's, was in this sense, even more romantic—and certainly more religious—than Blok's. See B. Pasternak, *Kogda razguliaetsia* (Moscow: unpub. MS, 1957) and N. Zabolotskii, "Kogda vdali ugasnet svet dnevnoi," in M. Aliger *et al.* (eds.), *Literaturnaia Moskva*, II, 415. The change is most interesting.

12. Cf. F. Nietzsche, *The Birth of Tragedy* (*Complete Works*, W. A. Haussman, trans. [Edinburgh, 1910–1927]), p. 161: "I ask the question of genuine musicians: whether they can imagine a man capable of hearing the third act of *Tristan* without expiring by a spasmodic distension of all the wings of the soul? A man who has thus, so to speak, put his ear to the heart chamber of the cosmic will... would he not collapse at once?"

13. On August 27, 1909, Blok wrote two poems: "Den' prokhodil kak vsegda" and "Chem bol'she khochesh' otdokhnut'," at first called "Ustalost'" (Fatigue). The latter was revised in 1911, and a few of its lines were transferred to the other poem. The other poem was revised definitively in 1914 and bears the date May 24, 1914. See the variant readings in Blok, *Sobr. soch.*, II, 450 and 454, and Orlov's notes in *Sobr. stikh.*, I, 647–48.

14. In the manuscript and the first published version, there were four lines between this line and the one before it (see Blok, *Sobr. stikh.*, II, 450):

Khlebnikov i Maiakovskii
Nabavili tsenu za knigi,
Tak chto prikashchik u Vol'fa
Ne mog ikh prodat' bez ulybki.

Khlebnikov and Maiakovskii
Raised the prices of [their] books,
So the salesman at Wolff's
Couldn't sell them without smiling.

Also cut were four lines dealing not with the poet's business affairs but with his dreams:

Takzhe, odnako, ne vsë v nikh
Svetlo i blazhenno,
Kak polagaetsia v snakh,
Kotorye sniatsia poetam.

However, not everything in them [dreams]
Is bright and blissful,
As it should be in the dreams
Poets dream.

15. "Golos iz khora". The first two lines in the MS are (*Sobr. stikh.*, II, 453):

Tol'ko deti, da glupye znaiut
Mrak i kholod griadushchikh dnei.

Only children and fools know
The darkness and cold of coming days.

16 "Shagi komandora" (1910–12). Briusov wrote Blok (September 29, 1912): "I must confess that the 'motorcar' of Don Juan disturbs me a bit, and I'm not completely sure whether or not it's good." Blok replied (September 30, 1912): "As regards the 'motorcar,' you are, of course, right; it has seemed jarring to me, too, sometimes; but this stanza is almost two years old now, and I've still not succeeded in changing it, I still haven't found anything better." (*Sobr. stikh.*, I, 648).

17. V. P. Burenin, "Kriticheskie ocherki," *Novoe Vremia*, November 23/December 6, 1912, p. 5.

Burenin said that modern artists "are deeply convinced that the 'new style' means precisely writing clumsy nonsense.... Allow me to give a little example of the verse nonsense of this kind. The stuff is entitled: 'The Steps of the Commander.'" He then quotes Blok's poem in its entirety and adds: "You can read the whole poem or each stanza separately any way you want—from the beginning forward, or from the end backward—the same obvious rubbish shows up, nothing more." He prints the poem, beginning with the next-to-last stanza, line for line backwards. Anyone can write it endlessly, he says, and then offers his own parody:

V spal'ne svet. Gotova vanna.
  Noch', kak teterev glukha.
Spit raskinuv ruki donna Anna
  I pod neiu prygaet blokha.

Don Zhuan letit v avtomobile,
  Na motore mchitsia Komandor.

Trëkh starukh dorogoi zadavili...
  Chërnyi, kak sova, otstal motor...

Nastezh' dver' — i Don Zhuan sel v vannu.
  Fyrkat' nachal, budto ryzhii kot.
Vdrug shagi. — "Podai mne donnu Annu!" —
  Komandor neistovo orët.

No duratskim krikom ne skonfuzhen,
  Don Zhuan vsë fyrkaet v vode.
— Ia ved' k Anne zvan toboi na uzhin:
  Gde zhe donna Anna, gde?

Na vopros zhestokii net otveta.
  Fyrkaet sred' vanny Don Zhuan.
Donna Anna dremlet do rassveta.
  Komandor stoit kak istukan i t. d.

A light in the bedroom. The bath is ready.
  The night is noiseless like a black grouse.
Donna Anna sleeps, her arms spread out,
  And a flea jumps underneath her.

Don Juan flies on in an automobile,
  The Commander speeds on in a motorcar.
They run over three old women on the way...
  Black, like an owl, the motorcar is slow...

The door's wide open—and Don Juan gets in the bathtub.
  He begins to snort, like a red tomcat.
Suddenly steps — "Give me Donna Anna!" —
  The Commander violently roars.

Undismayed by the idiotic shout,
  Don Juan keeps snorting in the water.
"Am I not called by you to dine at Anna's:
  Where then is Donna Anna, where?"

There is no answer to the cruel question.
  Don Juan is snorting in the bathtub.
Donna Anna dozes until dawn.
  The Commander stands like a graven image, and so on.

Blok's poem appeared in *Russkaia Mysl'* (Russian Thought), whose editor, Peter Struve, Burenin said, should have known better. "The author of 'The Steps of the Commander' is a certain Mr. Blok," he added, "one of the brightest luminaries of the Bedlamites, accepted by Bedlamite criticism as almost the equal of Briusov and Bal'mont, and perhaps even higher than they, who have already become antiquated representatives of rhyming absurdity."

18. "Slabeet zhizni gul upornyi" (August 1909). Merezhkovskii published

in his book *Simvoly* in 1892 a poem called "Addio Napoli," which contains the line "The farewell rumble of the sea grows fainter." The image of the poet as a child at the foot of the lion's column occurs also in the second poem of the series, "Kholodnyi veter ot laguny" (August 1909).

19. "Ravenna." Ravenna rhymes with the Russian word here translated as "mortal." Blok first thought of the poem in Ravenna in 1909 (*Zapisnye knizhki*, May 10, 1909, p. 107):

Vsë, chto..., vsë, chto brenno,
Ia zabyvaiu sred' tvoikh, Ravenna...

20. *Pis'ma Aleksandra Bloka*, p. 36. Pushkin's "Gavriliada" is an anti-religious poem, written in 1821 and circulated in manuscript but not published until after the 1917 Revolution. It is a mock love poem, based on the episode of the Annunciation, in which Joseph is presented as cuckolded by Gabriel and the devil, who war for, and both win, the delights of the Jewess Mary.

21. Cf. W. H. Auden's "Danse Macabre":

The star in the West shoots its warning cry:
"Mankind is alive, but Mankind must die."

22. "Korrespondentsiia Bal'monta iz Meksiki" (1905, 1908), signed "Grigorii E." (the name of the hedgehog at Shakhmatovo in the summer of 1905, to whom Blok dedicated the poem "The Old Woman and the Little Devils"), *Sobr. stikh.*, II, 230–31 and footnote, 554.

23. "Za suchok sukhoi berëzy mesiats zatsepilsia," *Sobr. stikh.*, II, 232. The other poem (*ibid.*, pp. 232–33) is "Mne snilos' nedavno. Kak budto v teatral'nom...." Blok also wrote a parody of his own "puppet shows" using the idea of Shakespeare's *The Taming of the Shrew* and called "Ukroshchenie stroptivoi" (*ibid.*, pp. 233–38).

24. "Zhenshchina" (1914). A structure and attitude involving a shift between the narrator's action and judgment by the narrator-protagonist may be found in Nekrasov's work, by which Blok was "deeply influenced." See Blok, *Pol. sobr. soch.*, XI, 424. For the relation between Blok's work and Nekrasov's, see V. Orlov, "Aleksandr Blok i Nekrasov," *N. A. Nekrasov, Nauchnyi biulleten' Leningradskogo universiteta*, 16/17.

25. For the beginning, see *La Table Ronde*, 97 (January 1956), especially Dennis de Rougemont, "Tableau du phénomène courtois" and Henry Corbin "Soufisme et Sophiologie."

26. "*O, da, liubov' vol'na, kak ptitsa*" (March 1914). The poem, particularly the second stanza, makes use of assonance and alliteration for thematic purposes, as Nikitina and Shuvalov have pointed out (*Poeticheskoe iskusstvo Bloka*, p. 106). The theme, or image, is manipulated by mutually imitative sounds, a definite musico-emotional effect being produced by the use of the four consonants K, R, M, N of the lady's name:

Da, v khishch*n*oi sile *ruk* p*rek*ras*n*ykh,
V ochakh, gde g*r*ust' iz*men*,
Ves' b*r*ed *m*oikh st*r*astei *nap*ras*n*ykh,
*M*oikh *n*ochei, *Karmen*!

See also Andrei Belyi, "O zhizni i tvorchestve A. A. Bloka," Belyi archive, TSGALI, Moscow, 53–1–91, and "Gogol' i Blok," *Masterstvo Gogolia* (Moscow, 1934).

27. "Net, nikogda moei, i ty nich'ei ne budesh'" (1914). One might point out in the second stanza the kind of enjambment characteristic of Blok: the first line, but especially the third, runs on into the next and is stopped abruptly after the first phrase or word. The run-on line and the syntactic pause that follows excellently control the reader's response. Blok felt that this poem was "important" (*Sobr. stikh.*, II, 665).

28. "Rozhdënnye v goda glukhie" (September 1914). The sense of the historic chaos out of which the present has come is given also in the poem "Rus' moia, zhizn' moia, vmeste l' nam maiat'sia?" (February 1910), in which the archaic chaos is given in the figure of the old Finnish tribes "behaving strangely."

VII: RETRIBUTION

A NARRATIVE

1. The difference of ideas in the following two lines, Blok says—lines which suggest a common notion—follows directly from their formal differences. How a poet perceives directly determines what is perceived: "*Chtob on, voskresnuv, vstat' ne mog* [That he, risen from the dead, could not arise] (mine), *Chtob vstat' on iz groba ne mog* [That he could not rise from the grave] (Lermontov, I remember now)—completely different ideas. What's common to them is the 'content,' which only shows once again that outside form content in itself does not exist, carries no weight." (Blok, *Zapisnye knizhki*, p. 197.)

2. Gol'tsev even says (V. Gol'tsev, "Problema realizma v tvorchestve Bloka," *Pechat' i revoliutsiia*, No. 4 [1926], p. 30) that "... the grand design of *Retribution* makes Blok akin to Emile Zola.... Blok himself called the representatives of the generation he describes... his 'Rougon-Macquarts.'"

3. N. Pavlovich, "Iz vospominanii ob A. Bloke," *Feniks*, I, 157.

4. The best available study of the poem's expansion is in P. Medvedev, *Dramy i poemy Al. Bloka.*

There were four chief stages of work on the poem covering twelve years: 1910–11, 1914, 1916, 1919–21. Blok's *obsession*, which became the poem, was first expressed as a poem to his half-sister, Angelina, that he began on the train to Warsaw going to his father's funeral and that he called "December 1, 1909." The present title *Retribution* dates from 1911, a version which is a revision of "December 1, 1909," included in the final text as chapter three, and in which the original, autobiographical "I" referring to the hero has been raplaced by "he." The prologue was begun in 1911 and called "The People and the Poet." The second chapter, dealing with the reign of Alexander III (1881–94), was begun in March 1911 and tentatively titled "Petersburg," but was never finished except for a long introduction.

In February 1911 he wrote his mother a letter in which he said: "I feel that, finally, at thirty-one, a very important change has happened to me, which is reflected in the poem and in my attitude to the world. I think that the last trace of 'decadence' has disappeared. I definitely want to live and foresee many simple, good and attractive possibilities—in things I didn't see before."

During the following couple of years Blok read widely for the poem—histories, biographies, sketches, and materials of all sorts on the period. His historical and archival researches for the poem are contained in a notebook published in *Pol. sobr. soch.*, V, 146–57. In 1916 he completed the first chapter, previously only in outline form. That is, he built the outer ring, the epic frame of reference, in the center of which was to be his epic hero's life and death. Part of an earlier version of the first chapter was published in 1914 under the title "Two Centuries." That Blok *planned* an epic-dramatic poem is suggested by a comment in the manuscript: "This is the essence—the dependence of one's own life on life in general."

The final stage of work on the poem is represented by the reworking of the draft of the second chapter in January 1921, by work on the scene of the son's meeting with the "simple girl," and by the effort at continuation of the second chapter in July 1921, although Blok lay dying. His effort clearly was to define "the hero of a new time."

The prologue and the first chapter were published in 1917; the introduction to the second chapter in 1918; the third chapter and the introduction to the whole poem in 1921. This material, plus other fragments published in Blok's lifetime, is the basis for the definitive edition. As Blok was aware, the later (post—1919) additions do not fit into the poem. Either they move against the poem—for example, a passage included in the 1922 edition as part of the introduction to the second chapter (beginning *Naprasno Angel okrylënnyi* and ending *No uzh sud'ba davala znak*) is unpleasant, debilitating rhetoric—or they are incomplete continuations and modulations of the thematic material—for example, the proposed additions to the third chapter. Some of the variants contain excellent lyric passages, particularly parts of the proposed second chapter, but in general they are useless digressions. They stand to the poem as interpolations rather than as integral parts.

5. See Blok, "O teatre," *Zolotoe Runo*, 3–4 (1908), p. 53: "Our dreams are close to reality. Our speech is ready to be enacted.... The words of the heroine of Ostrovskii's great symbolist drama are come true, for the storm comes on us.... We will never forget the timely words of the great builder Solness, shot through with a prophetic, dreadful anxiety: The younger generation—it means retribution."

6. *Brand* was not written for the stage. Blok's attitude was similar to Ibsen's, who later said, with *Brand* in mind: "I should like my last drama to be in verse—if only one knew beforehand which was going to be the last!" *Brand*, C. H. Herford, trans. (London, 1903), p. xv.

7. Blok, *Zapisnye knizhki*, p. 181 (June 3, 1916): "Conscious of myself as an artist, I again speak as if using the general language. May reality confirm the accuracy of my formulas.

"Many of the personal elements have remained in me.... I have ambition and sensuality; these are the most important of what remains—and will last the longest.

"But already on the *first levels* of the psyche new modes of thought have taken shape, of feeling, of attitudes to the world. May God help me cross the desert, organically introduce something fresh and general into that organic and individual whole which is the content of my first four books."

8. Cf. Ezra Pound ("Vorticism," *Fortnightly Review*, 71:461 [1914]): "I believe that every emotion and every phase of emotion has some toneless phrase, some rhythm-phrase to express it." Also: *Literary Essays of Ezra Pound* (Norfolk, Conn., 1954), p. 9: "I believe in an 'absolute rhythm,' a rhythm, that is, in poetry which corresponds exactly to the emotion or shade of emotion to be expressed."

Blok asks that his "angry iamb smash the stones!" Moses Hadas has pointed out that Archilochus (7th century B.C.) invented the iamb as a verse of abuse and that he speaks about "throwing the iamb," sometimes with terrible effectiveness. See M. Hadas, *Ancilla to Classical Reading* (New York, 1954), pp. 158 ff.

9. Hertz said that to avoid unpleasant consequences of the operations of things and to achieve some good we must construct "images or symbols of external objects, in such a way that the logically necessary consequents of the images are always of the causally necessary resultants in the nature of the things our images represent.... As a matter of fact, we do not know, nor do we have any means of knowing, whether our conceptions of things are in conformity with them in any other than this *one* fundamental respect." (*Principles of Mechanics*, quoted in E. Nagel, "Symbolism and Science," *Symbols and Values* [New York, 1954], p. 58).

10. Cf. W. B. Yeats, *A Vision*, in which Yeats presents his geometry of the movement of history.

11. Wife of False Dmitrii; in folk epos, a symbol of evil witchery.

12. Cf. W. B. Yeats, *Ideas of Good and Evil* (London, 1903), pp. 243–44: "All sounds, all colors, all forms, either because of their pre-ordained energies or because of long association, evoke indefinable and yet precise, emotions, or as I prefer to think, call down among us certain disembodied powers, ...and when sound and color and form are in a musical relation, a beautiful relation to one another, they become as it were one sound, one color, one form, and evoke an emotion that is made out of their distinct evocations, and yet is one emotion."

13. Blok, *Pol. sobr. soch.*, V, 161: "I stand at night by the fence of the Saxon Garden and hear the howling of the wind, the ringing of spurs and the snorting of a horse. Soon everything runs together and grows into a definite music. Battle sounds flutter over Warsaw—a light mazurka."

14. There are quite a few Byronic elements in *Retribution*, but not so many as in *Evgenii Onegin*. That Blok was quite familiar with Byron's poetry is attested by the fact that he translated fifteen of Byron's lyrics.

15. In a description of the father in the third chapter, the line "One is sorry for the father, endlessly sorry" rhymes with the title of one of Flaubert's books: "*I zhal' otsa, bezmerno zhal'... Education sentimentale.*"

16. Blok's letters to his mother of December 1, December 4, and December 9, 1909, in connection with his father's death speak of his father's "loneliness," "high-mindedness," and "strong nature," of Blok's identification with his father through a kind of guilt, and of his discovery that his half-sister Angelina had, like himself, a sense of "irony" (*Pis'ma k rodnym*, I, 292–94)

17. The theme of Peter the Great and his city occurred in Blok's poetry explicitly as early as 1904 in the poem "Pëtr" (Peter) dated February 22, 1904 (*Pol. sobr. soch.*, II, 106; see MS facsimile, p. 107). The theme is much like that of "The Bronze Horseman." N. Antsiferov in fact has said ("Nepostizhimyi gorod," *Ob Aleksandre Bloke* p. 287) that "Blok, like Pushkin, was a poet of Petersburg."

18. Blok, *Zapisnye knizhki*, p. 181. See also, *ibid.*, p. 188: "In Mama's letter there's a review of *Retribution* from *The New Life* (the first response to it which I read in free Russia—it delights me, the poem is called 'socially pertinent')...

"Should they ask me, 'What did you do during the Great War?' I can answer, however, that I was really doing something: I edited A. Grigor'ev, I presented *The Rose and the Cross*, and I wrote *Retribution.*"

19. The limits to nationalistic political or social interpretation are given by Blok in the introduction to *Retribution:* "A generation, having experienced the retribution of history, of environment, of the times, in its turn begins to take retribution; the last first-born... is ready with his little human hand to grab at the wheel by means of which the history of mankind revolves."

In a note on "On the Battlefield of Kulikovo" cycle, he raises what he considers the basic question, "What for?" (*Pol. sobr. soch.*, III, 220): "The Kulikovo Battle belongs, the author is convinced, to the symbolic events of Russian history. Such events are fated to recur. Understanding of them is still ahead."

20. Blok's attitude in the year before his father's death (1908) was straightforward. This later, serious, tormenting perception was only still later treated ironically. The failure of Blok's plays is that they are essentially pseudo-philosophical, romantic monologues. Cf. *The Song of Fate:* "Everything that was, everything that will be has surrounded me: right now I live the life of all time."

21. The "New World" (Nowy swiat) is a Warsaw street.

VIII: THE TWELVE

THE 'POEM OF THE REVOLUTION"

1. On January 7, 1918, Blok put down in his diary (*Dnevnik Al. Bloka, 1917–1921*, pp. 94–96), along with the comment that "the idea of popular representation may, like any 'distraction,' be interesting for an artist only as a passing whim, but fundamentally it is odious," an outline for a play on the life of Christ. Christ is described as being "neither a man nor a woman." His life is to be reacted, partly as if he were a contemporary of Blok's and partly following Renan's *Vie de Jesus*, which Blok had read. "How is he resurrected?" Blok asks himself. And quotes Plato: χαλεπά τὰ καλά (*Protagoras*, Protagoras quoting Simonides).

He is, also, the "Christ-artist." "He receives everything from the people (a feminine receptivity)." The Sermon on the Mount is a "meeting." Christ is arrested, but someone remains. "That is the greater truth," even among the prostitutes, he says.

2. K. Chukovskii, *Aleksandr Blok kak chelovek i poet*, p. 27. In the January-February 1921 issue of *Russkaia Mysl'*, P. Struve published a review of *The Twelve* which Blok copied into his diary (*Dnevnik Al. Bloka, 1917–1921*, pp. 236–39). Struve called Blok's poem "a monument of the revolutionary period," said that Blok's attitude to the revolution was "cynical and sacrilegious," attacking it as immoral and using Blok's historical poetry as paragon. Blok quietly observes at the end of the article he has copied down that "each issue of *Russkaia Mysl'* [in Bulgaria] costs 50 leva (10 French francs, 40 German marks, 4 shillings)."

3. S. G. Margolin, "Psychoanalysis and Symbols," *Symbols and Values*, p. 509.

4. In conversation with S. M. Alianskii on August 12, 1918, Blok elaborated on his letter to Annenkov: "Have you ever happened to walk the city streets on a dark night, in a snowstorm or driving rain when a frenzied wind tears and pulls at everything all around, when you can hardly keep on your feet and think only about not being knocked down, swept away.... At such times the wind rocks the heavy, hanging street-lamps with such force that it seems they'll be torn down and smashed to pieces. And the snow drives on harder and harder; the storm has no place to hide in the narrow streets; it feels hemmed in, strikes on all sides, gathering force to burst out into the open, but there is no open space, and so it starts whirling madly, forming a white sheet. Everything around becomes indistinct and seems to melt into it.

"Suddenly, in the nearest side-street, there flashes a bright or brightly lit spot. It sways and irresistibly draws things toward itself. Maybe it's a big, flapping flag or a poster torn loose by the wind?

"The bright spot quickly grows bigger, becomes enormous, and suddenly takes on an unexpected shape, turning into the silhouette of someone walking along or swimming through the air.

"Stunned and entranced, you're drawn along after this marvelous spot and you haven't the power to tear yourself away from it.

"I like walking around on such nights when nature rises up—it purges you.

"On one such unusually stormy winter night I had a vision of such a bright spot; it grew bigger and became enormous; it excited me and drew me toward itself. Around this enormous thing, both the twelve and Christ came to my mind.

"Some critics have told me that Christ is not successful in the poem; possibly this is so, but I can't reject him." (S. M. Alianskii, "Obraz Khrista v poeme 'Dvenadtsat'.'")

5. Kamenev told Blok's wife once that Blok's poetry was extremely talented, a brilliant expression of actuality. He said that Lunacharskii would write an article about it, "but that one need not read it aloud because it celebrates what we, old socialists, fear most of all." To which Blok added (*Zapisnye knizhki* p. 199): "The Marxists are clever, perhaps, and right. But where does that leave the artist again and his unshelterable work?" Blok could not help being worried by his terrible loneliness.

The Works of Aleksandr Blok

Verse

Stikhi o prekrasnoi Dame. Moscow, 1905.
Nechaiannaia Radost'. Moscow, 1907.
Snezhnaia Maska. St. Petersburg, 1907.
Zemlia v snegu. Moscow, 1908.
Nochnye chasy. Moscow, 1911.
Sobranie stikhotvorenii. 3 vols: *Stikhi o prekrasnoi Dame; Nechaiannaia Radost'; Snezhnaia noch'*. Moscow, 1911–12.
Kruglyi god. Moscow, 1913.
Skazki. Moscow, 1913.
Stikhi o Rossii. St. Petersburg, 1916.
Stikhotvoreniia. 3 vols (a reissue of the 1911–12 collection). Moscow, 1916.
Dvenadtsat' (*poema*). *Skify* (*stikhotvorenie*). St. Petersburg, 1918.
Solov'inyi sad (*poema*). Petersburg, 1918.
Dvenadtsat' (*poema*). Petersburg, 1918 (2d and 3d eds.); 1921 (4th ed.).
Stikhotvoreniia. 3 vols. Petersburg, 1918–19 (only first two vols. reissued).
Iamby, sovremennye stikhi (*1907–1914*). Petersburg, 1919.
Za gran'iu proshlykh dnei. Petersburg, 1920.
Sedoe utro (*piatyi sbornik stikhov*). Petersburg, 1920.
Dvenadtsat'. *Skify*. Paris, 1920.
Stikhotvoreniia. Vol. III, 3d ed. Petersburg, 1921.

Drama

Liricheskie dramy. St. Petersburg, 1908.
Teatr. Moscow, 1916 (includes *Liricheskie dramy*, *Deistvo o Teofile*, and *Roza i krest*).
Teatr. Petersburg, 1918 (same, without *Deistvo o Teofile*).
Pesnia sud'by (*dramaticheskaia poema*). Petersburg, 1919.

Prose (*collections of critical articles*)

Rossiia i intelligentsiia. Moscow, 1918.
Katilina. Petersburg, 1918.
Rossiia i intelligentsiia (*1907–1918*). 2d ed. Petersburg, 1919.
O simvolizme. Petersburg, 1921.

Some Posthumous Editions of Blok's Work

"Iz neizdannykh tekstov Aleksandra Bloka," ed. by V. Orlov, *Literaturnoe nasledstvo*, XXVII/XXVIII (1937).
Neizdannye stikhotvoreniia (*1897–1919*). Ed. by P. N. Medvedev. Leningrad, 1926.
Poeziia, stat'i i p'esy i teatral'nye zamysly. In *Russkii sovremennik.* Vol. III. Leningrad-Moscow, 1924.
Polnoe sobranie stikhotvorenii v dvukh tomakh. Ed. by V. Orlov. 2 vols. Leningrad, 1946.
Sobranie sochinenii. 12 vols. Moscow-Leningrad, 1932–36.
Sobranie sochinenii. 4 vols. Berlin, 1923.
Sobranie sochinenii. 8 vols. Moscow, 1960–.
Sochineniia v odnom tome. Ed. by V. Orlov. 1st ed. Leningrad, 1936. 2d ed. Moscow-Leningrad, 1946.

Diaries and Notebooks

Dnevnik Al. Bloka, 1911–1913. Ed by P N Medvedev. Leningrad, 1928.
Dnevnik Al. Bloka, 1917–1921. Ed. by P. N. Medvedev. Leningrad, 1928.
"Iunosheskii dnevnik Aleksandra Bloka," *Literaturnoe nasledstvo*, XXVII/XXVIII (1937).
Zapisnye knizhki Al. Bloka. Ed. by P. N. Medvedev. Leningrad, 1930.

Correspondence

Aleksandr Blok, Andrei Belyi: Perepiska. Ed. by V. Orlov. *Letopisi gosudarstvennogo literaturnogo muzeia.* Vol. VII. Moscow, 1940.
Pis'ma Aleksandra Bloka. Leningrad, 1925.
Pis'ma Al. Bloka k E. P. Ivanovu. Moscow-Leningrad, 1936.
Pis'ma Aleksandra Bloka k rodnym. 2 vols. Moscow-Leningrad, 1927, 1932.
"Pis'ma k Andreiu Belomu," *Zapiski Mechtatelei*, 6 (1922).

Selected Bibliography

Adamovich, G. "Aleksandr Blok," *Sovremennye zapiski*, XLVII (1931).
——. "Dva slova o rifme," *Tsekh poetov*, 1922, No. 3.
——. "Iz zapisnoi knizhki," *Novosel'e*, 1949, No. 39–41.
——. Review of Blok's *Nechaiannaia Radost'*, in *Obrazovanie* 1907, No. 2.
Aikhenval'd, Iu. *Poety i poetessy*. Moscow, 1922.
——. "Poeziia Bloka," *Slovo o kul'ture*. Moscow, 1918.
Alfonsov, V. "Blok i zhivopis' Ital'ianskogo vozrozhdeniia," *Russkaia literatura*, 1959, No. 3.
Alianskii, S. M. "Obraz Khrista v poeme 'Dvenadtsat'." Unplubished work in author's possession. Moscow, 1961.
Andreev, V. "Stat'ia o Mandel'shtame." Unpublished work in author's possession, New York, 1958.
Anichkov, E. *Novaia russkaia poeziia*. Berlin, 1923.
Annenkov, Iu. "Ob Aleksandre Bloke," *Novyi zhurnal*, 1959, No. 1.
——. "Smert' Bloka, "*Zhizn' iskusstva*, 1921, No. 804.
Annenskii, I. F. *Kniga otrazhenii*. St. Petersburg, 1906.
Antsiferov, N. "Nepostizhimyi gorod. Petersburg v poezii A. Bloka," *Ob Aleksandre Bloke*. Petersburg, 1921.
Ashukin, N. S. *Aleksandr Blok*. Moscow, 1923.
Asmus, V. "Filosofiia i estetika russkogo simvolizma," *Literaturnoe nasledstvo*, XXVII/XXVIII (1937).
Babenchikov, M. B. *Al. Blok i Rossiia*. Moscow-Petrograd, 1923.
Bakulin, V. [Briusov, V.] "Torzhestvo pobeditelei," *Vesy*, 1907, No. 9.
——. "Proekt vseobshchego primireniia," *Vesy*, 1908, No. 4.
Bal'mont, K. *Gornye vershiny*. Moscow, 1904.
——. *Poeziia kak Volshebstvo*. Moscow, 1915.
Beketova, M. A. *Aleksandr Blok*. Petrograd, 1922.
——. *Aleksandr Blok i ego mat'*. Leningrad-Moscow, 1924.
——. "O risunkakh Aleksandra Bloka," *Literaturnoe nasledstvo*, XXVII/XXVIII (1937).
——. "Vesëlost' i iumor Bloka," in Nikitina, E. F. (ed.). *O Bloke*. Moscow, 1929.
Belousov, I. A. *Literaturnaia sreda. Vospominaniia 1880–1928*. Moscow, 1928.
Belyi, A. "Apokalipsis v russkoi poezii," *Vesy*, 1905, No. 4.
——. *Arabeski*. Moscow, 1911.
——. "Blok i Merezhkovskie," *Posledniia Novosti*, April 7, 1922.
——. "Blok v iunosti," *Golos Rossii*, February 26, 1922.

——. "Charles Baudelaire," *Vesy*, 1909, No. 6.
——. "Iz vospominanii o Bloke," *Golos Rossii*, April 2, 1922.
——. "Krititsizm i simvolizm," *Vesy*, 1904, No. 2.
——. "Lug zelënyi," *Vesy*, 1905, No. 8.
——. "Maska," *Vesy*, 1904, No. 6.
——. *Masterstvo Gogolia*. Moscow, 1934.
——. *Mezhdu. dvukh revoliutsii* Leningrad, 1934.
——. *Nachalo veka*. Moscow, 1933.
——. *Na rubezhe dvukh stoletii*. Moscow, 1930.
——. "Nastoiashchee i budushchee russkoi literatury," *Vesy*, 1909, Nos. 2, 3.
——. *O smysle poznaniia*. Petersburg, 1922.
——. "O tselesoobraznosti," *Novyi Put'*, 1904, No. 9.
——. *Poeziia slova*. Petersburg, 1922.
——. *Revoliutsiia i kul'tura*. Moscow, 1917.
——. "Simvolizm," *Vesy*, 1908, No. 12.
——. *Simvolizm*. Moscow, 1910.
——. "Simvolizm kak miroponimanie," *Mir iskusstva*, 1904, No. 5.
——. "Venok ili venets," *Apollon*, 1910, No. 11.
——. "Vospominaniia, t. III, ch. II (1910–1912)," *Literaturnoe nasledstvo*, XXVII/XXVIII (1937).
——. "Vospominaniia o Bloke," *Epopeia*, 1922/23, Nos. 1, 2, 3, 4.
Belyi, A. and Briusov, V. "Pis'ma," *Literaturnyi kritik*, 1939, No. 10–11.
Berberova, Nina. *Alexandre Blok et son temps, suivi d'un choix de poémes*. Paris, 1947.
Blagoi, D. "Aleksandr Blok i Apollon Grigor'ev," in Nikitina, E. F. (ed.). *O Bloke*. Moscow, 1929.
Blium, E. and Gol'tsev, V. "Literatura o Bloke za gody revoliutsii," in Nikitina, E. F. (ed.). *O Bloke*. Moscow, 1929.
Blok, G. P. "Geroi 'Vozmezdiia'," *Russkii sovremennik*, 1924, No. 3.
Bogdanov, E. "Na pole Kulikovom," *Sovremennye zapiski*, XXXII (1927).
Bonneau, Sophie. *Examen critique du drame lyrique d'Alexandre Blok*. Paris, 1946.
——. *L'univers poétique d'Alexandre Blok*. Paris, 1946.
Bowra, C. M. *The Heritage of Symbolism*. London, 1951.
——. "The Position of Alexander Blok," *The Criterion*, 1932, No. 4.
Brainina, B Ia. "Pravo na zhizn'. Pervaia kniga Aleksandra Bloka," in Nikitina, E. F. (ed.). *O Bloke*. Moscow, 1929.
Briusov, V. *Dnevniki 1891–1910*. Moscow, 1927.
——. *Izbrannye sochineniia*. 2 vols. Moscow, 1955.
——. "Iz literaturnogo nasledstva Valeriia Briusova," *Literaturnoe nasledstvo*, XXVII/XXVIII (1937).
——. "K istorii simvolizma," *Literaturnoe nasledstvo*, XXVII/XXVIII (1937).
——. "Kliuchi tain," *Vesy*, 1904, No. 1.
——. *Kratkii kurs nauki o stikhe*. Moscow, 1919.
——. "Ob odnom voprose ritma," *Apollon*, 1910, No. 11.
——. *O iskusstve*. Moscow, 1899.

——. *Opyty*. Moscow, 1918.
——. "O 'rechi rabskoi,' v zashchitu poezii," *Apollon*, 1910, No. 9.
——. "O rifme," *Pechat' i revoliutsiia*, 1924, No. 1.
——. *Osnovy stikhovedeniia*. Moscow, 1924.
——. *Pis'ma k P. P. Pertsovu 1894–1895*. Moscow, 1927.
——. "Poeziia i proza," *Sofiia*, 1914, No. 6.
——. (ed.). *Problemy poetiki*. Moscow-Leningrad, 1925.
——. "Strast'," *Vesy*, 1904, No. 8.
——. "Svoboda slova," *Vesy*, 1905, No. 11.
Briusov, V. and Miropol'skii, A. L. *Russkie simvolisty*. 3 vols. Moscow, 1894–95.
Brodskii, B. (ed.). *Erotika v russkoi poezii*. Berlin, 1922.
Brodskii, N. L., N. P. Sidorov, and L'vov-Rogachevskii, V. (eds.). *Literaturnye manifesty ot simvolizma k oktiabriu*. Moscow, 1929.
Brunetière, F. *L'Evolution de la poésie lyrique en France au XIX siècle*. 2 vols. Paris, 1906.
Bugaev, Boris [Belyi, A.]. "Na perevale," *Vesy*, 7, 8, 9, 10 (1906); also, 2, 4, 5, 9 (1908), 2 (1909), and 9 (1909).
Bugaeva, K. and Petrovskii, A. "Literaturnoe nasledstvo Andreia Belogo," *Literaturnoe nasledstvo*, XXVII/XXVIII (1937).
Burgi, R. T. "The Plays of Alexander Blok." Master's thesis, Columbia University, 1947.
Castex, P. G. (ed.). *Autour du symbolisme*. Lille-Paris, 1955.
Chukovskii, K. *Aleksandr Blok kak chelovek i poet*. Petersburg, 1924.
——. "Iz vospominanii ob Aleksandre Bloke," in M. Aliger, *et al.* (eds.). *Literaturnaia Moskva*. Vol. I. Moscow, 1956.
——. *Kniga ob Aleksandre Bloke*. Berlin, 1922.
——. "Poslednie gody Bloka," *Zapiski Mechtatelei*, VI (1922).
Chulkov, G. "Iz istoriii Balaganchika," *Kul'tura Teatra*, 1921, Nos. 7, 8.
——. "Vesy," *Apollon*, 1910, No. 7.
——. *O misticheskom anarkhizme*. St. Petersburg, 1906.
Derman, A. "Ob Aleksandre Bloke," *Russkaia Mysl'*, July 1913.
Desnitskii, V. A. "A. Blok, kak literaturnyi kritik," in Blok, A. *Sobranie sochinenii*. Vol. X. Leningrad, 1935.
——. "Sotsial'no-psikhologicheskie predposylki tvorchestva A. Bloka," in *Pis'ma Aleksandra Bloka k rodnym*. Vol. II. Moscow-Leningrad, 1932.
Dobroliubov, A. *Iz knigi nevidimoi*. Moscow, n.d.
Dolgopolov, L. K. "'Dvenadtsat' Al. Bloka (Ideinaia osnova poemy)," *Voprosy sovetskoi literatury*, VIII. Moscow-Leningrad, 1959.
——. "'Vozmezdie,' nezavershennaia poema Bloka," *Russkaia literatura*, 1959, No. 4.
Donchin, Georgette. *The Influence of French Symbolism on Russian Poetry*. The Hague, 1958.
Dukor, I. "Problemy dramaturgii simvolizma," *Literaturnoe nasledstvo*, XXVII/-XXVIII (1937).
Eikhenbaum, B. "Blok i Gorky," in his *Moi vremennik*. Leningrad, 1929.

——. "Sud'ba Bloka," in *Ob Aleksandre Bloke*. Petersburg, 1921.

Ellis. "Itogi simvolizma," *Vesy*, 1909, No. 7.

——. "Kul'tura i simvolizm," *Vesy*, 1909, No. 10–11.

——. *Russkie simvolisty*. Moscow, 1910.

Engel'gardt, B. "V puti pogibshii," in *Ob Aleksandre Bloke*. Petersburg, 1921.

Erenburg, I. *Portrety russkikh poetov*. Berlin, 1922.

Erlich, V. "Russian Poets in Search of a Poetics," *Comparative Literature* 1952, No. 4.

Fidler, F. F. (ed.). *Pervye literaturnye shagi. Avtobiografii sovremennykh russkikh pisatelei*. Moscow, 1911.

Ghil, R. *Traité du verbe*. Paris, 1887.

Gippius, Z. N. *Literaturnyi dnevnik*. St. Petersburg, 1908.

——. "My i oni," *Vesy*, 1907, No. 6.

——. "Notes sur la littérature russe de notre temps," *Mercure de France*, January 1, 1908.

——. *Zhivye litsa*. 2 vols. Prague, 1925.

Gofman, M. (ed.). *Kniga o russkikh poetakh poslednego desiatiletiia*. St. Petersburg-Moscow, 1908.

Gofman, M. and Gofman, R. *Les symbolistes russes*. Paris, n.d.

Gofman, V. "Iazyk simvolistov," *Literaturnoe nasledstvo*, XXVII/XXVIII (1937).

Gollerbakh, E. "Obraz Bloka," *Vozrozhdenie*, 1923, No. 1.

Gol'tsev, V. V. "Briusov i Blok," *Pechat' i revoliutsiia*, 1928, Nos. 4, 5.

——. "O muzykal'nom vospriiatii mira u Bloka," in Nikitina, E. F. (ed.). *O Bloke*. Moscow, 1929.

——. "O preodolenii liriki v tvorchestve Bloka," *Novyi mir*, 1927, No. 5.

——. "Problema realizma v tvorchestve Bloka," *Pechat' i revoliutsiia*, 1926, No. 4.

Goodman, Th. *Alexander Block, eine Studie zur neueren russischen Literaturgeschichte*. Königsberg, 1936.

Gorbachëv, G. E. *Kapitalizm i russkaia literatura*. Leningrad, 1925.

Gor'kii, M. *O pisteliakh*. Moscow, 1928.

Gorodetskii, S. "Aleksandr Blok. Liricheskie dramy. Kritika," *Obrazovanie*, 1908, No. 8.

——. "Bor'ba za Bloka," *Izvestiia*, 1926, No. 180.

——. "Manifest ob Akmeizme," *Apollon*, 1913, No. 1.

Gromov, P. *Geroi i vremia*. Leningrad, 1961.

Grossman, Leonid. *Ot Pushkina do Bloka. Etiudy i portrety*. Moscow, 1926.

Gudzii, N. K. "Iz istorii rannego russkogo simvolizma," *Iskusstvo*, 1928, Vol. III, No. 4.

——. "Tiutchev v poeticheskoi kul'ture russkogo simvolizma," *Izvestiia po russkomu iazyku i slovesnosti Akademii Nauk S.S.S.R.*, 1930, Vol. III.

Guenther, J. von. *Alexander Block. Der Versuch einen Darstellung*. Munich, 1948.

Gumilëv, N. S. *Pis'ma o russkoi poezii*. Petrograd, 1923.

——. "Poeziia v 'Vesakh'," *Apollon*, 1910, No. 9.

——. "Zhizn' stikha," *Apollon*, 1910, No. 7.

Haumant, Émile. *La culture française en Russie 1700–1900*. Paris, 1913.
Ivanov, Georgii. *Peterburgskie zimy*. New York, 1952.
Ivanov, Viacheslav. "Aleksandr Blok. Stikhi o Prekrasnoi Dame," *Vesy*, 1904, No. 11.
——. *Borozdy i mezhi*. Moscow, 1916.
——. "Dve stikhii o sovremennom simvolizme," *Zolotoe Runo*, 1908, No. 3–4.
——. "Estetika i ispovedanie," *Vesy*, 1908, No. 11.
——. "Kop'ë Afiny," *Vesy*, 1904, No. 10.
——. "Mysli o simvolizme," *Trudy i dni*, 1912, No. 1.
——. "Nietzsche i Dionis," *Vesy*, 1904, No. 5.
——. "O noveishikh teoreticheskikh iskaniiakh v oblasti khudozhestvennogo slova," *Nauchnye Izvestiia*, II (1922).
——. "Poet i chern'," *Vesy*, 1904, No. 3.
——. *Po zvëzdam. Opyty filosofskie, esteticheskie i kriticheskie*. St. Petersburg, 1909.
——. "Sporady," *Vesy*, 1908, No. 8.
——. "Zavety simvolizma," *Apollon*, 1910, Nos. 8 and 9.
Ivanov-Razumnik, R. V. *Aleksandr Blok. Andrei Belyi*. Petersburg, 1919.
——. *Pamiati Aleksandra Bloka*. Petersburg, 1922.
Izmail'skaia, V. D. "Problema 'Vozmezdiia'," in Nikitina, E. F. (ed.). *O Bloke*. Moscow, 1929.
Jakobson, Roman. "Briusovskaia stikhologiia i nauka o stikhe," *Nauchnye Izvestiia*, II (1922).
Kahn, Gustave. *Symbolistes et décadents*. Paris, 1902.
Khodasevich, V. *Literaturnye stat'i i vospominaniia*. New York, 1954.
——. *Nekropol'*. Brussels, 1939.
Kniazhnin, V. N. *Aleksandr Aleksandrovich Blok*. Petersburg, 1922.
Knipovich, E. F. "Blok i Geine," in Nikitina, E. F. (ed.). *O Bloke*. Moscow, 1929.
——. "O literaturnom nasledii Bloka," *Kniga o knigakh*, 1924, No. 7–8.
Kogan, P. "Drama Bloka," *Pechat' i revoliutsiia*, 1923, No. 8–9.
Kolpakova, E., P. Kupriianovskii, and D. Maksimov. "Bibliografiia A. Bloka," *Uchënye zapiski Vil'niusskogo gosudarstvennogo pedagogicheskogo instituta*, Vol. VI, 1959.
Komarovskaia, N. I. "Aleksandr Blok v Bol'shom dramaticheskom teatre," in *Teatr i zhizn'*. Leningrad-Moscow, 1957.
Kovalëv, V. "Pis'ma Bloka M. F. Andreevoi," *Russkaia literatura*, 1960, No. 4.
Kuzmin, M. "Khudozhestvennaia proza 'Vesov'," *Apollon*, 1910, No. 9.
——. "O prekrasnoi iasnosti," *Apollon*, 1910, No. 4.
Labry, Raoul. "Alexandre Blok et Nietzsche," *Revue des Études Slaves*, XXVII (1951).
Lanz, Henry. *The Physical Basis of Rime*. Stanford, 1931.
Lebedev, V. I. "Uteriannye stikhi A. Bloka," *Novosel'e*, 1942, No. 1.
Lednicki, W. "Pol'skaia poema Bloka," *Novyi zhurnal*, 1942, Nos. 2, 3.
Lehmann, A. G. *The Symbolist Aesthetic in France, 1885–1895*. Oxford, 1950.
Lenin, V. I. *Filosofskie tetradi*. Moscow, 1934.

——. "Partiinaia organizatsiia i partiinaia literatura," *Novaia zhizn'*, 1905, No. 12.

Lirondelle, André. "La poésie russe de l'art pour l'art et sa destinée," *Revue des Études Slaves*, I (1921).

Loks, K. "Briusov-teoretik simvolizma," *Literaturnoe nasledstvo*, XXVII/XXVIII (1937).

Lozovskii, Lev. "Blok v otsenke kritikov," in Nikitina, E. F. (ed.). *O Bloke*. Moscow, 1929.

Lunacharskii, A. "Aleksandr Blok," in Blok, A. *Sobranie sochinenii*. Vol. I. Leningrad, 1932.

L'vov-Rogachevskii, V. *Poet—prorok*. Moscow, 1921.

Maiakovskii, V. "Umer Aleksandr Blok," *Polnoe sobranie sochinenii*. Vol. II. Moscow, 1939.

Makashin, S. "Literaturnye vzaimootnosheniia Rossii i Frantsii XVIII–XIX vv.," *Literaturnoe nasledstvo*, XXIX/XXX (1937).

Makovskii, S. K. "Aleksandr Blok." Unpublished work in author's possession, Paris, 1955.

——. *Portrety sovremennikov*. New York, 1955.

Maksimov, D. E. "Iz arkhivnykh materialov o Bloke," *Uchënye zapiski Leningradskogo gosudarstvennogo pedagogicheskogo instituta*, 1956, Vol. XVIII, No. 1.

——. "Materialy iz biblioteki Al. Bloka," *Uchënye zapiski Leningradskogo gosudarstvennogo pedagogicheskogo instituta*, 1958, Vol. 184, No. 6.

——. *Poeziia Valeriia Briusova*. Leningrad, 1940.

——. "Tvorcheskii put' A. Bloka," *Literaturnaia uchëba*, 1935, No. 6.

Malinka, E. "Al. Blok i V. Maiakovskii," *Literaturnyi kritik*, 1938, Nos. 9, 10.

Mallarmé, S. "Définition de la poésie," *Vogue*, April 18, 1886.

——. *Divagations*. Paris, 1897.

Mandel'shtam, O. "A. Blok," *Rossiia*, 1922, No. 1.

——. *Sobranie sochinenii*. New York, 1955.

Mashbits-Verov, I. "Al. Blok i pervaia revoliutsiia," *Zvezda*, 1926, No. 3.

Maslenikov, O. *The Frenzied Poets*. Berkeley and Los Angeles, 1952.

Matlaw, R. E. "The Manifesto of Russian Symbolism," *The Slavic and East European Journal*, 1957, No. 3.

Medvedev, P. N. "Dni i dela A. A. Bloka," in Medvedev, P. N. (ed.). *Pamiati Bloka*. Petersburg, 1922.

——. *Dramy i poemy Al. Bloka*. Leningrad, 1928.

——. "Iz istorii sozdaniia proizvedenii A. Bloka," *Zvezda*, 1 (1926).

——. (ed.). *Pamiati Bloka*. Petersburg, 1922.

——. *Pometki Al. Bloka v tetradiakh stikhov*. Leningrad, 1926.

Meierhold, V. "Iz pisem o teatre," *Vesy*, 1907, No. 6.

Meilakh, B. *Lenin i problemy russkoi literatury*. 2d ed. Moscow, 1951.

——. "Simvolisty v 1905 godu," *Literaturnoe nasledstvo*, XXVII/XXVIII (1937).

Merezhkovskii, D. S. *O prichinakh upadka i o novykh techeniíakh sovremennoi russkoi literatury*. St. Petersburg, 1893.

——. *Simvoly*. Moscow, 1892.
——. "Umytye ruki," *Vesy*, 1905, No. 9–10.
Messer, R. "Simvolisty v epokhu imperialisticheskoi voiny," *Leningrad*, 1932, No. 7.
Miasnikov, A. S. *A. A. Blok*. Moscow, 1949.
——. "Blok," *Bol'shaia sovetskaia entsiklopediia*. Vol. V. 2d ed. Moscow, 1950.
Michaud, Guy. *Message poétique du symbolisme*. 4 vols. Paris, 1951–55.
Mikhailovskii, B. V. *Russkaia literatura xx veka*. Moscow, 1939.
Minskii, N. M. *Na obshchestvennye temy*. St. Petersburg, 1909.
——. *Ot Dante k Bloku*. Berlin, 1922.
Mochul'skii, K. V. *Aleksandr Blok*. Paris, 1948.
Mohrenschild, D. von. "The Russian Symbolist Movement," *PMLA*, 1938, No. 4.
Nemerovskaia, O. and Vol'pe, Ts. (eds.). *Sud'ba Bloka*. Leningrad, 1930.
Nikitina, E. F. (ed.). *O Bloke. Sbornik*. Moscow, 1929.
——. *Russkaia literatura ot simvolizma do nashikh dnei*. Moscow, 1926.
Nikitina, E. F. and Shuvalov, S. V. *Poeticheskoe iskusstvo Bloka*. Moscow, 1926.
Ob Aleksandre Bloke. Petersburg, 1921.
Orlov, V. N. *Aleksandr Blok*. Moscow, 1956.
——. "Aleksandr Blok," in Blok, A. *Sochineniia v odnom tome*. Moscow-Leningrad, 1946.
——. "Aleksandr Blok i Andrei Belyi v 1907 godu," *Literaturnoe nasledstvo*, XXVII/XXVIII (1937).
——. "Aleksandr Blok. K 60-letiiu so dnia rozhdeniia," *Pravda*, November 29, 1940.
——. "Aleksandr Blok i Nekrasov," *N. A. Nekrasov, Nauchnyi biulleten' Leningradskogo universiteta*, 1947, No. 16/17.
——. "Aleksandr Blok i p'esa Sem Benelli," *Uchënye zapiski gosudarstvennogo nauchno-issledovatel'skogo instituta teatra i muzyki*, 1958, Vol. I.
——. "Aleksandr Blok i Rossiia," in Blok, A. *O rodine*. Moscow, 1945.
——. "Literaturnoe nasledstvo Aleksandra Bloka," *Literaturnoe nasledstvo*, XXVII/XXVIII (1937).
——. "Neosushchestvlënnyi zamysel Aleksandra Bloka—drama 'Nelepyi chelovek'," *Uchënye zapiski Leningradskogo gosudarstvennogo pedagogicheskogo instituta*, 1948, No. 67.
Otzoupe, Nicolas. "N. S. Goumilev." Doctorat d'Université présenté à la Faculté des Lettres de l'Université de Paris, 1952.
Ovsianiko-Kulikovskii, D. N. (ed.). *Istoriia russkoi literatury XIX v*. 5 vols. Moscow, 1911.
Pamiati Aleksandra Bloka: LXXXIII otkrytoe zasedanie Vol'noi Filosofskoi Assosiatsii, 28 avgust 1921. (Speeches by Andrei Belyi, Ivanov-Razumnik, and A. Z. Shteinberg.) Petersburg, 1921.
Pavlovich, N. "Iz vospominanii ob A. Bloke," *Feniks*. Vol. I. Moscow, 1921.
——. "Ob Aleksandre Bloke," *Ogonëk*, July 1946.
Perets, V. N. *Ocherki po istorii poeticheskogo stilia v Rossii*. St. Petersburg, 1905.

Pertsov, P. *Literaturnye vospominaniia 1890–1902 gg.* Moscow, 1933.

——. *Rannii Blok.* Moscow, 1922.

Piast, V. "Dva slova o chtenii Blokom stikhov," in *Ob Aleksandre Bloke.* Petersburg, 1921.

——. "O 'Pervom tome' Bloka," in *Ob Aleksandre Bloke.* Petersburg, 1921.

——. *Vospominaniia ob A. Bloke.* Petersburg, 1923.

Poggioli, R. *The Poets of Russia, 1890–1930.* Cambridge, Mass., 1960.

Poiarkov, N. *Poety nashikh dnei.* Moscow, 1907.

Polianskii, V. "Sotsial'nye korni russkoi poezii ot simvolistov do nashikh dnei," in Ezhov, I. (ed.). *Russkaia poeziia XX veka.* Moscow, 1925.

Raymond, Marcel. *De Baudelaire au surréalisme.* Paris, 1952.

Remenik, G. *Poemy Aleksandra Bloka.* Moscow, 1959.

Remizov, A. "Moskva," *Novosel'e*, 1949, No. 39–41.

Retté, Adolphe. *Le symbolisme. Anecdotes et souvenirs.* Paris, 1903.

Roland-Manuel. "La musique et l'amour courtois," *La Table Ronde*, 1956, No. 97.

R[oskin], A. "Aleksandr Blok obrashchaetsia k Chekhovu," *Literaturnyi kritik*, 1939, No. 2.

Rozanov, Ivan. "Blok–redaktor poetov," in Nikitina, E. F. (ed.). *O Bloke.* Moscow, 1929.

Rozanov, Matvei. "Motivy 'mirovoi skorbi' v lirike Bloka," in Nikitina, E. F. (ed.). *O Bloke.* Moscow, 1929.

Rozanov, V. "Nechto iz tumana "obrazov: "podobii," *Vesy*, 1909, No. 3.

Ruff, Marcel-A. "Baudelaire et l'amour," *La Table Ronde*, 1956, No. 97.

Russkoe Bogatsvo, August 1894. Anonymous review of Briusov's *Russkie simvolisty.* Vol. I.

Rybnikova, M. A. *A. Blok—Gamlet.* Moscow, 1923.

Seferiants, A. "Nepostizhimaia. K eidologii Bloka," in Nikitina, E. F. (ed.). *O Bloke.* Moscow, 1929.

Selivanovskii, A. "Raspad simvolizma," *Literaturnaia uchëba*, 1934, No. 7.

Shengeli, G. "O liricheskoi kompozitsii," in Briusov, V. (ed.). *Problemy poetiki.* Moscow-Leningrad, 1925.

——. *Traktat o ruskkom stikhe.* Moscow-Petrograd, 1923.

Shklovskii, V. "Blok i Rozanov," in Nikitina, E. F. (ed.). *O Bloke.* Moscow, 1929.

——. *Khod konia.* Berlin, 1923.

Shtut, S. "'Dvenadtsat' A. Bloka," *Novyi mir*, 1959, No. 1.

Shubin, E. "Poema A. Bloka 'Dvenadtsat'," *Filologicheskii sbornik studenchesko-go nauchnogo obshchestva Leningradskogo universiteta*, 1959.

Shuvalov, S. V. "Blok i Lermontov," in Nikitina, E. F. (ed.). *O Bloke.* Moscow. 1929.

Slonimskii, A. "Blok i Solov'ëv," in *Ob Aleksandre Bloke.* Petersburg, 1921.

Solov'ëv, S. *Crurifragium.* Moscow, 1908.

——. "Simvolizm i dekadenstvo," *Vesy*, 1909, No. 5.

Solov'ëv, V. *Sobranie sochinenii.* 2d ed. St. Petersburg, 1911.

Strémooukhoff, D. "Echos du symbolisme français dans le symbolisme russe," in Castex, P-G. (ed.). *Autour du symbolisme*. Paris, 1955.
Struve, P. B. "In memoriam Blok—Gumilëv," *Rul'*, September 12/25, 1921.
Symons, Arthur. *The Symbolist Movement in Literature*. London, 1899.
Tager, Iu. *Aleksandr Blok*. Moscow, 1946.
Taupin, René. *Influence du symbolisme français sur la poésie américaine de 1910 à 1920*. Paris, 1929.
Teatr. Sbornik statei. St. Petersburg, 1908.
Thorel, J. "Les Romantiques allemands et les Symbolistes français," *Entretiens Politiques et Littéraires*, III (September 18, 1891).
Tikhonov, N. "Aleksandr Blok," *Pravda*, August 7, 1946.
Timofeev, L. I. *Aleksandr Blok*. Moscow, 1946.
——. "Poema Bloka 'Dvenadtsat' i eë tolkovateli," *Voprosy literatury*, 1960, No. 7.
Tomashevskii, B. *Russkoe stikhoslozhenie*. Petrograd, 1923.
Trotsky, L. *Literatura i revoliutsiia*. Moscow, 1923.
Tsekhnovitser, O. "Simvolizm i tasrskaia tsenzura," *Uchënye zapiski, Leningradskogo gosudarstvennogo universiteta*, 1941, No. 76.
Tsenzor, D. "Vospominaniia ob Aleksandre Bloke," *Leningrad*, 1946, No. 5.
Tsingovatov, A. *A. A. Blok*. Moscow-Leningrad, 1926.
——. "Blok," *Bol'shaia sovetskaia entsiklopediia*. Vol. VI. Moscow, 1927.
Tsvetaeva, M. "Plennyi dukh. Moia vstrecha s Andreem Belym," *Sovremennye zapiski*, LV (1934).
Tynianov, Iu. "Blok i Geine," in *Ob Aleksandre Bloke*. Petersburg, 1921.
——. *Problema stikhotvornogo iazyka*. Leningrad, 1924.
Unbegaun, B. O. *Russian Versification*. New York, 1956.
Valéry, P. *Variété*. Paris, n.d.
Vanor, G. *L'art symboliste*. Paris, 1886.
Vengerov, S. S. (ed.). *Russkaia literatura XIX veka*. 3 vols. Moscow, 1914–16.
——. (ed.). *Russkaia literatura XX veka*. 2 vols. Moscow, 1917.
——. (ed.). *Biblioteka velikikh pisatelei*. Vol. VI.: *Pushkin*. Petersburg, 1915.
Vengerova, Z. "Poety-simvolisty," *Vestnik Evropy*, 1892, No. 9.
Verkhovenskii, Iu. "Voskhozhdenie. K poetike Aleksandra Bloka," in *Ob Aleksandre Bloke*. Petersburg, 1921.
Voitolovskii, L. "Sumerki iskusstva," *Literaturnyi Raspad*, 1908, Nos. 1, 2.
Volkov, A. "Aleksandr Blok," *Novyi mir*, 9 (1936).
——. *Ocherki russkoi literatury kontsa XIX i nachala XX vekov*. Moscow, 1952.
Volkov, N. *Aleksandr Blok i teatr*. Moscow, 1926.
Voloshin, M. *Liki tvorchestva*. St. Petersburg, 1914.
——. "Magiia tvorchestva," *Vesy*, 1904, No. 11.
——. "Skelet zhivopisi," *Vesy*, 1904, No. 1.
Volynskii, A. *Bor'ba za idealizm*. St. Petersburg, 1900.
Vospominaniia o Bloke. 1. E. M. Tager, "Blok v 1915 g." 2. "Teatral'nye vospominaniia o Bloke V. P. Veriginoi i N. N. Volokhovoi." *In Trudy po russkoi i slavianskoi filologii. Uchënye zapiski Tartuskogo gosudarstvennogo universiteta*. 1961, Vol. IV, Vypusk 104.

Whitehead, A. N. *Symbolism, its Meaning and Effect.* New York, 1927.
Zamiatin, E. "O Bloke," *Russkii sovremennik*, 1924, No. 3.
Zenkovskii, V. V. *Istoriia russkoi filosofii.* 2 vols. Paris, 1950.
Zhirmunskii, V. M. "Dva napravleniia sovremennoi poezii," *Zhizn' iskusstva*, 339–40 (1919).
——. "Iz istorii teksta stikhotvorenii A. Bloka," *Zapiski Peredvizhnogo Teatra*, 1923, No. 45.
——. *Poeziia Aleksandra Bloka.* Petrograd, 1922.
——. "Preodolevshie simvolizm," *Russkaia Mysl'*, 1916, No. 12.
——. *Nemetskii romantizm i sovremennaia mistika.* St. Petersburg, 1914.
——. *Rifma: eë istoriia i teoriia.* Petrograd, 1923.
——. *Valerii Briusov i nasledie Pushkina.* Petersburg, 1922.
Zonov, A. (ed.). *Sbornik pamiati Kommissarzhevskoi.* St. Petersburg, 1911.
Zorgenfrei, V. A. "Aleksandr Aleksandrovich Blok. Po pamiati za 15 let, 1906–1921 gg.," *Zapiski Mechtatelei*, 1922, No. 6.
Zundelovich, Ia. "Poetika groteska," in Briusov, V. (ed.). *Problemy poetiki.* Moscow-Leningrad, 1925.

Index